THE REALM OF
TIBETAN BUDDHISM

THE REALM OF
TIBETAN

BUDDHISM

Text: Li Jicheng   Photos: Gu Shoukang and Kang Song
Editors: Xiao Shiling and An Chunyang   Translation: Wang Wenjiong

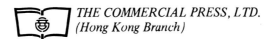

THE COMMERCIAL PRESS, LTD.
(Hong Kong Branch)

THE REALM OF TIBETAN BUDDHISM

© 1984, 1985 The Commercial Press, Ltd., Hong Kong Branch

First co-published in Chinese by:
The Commercial Press, Ltd., Hong Kong Branch
4/F., Kiu Ying Building, 2D, Finnie Street, Quarry Bay, Hong Kong
and
Foreign Languages Press
24 Baiwanzhuang Road, Beijing, PRC

Authors: Li Jicheng, Ku Shoukang
Executive Editors: Xiao Shiling, An Chunyang, Teresa Ngai
Photographers: Ku Shoukang, Kang Song
Graphic Design: Arrow Productions Ltd.

Printed in Hong Kong
by C & C Joint Printing Co., (H.K.) Ltd.

English edition first co-published in 1985
Reprinted 1988
by The Commercial Press, Ltd., Hong Kong Branch
and Foreign Languages Press
ISBN 962 07 5020 9

Publisher's Note

Since it was introduced into Tibet, Esoteric Buddhism, which originated in ancient India, has evolved in a different social and historical environment into a unique sect known as Tibetan Esoteric Buddhism. This belief, which belongs to the Mahayana faith, calls for monastic study of both the Exoteric and the Esoteric doctrines. The study of the latter comes at the most advanced stage, and the text that demands the most attention is the Anuttara Yoga Tantra.

The Esoteric doctrine has a long tradition in Tibet and its influence on Tibetan history and the life of the people has been very strong. Tibetan Buddhists regard Esoteric Buddhism as "the essence of the sacred religion". The study of its doctrine has become so important that its understanding is thought to be the key to a complete and thorough comprehension of Tibetan Buddhism. To gain a true understanding of Tibetan Esoteric Buddhism, one has to study not only its canonical texts, but its works of art related to the religious beliefs. These works, in their various forms and expressions, will bring one into visual contact with the religious order.

The Realm of Tibetan Buddhism outlines the origin, development, canonical texts, meditative practices and, in particular, the works of art related to Tibetan Esoteric Buddhism. The book contains 159 pictures which amply show these works in their traditional style. Many of the objects shown in the pictures are cultural relics and are rare items of art in Tibet. The scholarly introduction and these pictures will be of enormous value to artists, students and scholars of Tibetan Buddhism.

The text is written by Li Jicheng, who is an assistant researcher at the Institute of World Religions of the Chinese Academy of Social Sciences. He is also a member of the board and deputy secretary-general of the Beijing Institute of Tibetan Buddhism. The pictures are provided by Gu Shoukang and Kang Song. Gu is one of the top journalists in China, and Kang Song is a distinguished Tibetan press photographer. Both Li Jicheng and Gu Shoukang have studied Esoteric Buddhism for many years in Tibet and are well versed in this religious belief.

Thanks are due to the various organizations and monastic communities in Tibet, and especially to Mr. Wang Furen, Tibetologist, for their help, advice and cooperation during the preparation of the book.

5

CONTENTS

A BRIEF HISTORY OF
TIBETAN ESOTERIC BUDDHISM

A BRIEF HISTORY OF TIBETAN ESOTERIC BUDDHISM

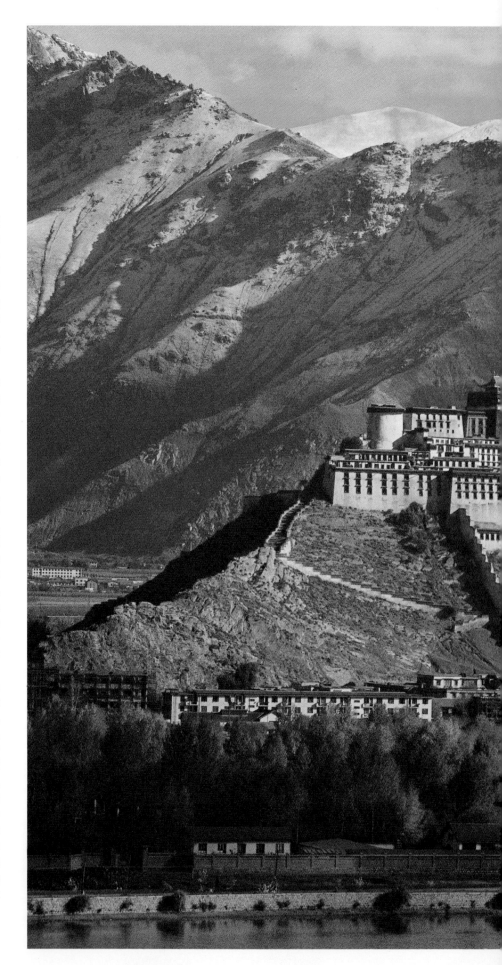

Tibetan Buddhism has a history of more than 1,000 years. It incorporates the doctrines of the Exoteric Sect with that of the more fully developed Esoteric Buddhism. Traditionally, the Esoteric doctrine has been regarded as containing the essence of the beliefs of Tibetan Buddhism, and it is studied at an advanced stage only after the doctrine of Exoteric Buddhism has been mastered.

The Tibetan term for Esoteric Buddhism is "gsang-sugags", meaning "the mystic truth". It is so called because the founders believed that it is the recipient of the profoundly secret doctrines of the Mahāvairocana, or the Dharmakāya Buddha (Buddha in the body of the law). These doctrines, according to their belief, constitute the true teaching of Esoteric Buddhism. All other sects of Buddhism are called "Exoteric" because their doctrines are what Śākyamuni, the Nirmānakāya (Buddha in the incarnation body), preached openly. According to Tibetan Buddhism, "Esoteric Buddhism is the essence of the sacred religion", representing the highest and the most difficult stage of monastic study.

Although it is of Indian origin, Tibetan Esoteric Buddhism has nevertheless developed its own system of succession, and is different from Indian Buddhism in its system, ceremonies, monastic study and points of emphasis in the study of canonical texts. The epithet "Tibetan", therefore, is used to distinguish it from the Esoteric doctrine practised by the Hans or that by the followers of Eastern Esoteric Buddhism in Japan, which is known as the Mantra (True Teaching Sect) or Mantrayāna (True Teaching Vehicle), a sect founded by the great master Kukai (774-835).

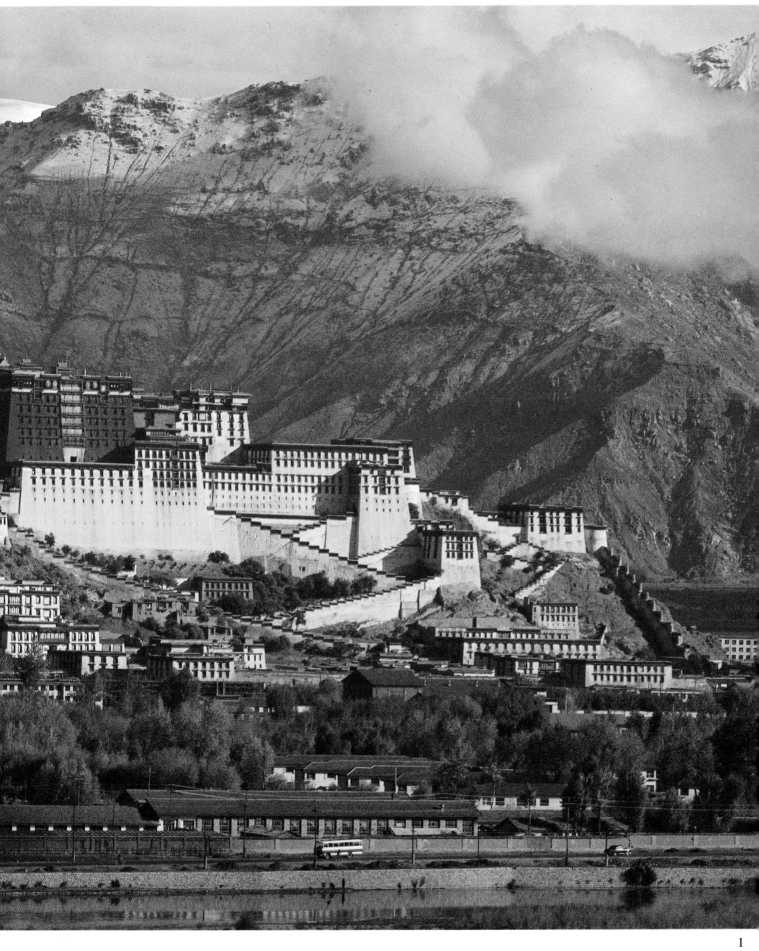

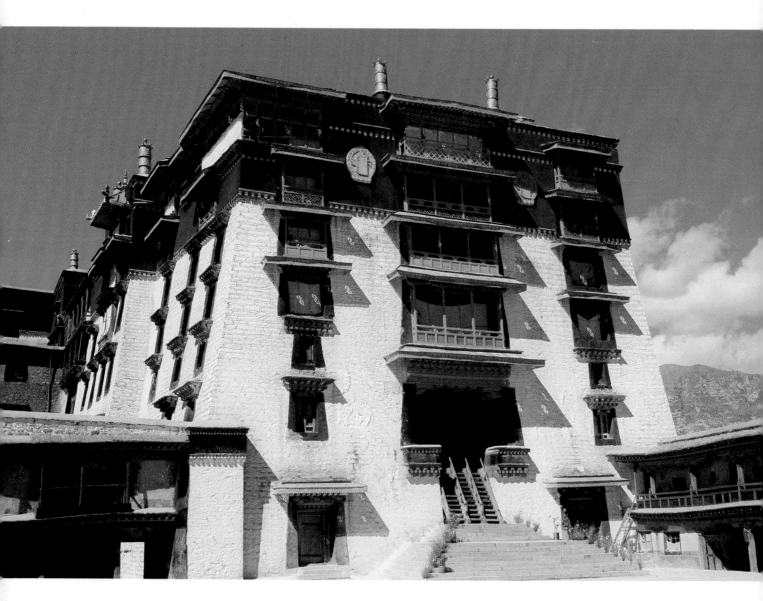

1. Full view of the Potala Palace. Covering an area of 130,000 sq.m., the palace stands majestically on the slope of Red Hill overlooking Lhasa. Badly damaged after it was built in the 7th century, the Potala Palace was reconstructed and extended 10 centuries later. It has two major sections, the White Palace and the Red Palace, and was the residence of 9 Tibetan kings and 10 Dalai Lamas. The Potala Palace, which is lavishly decorated with frescoes, *thang-kas,* carved Buddhist images, antiques and jewels, is a museum of Tibetan Buddhist culture.

2. The Hall of the Virtuous Summer Sun in the Potala Palace. Religious dances used to be performed on the platform in front of the hall while the Dalai Lama watched from one of its windows.

ORIGIN AND DEVELOPMENT

ORIGIN AND DEVELOPMENT

Bon-po, more commonly known as Bon, was an animistic religion in ancient Tibet. Its theory was based on the belief that "all things possess innate souls". In ancient Tibet Ban-po had a mass following.

In the early 7th century, Srong-btsan Sgam-po (?-650), after pacifying rivalling tribes in Tibet, founded the Turfan (Bod) Dynasty and a slave society first came into being. The liberal policy he followed in matters related to politics, economy and culture paved the way for the introduction of Buddhism into Tibet. After marrying Princess Khri-btsun, daughter of the Nepalese king Amsuvarman, he went into wedlock with Princess Wencheng, foster-daughter of Tai Zong, the Tang emperor, Khri-btsun arrived in Tibet with mi-bskyod rdo-rje, a life-size image of Śākyamuni at the age of eight, and Princess Wencheng brought to Lhasa jo-bo shvkya-mu-ni, a life-size image of Śākyamuni at the age of 12, as well as 360 volumes of Buddhist texts. The royal family realized that the Buddhist practice of idolatry and its notion of the supremacy of the divine right would help to con-

solidate the new dynasty. Not surprisingly, therefore, it made every effort to foster Buddhism.

Esoteric Buddhism came to Tibet with the introduction of Indian Buddhism. Ku Sara, Bram-za Sham Kara and Shi La Mangdra, Esoteric masters from India and other countries, were invited by Srong-btsan Sgam-po to Tibet to translate Esoteric texts such as the *Ratna-megha-sūtra* and *ratnakarandaka-sūtra*. In Lhasa, the Qoikang and Ramoqe monasteries were built, where the images of Tārā, Mahāmāya, Sarasvatī and Amṛtakuṇḍalin were also created. These were the events which marked the beginning history of Esoteric Buddhism in Tibet.

3. Shown in the picture is the Drepung Monastery. Located 15 km. northwest of Lhasa, the monastery, now covering an area of 250,000 sq.m., was first built in 1416. It used to be Tibet's largest monastery where the 2nd, 3rd and 4th Dalai Lamas ascended the throne.

4. The gilded roofs and metal reliefs on the walls of the Drepung Monastery.

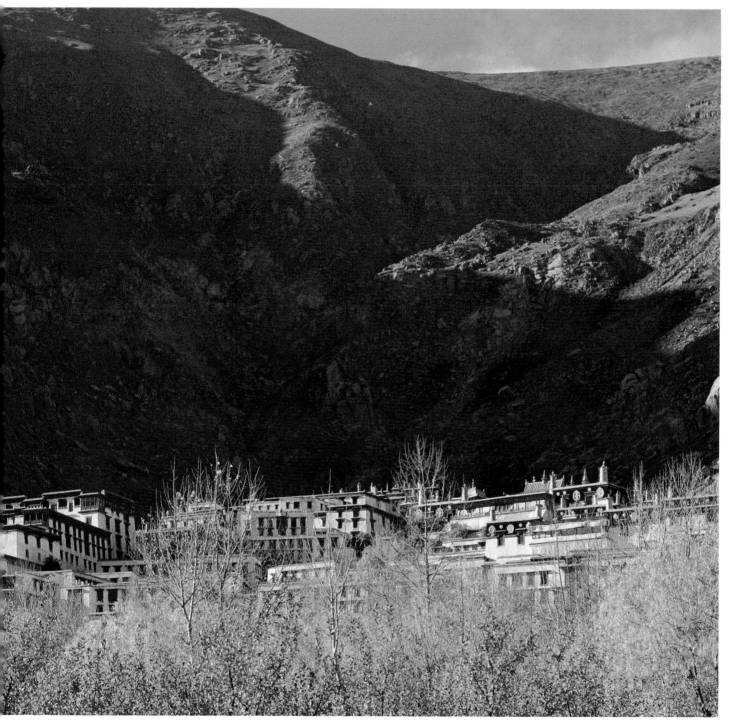

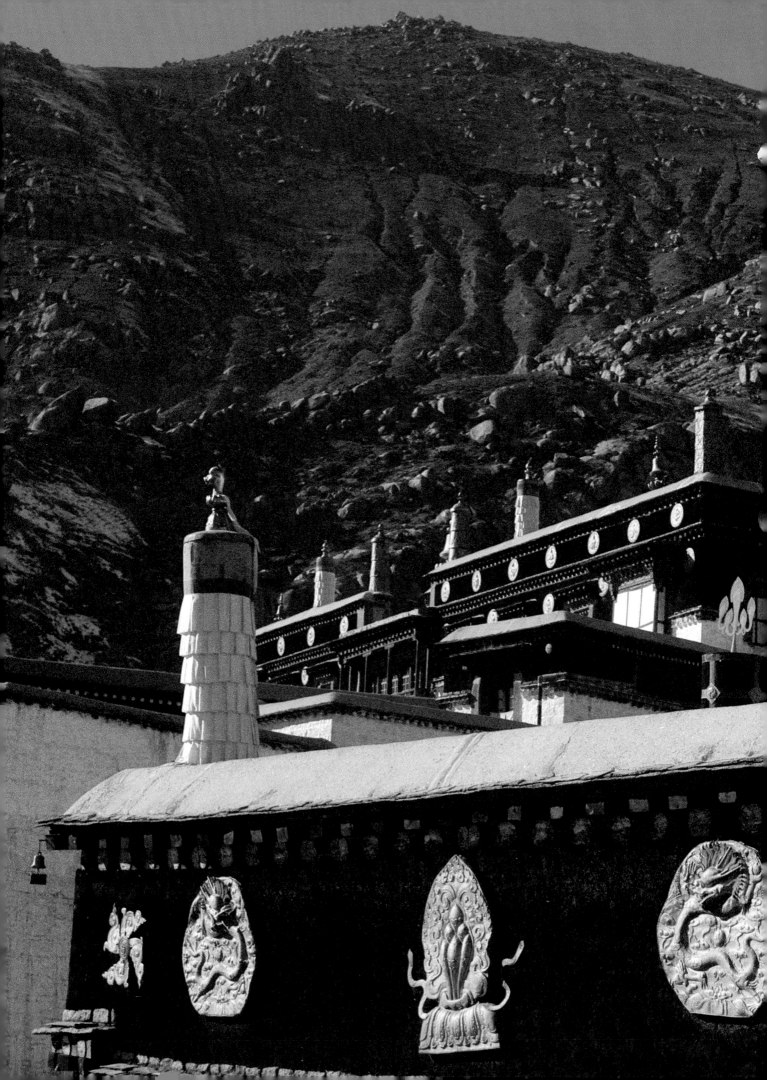

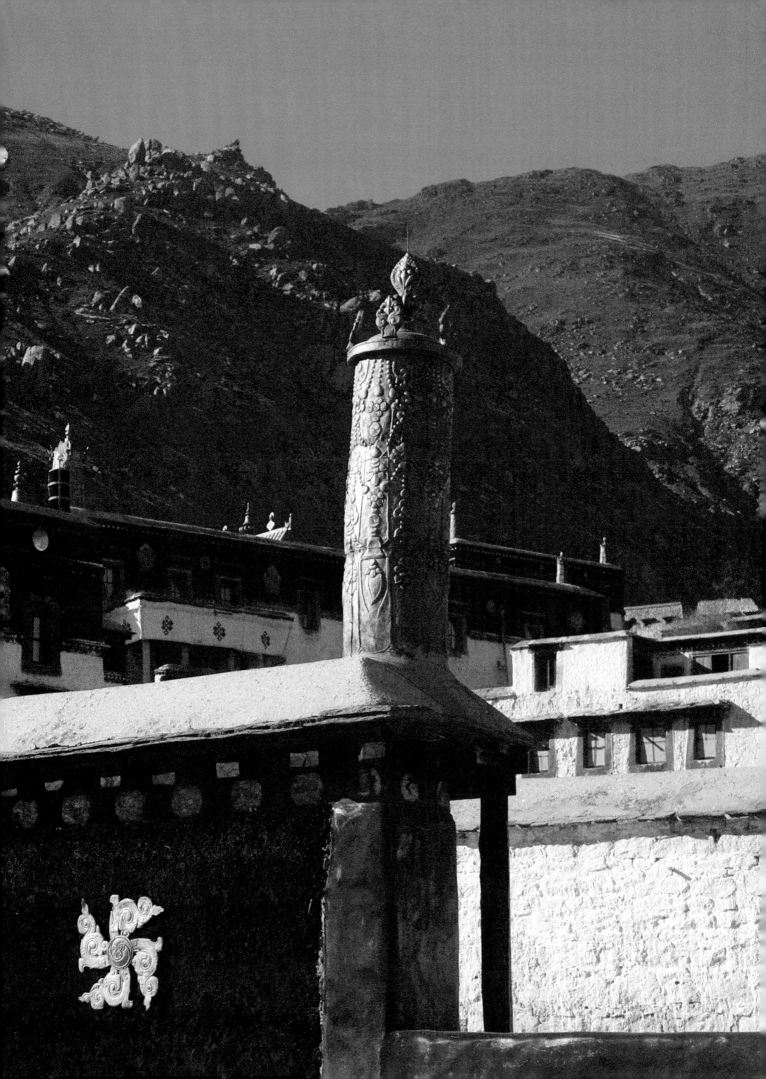

After the death of Srong-btsan Sgam-po, the two succeeding kings, Mang-srong Mang-btsan (650-676) and Khri-vdus-srong Mang-po-rje, who reigned from 676 to 704, were busily engaged in quelling rebellions and in wars of conquest. As a result, the spread of Buddhism in Tibet was arrested. In the early 8th century, Khri-lte Gtsug-btsan (704-755) came to the throne. During his reign, new monasteries were built, more Buddhist texts were translated, and foreign Buddhist monks were brought into Tibet. However, the Bon ministerial chiefs, taking advantage of an outbreak of small-pox, attributed it to the "gods' wrath at foreign monks". They expelled the Buddhist monks and closed the temples and monasteries, thus causing great damage to Buddhism in Tibet. The struggle between the two opposing factions lasted well over 100 years with many ups and downs for both sides. However, the pro-Buddhist force with the kings behind it, kept growing stronger and Esoteric Buddhism gradually became even more firmly established in Tibet.

In 755 the young Khri-srong Lde-btsan (742-797) succeeded to the throne and became the fifth king of the Bod Dynasty. When he had grown up and gained enough political power, he decided to crack down on the Bon nobles. With the support of his Buddhist ministers, he got rid of influential Bon-pos, declared that Buddhism was to be the compulsory religious faith for all his subjects. He sent special envoys to Nepal to bring into Tibet Santaraksita, the well-known Indian master of Exoteric Buddhism.

At Bsam-yes, Tibet, the king met with Santaraksita, who instructed him in Buddhist doctrines. What the king did triggered off a new wave of opposition from the Bon-pos. They took advantage of the natural disasters caused by light-ning strikes, floods and the outbreak of pestilence, and launched an even more violent attack on Buddhism. The great master Santaraksita, unable to repel the onslaught, returned to Nepal. Before his departure, however, he offered to send into Tibet Padmasambhava, the great Indian master, who, with the powers of Esoteric Buddhism, would be able to subdue the Bon-poist "demons".

Soon Padmasambhava arrived in Tibet. Armed with the doctrine and pro-found knowledge of Esoteric Buddhism, he launched a campaign against Bon-po. He explained to the people that natural disasters like lightning strikes and floods were the whims of the mountain gods and they had nothing to do with Buddhism. He ensured everybody that he could vanquish these gods responsible for the disasters. Every time he outraged a Bon sorcerer and subsequently defeated him, he would immediately proclaim the sub-jugation of a Bon deity. With the aim of extending the influence of Buddhism, he then announced that the vanquished Bon deity had been conferred the Buddhist title dharmapāla (defender of Buddhism).

Though a preacher of Exoteric Buddhism, Santaraksita was not able to do anything about the struggle between the two faiths. The king realized, however, that Esoteric Buddhism alone was not powerful enough, if Buddhism was to make any further progress in Tibet. So Santaraksita was brought into Tibet for the second time. He joined Padmasamb-hava in helping the king to spread Buddhism in Tibet. In 766, the Samye Monastery, the first proper Tibetan monastery, was built with Padmasamb-hava acting as the supervisor of the project and Santaraksita as its architect.

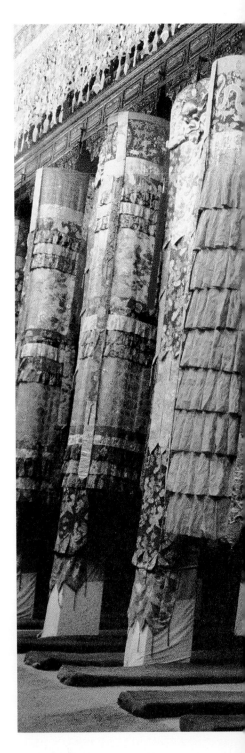

5. The Rtsho-chen Hall in the Drepung Monastery is big enough for an assembly of more than 7,000 lamas. In the hall are hung many works of exquisite embroidery and lavishly painted ornaments.

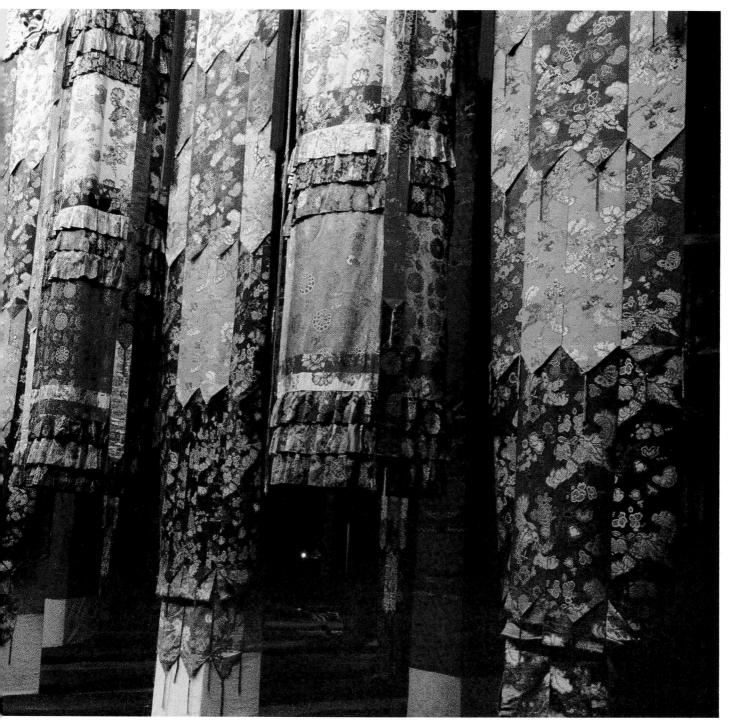

5

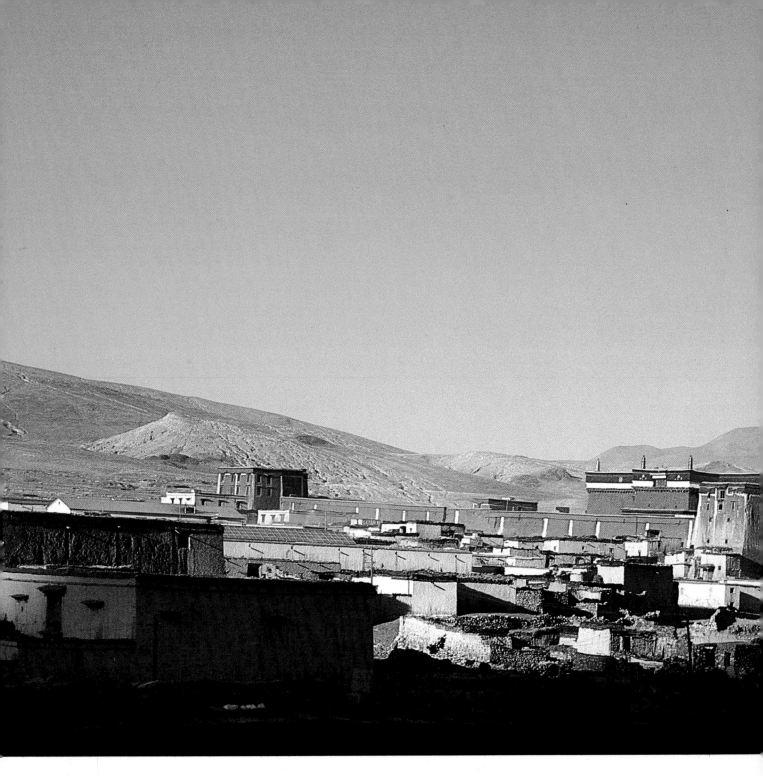

Three events which took place following the construction of the Samye Monastery were of great significance to the development of Tibetan Buddhism. The first was the ordination by Santaraksita of seven young monks from aristocratic families. Known as "the Seven Sadmis" or "the Seven Awakened", they were the first Tibetan monks ever ordained. The second event was the translation of the Exoteric and Esoteric Buddhist texts into the Tibetan language. They include *The Esoteric Essentials of Vajradhātu-maṇḍala and Others, The*

Guhyasamāja, Mahāmāyā and Caryātantra's Eight Kinds of Scriptures and Treaties and *The Essence of Guhyasamājatantra.* Copies of these texts in both Tibetan and the Sanskrit original, which are extremely rare, are well preserved in Tibet today. The third was the introduction of the practices of Esoteric Buddhism.

Padmasambhava carried the Indian secret doctrine of Vajrayāna with him whenever he preached Buddhism in different places in Tibet at a time when the Anuttara Yoga Tantra, a doctrine popular in India, had been brought into

the kingdom. According to legend, Padmasambhava had five women as companions for meditation – a practice called yab-yum (union of the two polarities). These women companions were: Mandārava, daughter of the Indian king, Knlasiddhi and Shakyadevi from Nepal, a Tibetan woman by the name of Bkra-shis Khye-dren, and Khri-srong Lde-btsan's queen Ye-shes Tsho-rgyal. They were called Mahāmāyā or devī or lokadākinī. Esoteric Buddhism believes that yab-yum will eventually change the female companions from being "earthly women"

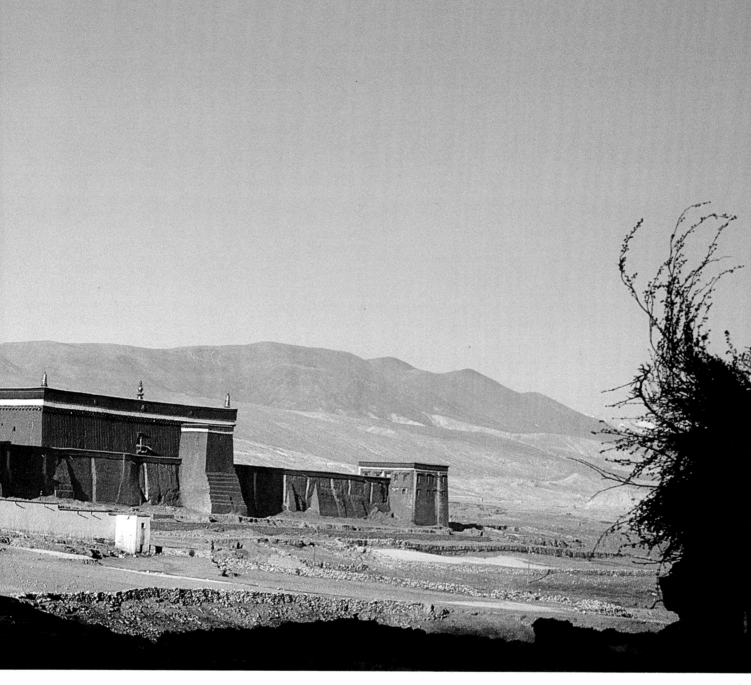

into revered "female deities". Once again, the Bon-pos lashed out, this time at yab-yum, but the king ignored them. He continued to send Tibetan monks to India to study the doctrine of Vajrayāna and he made himself always available for the ceremonies of welcoming their return from India.

During the span of more than a century beginning with Srong-btsan Sgam-po in the early 7th century to Khri-srong Lde-btsan in the 8th century, Tibetan Buddhism emerged in its initial form: a Buddhist faith based on the Exoteric theory with the ultimate aim of "achieving Buddhahood" through Esoteric practices which were based on the combined study of the two doctrines. Thus the foundation was laid for the future development of Buddhism in Tibet. However, the struggle between Bon-po and Buddhism was not yet over.

After the death of Khri-srong Lde-btsan, his son Mu-ne btsan-po became the sovereign. He reigned for only one year (797-798). From 798 to 815, Khri-lde Srong-btsan was on the throne. During the 18 years of their reigns the dispute between the royal family and the ministerial chiefs over Tibet's external policy never ceased. The royal family sought alliance with the Tang empire in order to consolidate its position while the chiefs were in favour of war with Tang for they thought they could wrestle material gains.

6. The Sagya Monastery in Sagya County. Built in the 11th century, it is the principal monastery of the Sa-gya-pa Sect. It is here that Hphags-pa, commissioned by Emperor Shi Zu of the Yuan Dynasty, formulated the new Mongolian language.

With the aim of strengthening their rule, the kings refuted the opposing chiefs with Buddhist anti-war teachings. It was against this background that we should see today why the royalty became enthusiastic sponsors of Buddhism.

From 815 to 835 Ral-pa-can was the Tibetan sovereign. Like the kings before him, he tried hard to promote Buddhism for he himself was a fervent follower of the religion. The Bon-poist nobles, in a conspiracy to isolate him, managed to strip him of all his loyal aides who believed in Buddhism. This done, they intoxicated him with spirits and murdered him, and in 838 put Dar-ma on the throne.

During Dar-ma's five-year reign Buddhism met its tragic fate. Buddhist images were buried, its canonical texts were burned, monks were ordered to break their vows and Buddhist masters fled. Many of the monks who refused to follow the orders were slaughtered. Temples and monasteries were closed and destroyed without warrant and were even reduced to cow-sheds. The frescos in the monasteries were either defaced or replaced with paintings showing monks indulged in boisterous drinking bouts. The attack was so violent and swift that the Buddhist monks were caught totally unprepared. The wave of persecution eventually subsided. Then a monk managed to sneak into Lhasa and assassinate Dar-ma. For over a hundred years afterwards Buddhism made no progress in Tibet. The crack-down had dealt a most severe blow to Exoteric Buddhism. However, Esoteric Buddhism survived, only because its staunch followers maintained their faith and observed its practices in secrecy. The period from Srong-btsan Sgam-po's propagation of Buddhism to Dar-ma's attempt to destroy the religion is referred to by scholars as the Pre-Propagation Period in the history of Tibetan Buddhism.

After the assassination of Dar-ma, the royal family split. When the Tibetan slaves rose in rebellion, the Bod Dynasty, founded on the slave system, collapsed, and Tibet was divided between rivalling clans. By 978, feudalism had emerged in Tibet, and the zeal for Buddhism was revived by the feudal lords. As the activities of the revivalists were increased and enthusiasm grew, many sects came into being such as Rnying-ma-pa, Bkah-gdams-pa, Sa-gya-pa, Bkah-brgyud-pa, Zhi-byed-pa, Gead-yul-pa, Jo-nang-pa and the most influential, Dge-lugs-pa. This period, from the destruction of Buddhism by Dar-ma to the renaissance of the religion with the subsequent emergence of its sects, is called by scholars of Tibetan history the Post-Propagation Period. During this period Buddhism returned to Tibet along two major routes: the upper route (Ngari) and the lower route (Mdo-khams); and the works of renowned translators gave a great impetus to the spread of the Esoteric doctrine. These translators were:

Rin-chen Bzang-po (958-1055), who was ordained at the age of 13 and went abroad three times to India and Nepal to study. He was a zealous propagator of the Exoteric doctrine of the Prajñā, and made much contribution to the spread of Esoteric Buddhism. He had many disciples and was a prolific translator. The translation of the yoga texts of Exoteric Buddhism was his major achievement.

Vbro-mi (994-1078), leading preacher in Tibet of the Lam-hbras (the result of the Buddha Way), an Indian Buddhist doctrine. He studied phonology in Nepal and Esoteric doctrines in India. He translated many Esoteric texts and founded the Myu-ku-lung Monastery. Many of his disciples were renowned Buddhist monks, among whom was Hkhom-dkon mchog-rgyal-po (1034-1102), founder of the Sa-gya-pa Sect.

7.   A courtyard in the Sagya Monastery.

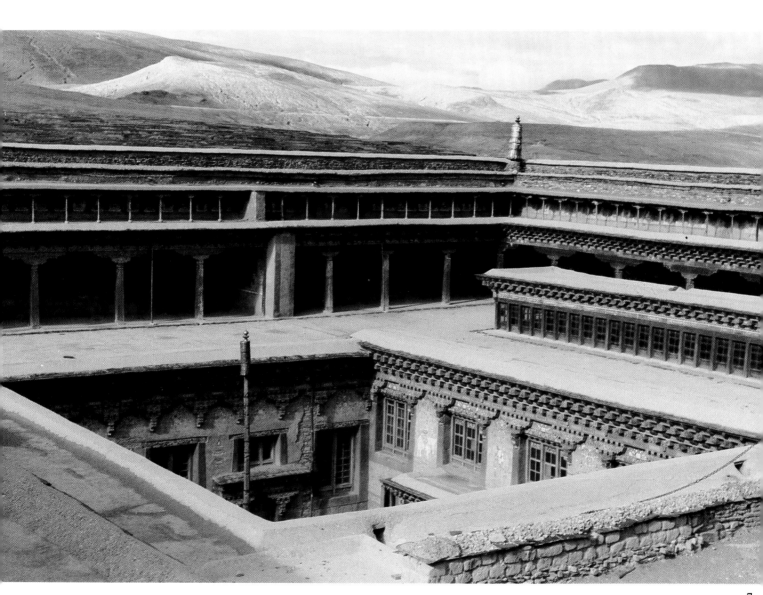

Mar-pa (1012-1097), who began to learn phonology from Vbro-mi at the age of 15. Later, he went to India three times and Nepal four times to study various Esoteric doctrines. When he returned to Tibet, he devoted himself to the translation of Buddhist texts and the teaching of his disciples. He was the founder of the Bkah-brgyud-pa Sect.

Atiśa (982-1054), born near what is now Dacca in Bangladesh, and ordained at the age of 29. He arrived in Tibet in 1042 and spent many years there as a Buddhist preacher. He devoted most of his work to the improvement of the monastic study system of Exoteric and Esoteric Buddhism, and of the relationship between the two doctrines. He was the author of the *Bodhimargapradipa,* which summarizes the essential beliefs of Exoteric and Esoteric Buddhism and he interpreted the meditative practices as a means of achieving bliss and wisdom. He regarded Anuttara Yoga Tantra as an important part of the "complete practice" and the most advanced stage of study. Being an extremely prudent teacher of the Esoteric doctrine, he transmitted its teachings to only one disciple of his — Vbrom-ston-pa` (1004-1064), who was to become the founder of the Bkah-gdams-pa Sect, a sect that influenced all other sects of Tibetan Buddhism, and provided the doctrinal basis for the Dge-lugs-pa Sect (Yellow Sect). That is why the Dge-lugs-pa Sect is also called the Neo-Bkah-gdams-pa Sect.

Tsong-kha-pa (1357-1419), formerly named Blo-bzang grags-pa, was the founder of the Dge-lugs-pa Sect. Ordained at the age of seven at the Qaqiong Monastery near Xining, his birth-place, he spent nine years at the monastery to study Buddhist texts. He went to Tibet at the age of 17 and studied all aspects of the Exoteric and Esoteric doctrines of all Buddhist orders in Tibet, practised them systematically and made remarkable achievements. A religious figure active in public life, he knew many people in the Buddhist community and often obliged others with sermons. His talent in writing, extensive knowledge and eloquence of speech won him great respect. On the basis of the *Bodhimargapradipa* by Atisa, he wrote the *Byan-chub lam-gyi rim-pa chenpo* and *Gsan-snags lam-rim,* thus laying the theoretic foundation of the Dge-lugs-pa Sect. He approached Esoteric Buddhism in his own way, paying particular attention to the explanation of Esoteric canonical texts rather than the practice of one single doctrine. In his approach, he emphasized that a systematic study of Esoteric Buddhism was possible only when one had become steeped in Exoteric Buddhism. The Esoteric doctrines of the Dge-lugs-pa Sect developed by Tsong-kha-pa were inherited by the two major orders of Lamaism, namely the Dalai and the Bainqen, and have been passed on to followers down to the present day. Because of the prominent position the Yellow Sect holds in Tibetan political and religious life, its Exoteric and Esoteric doctrines have stronger influence on Tibetan society than any other sect.

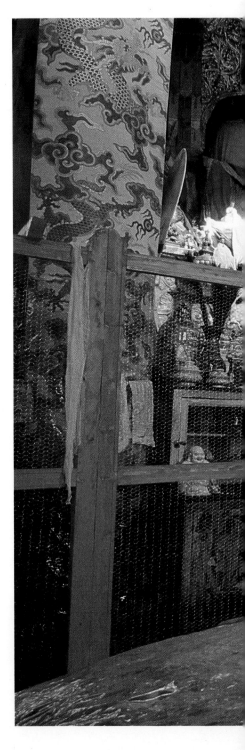

8. The Buddha Hall in the Sagya Monastery. The huge copper lamp in front of the shrine is among the treasures of the monastery.

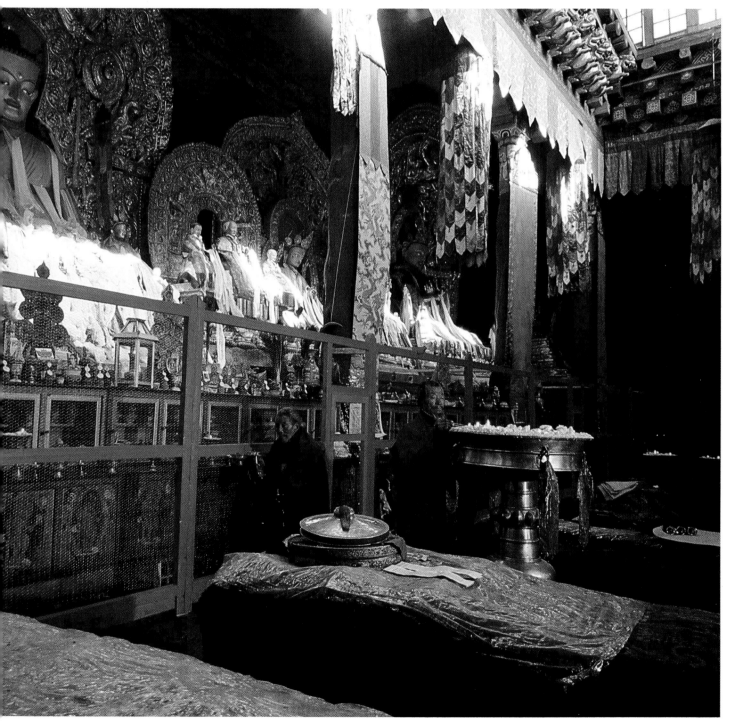

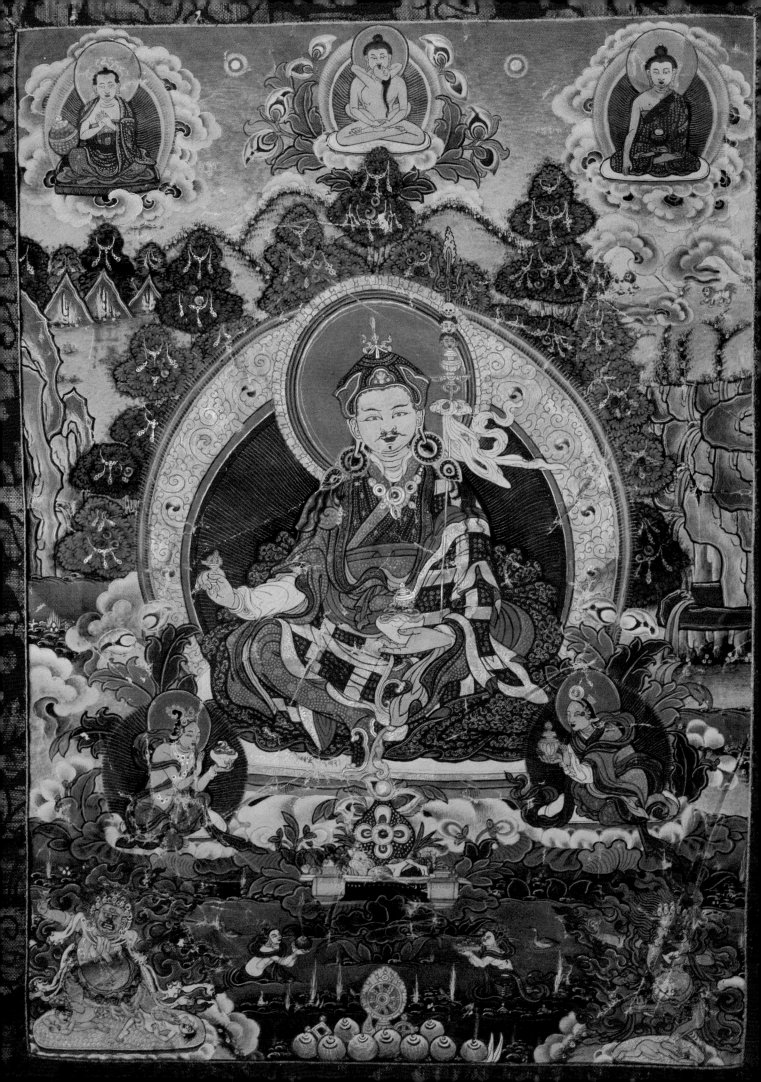

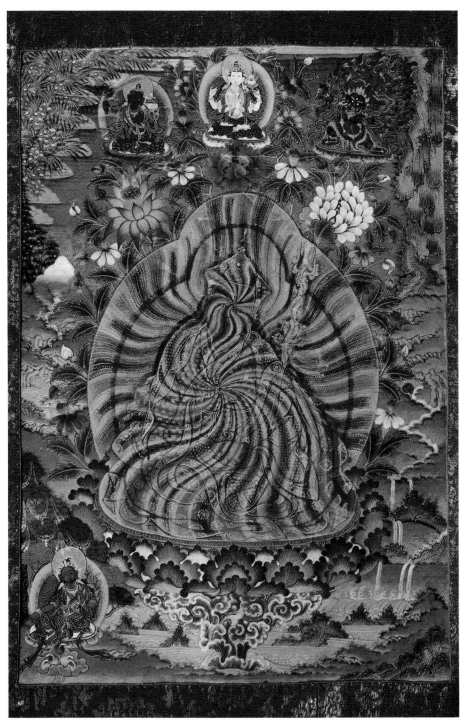

9. A portrait of Padmasambhava in the Sagya Monastery. The great tantric master arrived in Tibet in the 8th century, and was the principal figure in the defeat of Bon-po sorcerers. He contributed a great deal to the spread of the Esoteric doctrine.

10. Padmasambhava reveals himself in the form of a rainbow. According to Esoteric meditators, when they tried to recall the image of Padmasambhava during meditation, they would sometimes see in their imagination the master turning into a rainbow. In the Sagya Monastery.

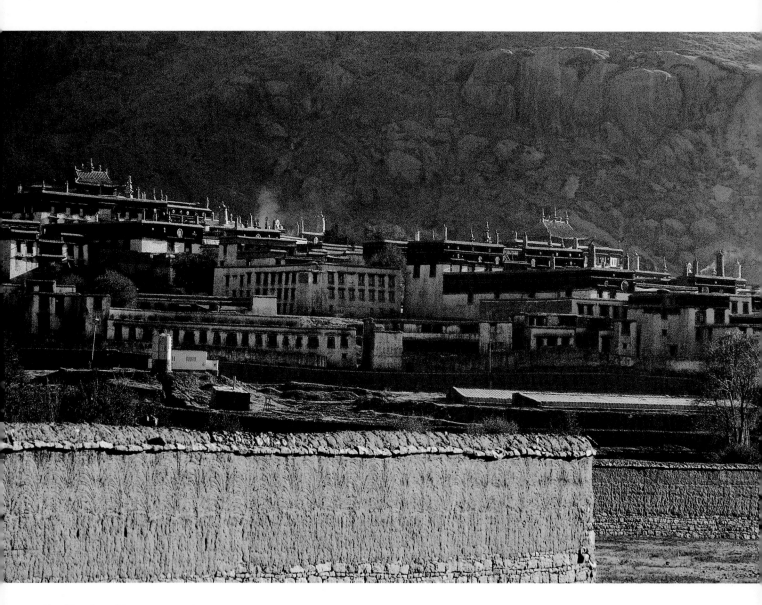

11. The Sera Monastery at the foot of a mountain 5 km. north of Lhasa. The construction of the monastery began in 1419.

THE CANONICAL TEXTS AND DOCTRINES
OF TIBETAN ESOTERIC BUDDHISM

THE CANONICAL TEXTS AND DOCTRINES OF TIBETAN ESOTERIC BUDDHISM

The many and varied canonical texts of Tibetan Esoteric Buddhism are included in the Tibetan language version of *The Tripitaka (The Collected Works of Buddhist Literature)*. Those of the Esoteric texts are included in the 7th category in the *Bkah-hgyur (Quotations from the Buddha)*. The *Bkah-hgyur* consists of 1,108 titles of books on discipline, Prajñā, Avataṁsa, Ratna-yasi, Sūtrasaingiti, Nirvāna, and Guhyayanā. The texts of the exegeser of tantras are to be found in the *Bstan-hgyur (Exposition)*. Collected in the *Bstan-hgyur* are 3,461 titles of books including the exposition and explanatory notes of Buddhist canons, ceremonies of the Esoteric school and miscellaneous writings of Pañcavidyā (five subjects for learning). This collection is divided into four major parts, namely eulogies, explanations of incantations, explanations of canonical texts and catalogues. Both the *Bkah-hgyur* and the *Bstan-hgyur* were compiled in the latter half of the 14th century.

In addition to the two collections, there is an encyclopedia of Esoteric doctrines: *Collections of the Important Methods of Esoteric Mahāyāna*. The encyclopedia — the number of volumes is not certain — deals with roughly three topics: 1. explanation of the quotations from the lam-hbras, which is the essential text for the doctrine of the Sa-gya-pa Sect; 2. the meditation exercises of the dhāranī maṇdala; 3. the upadesás of mahāmudrā (the path of the great seal). Through mahāmudrā, one of the practices of the Bkah-brgyud-pa Sect involving a series of breathing and body exercises the meditator will achieve Buddhahood in the present body after he has been thoroughly cleansed of all troubles and spiritual obstacles.

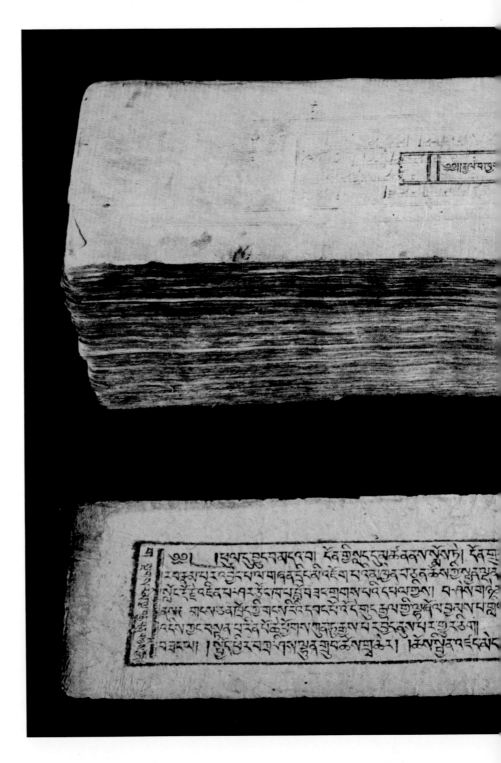

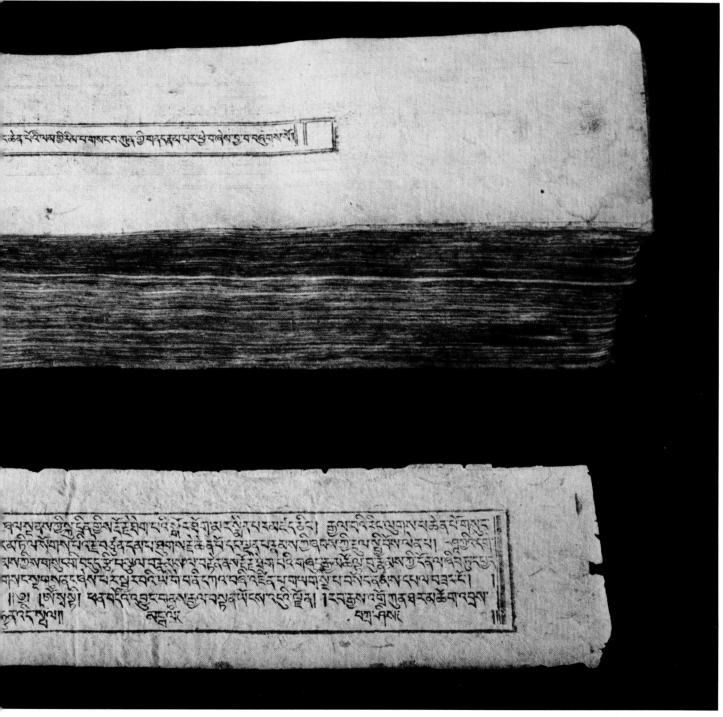

12. Tsong-kha-pa, founder of the Dge-lugs-pa Sect, wrote *Gsansnags lam-rim (A Complete Course of the Order of Tantric Buddhism)* in the 14th century. The picture shows a part of the book in woodblock print. In the Sagya Monastery.

12

The doctrine of Tibetan Esoteric Buddhism is based on the *Mahāvairocana-sūtra, Vajrasekhara-sūtra,* and *Kālacakraindriya-sūtra.* Its theory may be summarized as follows: "taking the six elements as essence", "five Buddhas and five wisdoms", "taking the four maṇḍalas as appearance", "taking the three secrets as means", " cause, base, final means" and "anger and fear".

"Taking the six elements as essence" is the Esoteric interpretation of the origin of the cosmos. According to Esoteric Buddhism, the six elements, the earth, water, fire, wind, air and ether (consciousness), make up the dharmakāya (cosmic body) of the Mahāvairocana. They provide the nature of all creation and are at once the source and foundation of the existance of all phenomena. As they are possessed by all beings in the universe, they exist in the minds of the laity. This is something that the Buddha shares with the laymen. However, according to Esoteric Buddhism, the laity are incapable of recognizing the nature of cosmic beings, "unless they are aided by the supreme benevolent power of the Tathāgata", which means that the practice of "the three secrets" is a necessity if one wishes to purify one's mind and recognize the nature of all cosmic beings.

"The three secrets" are: body secret, speech secret and mind secret. The follower must conform his body, speech and mind to those of the Buddha. "Taking the three secrets as means" refers to a form of meditation during which the meditator, with specified gestures and in specified sitting posture, recites the true teaching of the Satyadevatā or yidam (the most honoured of all Buddhas) while concentrating on evoking the deity's image before his inward eye. For the follower, it is not enough to do no evil, for he must impress the image of the Satyadevatā deeply in his mind. It is not enough not to use any coarse and foul language, for he must recite the deity's true teaching; it is not enough to entertain no wicked ideas, for he must never forget the vows and wishes of the Satyadevatā. By doing so, he will eventually be "purified", achieve "the perfect body of the Buddha", and "reach Buddhahood in the present body".

"The four maṇḍalas" refers to the different types of maṇḍala. The maṇḍala in Sanskrit (Tibetan: dkyil-vkhor) means "rostrum" or "rostrum ground". In ancient India, the maṇḍala was a round or square mud platform at a meditation site erected to ward off "demons" during meditation sessions of Esoteric Buddhists. When a king ascended to the throne, or when a monk was ordained, the ceremony would take place on a maṇḍala. To these ceremonies, all the deities representing the past, present and future from all the cosmic compass points (east, west, south, north, northeast, northwest, southeast and southwest from high above and down below) would be invited as witnesses to these occasions, and on the platform their images would be drawn. Later on, different types of maṇḍala were developed, of which the following four are the most common;

1. The Great Maṇḍala, at which the images of the deities from their respective areas are drawn in green, yellow, red, white and black to represent "the earth, water, fire, wind and air".

2. The Samādhi Maṇḍala at which the presence of the deities is shown not by the drawings of their images, but by those of the pearls, swords or wheels they carry so that the meditators may associate these objects with the images of the deities and practise visionary meditation.

3. The Dharma Maṇḍala, at which the deities are not represented by the drawings of their images or those of the objects they carry, for it is believed that the sight of the initial syllables in Sanskrit of their titles will invoke their images in the meditators.

4. The Karma Maṇḍala, where carved, sculptured or cast figures of the deities are set up to impress the meditators with the vivid, life-like sight of these deities.

The maṇḍala is the manifestation of the Mahāvairocana and the occasion on which he spreads his teachings to earthly beings so that worshippers of maṇḍalas, with the aid of the Tathāgata, will be able to "dispel the clouds of troubles and spiritual obstacles". As this spiritual communication with the deities can be done only by means of the four maṇḍalas and by reciting their true teachings, the practice is described as "taking the four maṇḍalas as appearance".

"Five Buddhas and five wisdoms" is one of the major doctrines of Tibetan Esoteric Buddhism. According to this doctrine, one will not "reach Buddhahood in the present body" just by reciting the true teachings and practising the mandala. He needs the five wisdoms of the Five Dhyāni-Buddhas (Vairocana, Aksobhya, Ratnasambhava, Amitābha and Amoghavajra), namely the wisdom of the universal law, the wisdom of the mirror, the wisdom of equality, the wisdom of the distinction and discernment, and the wisdom of accomplishing works. When a person has acquired the five wisdoms, he will be able to achieve Buddhahood without abstaining from meat, wine or sex. However, these wisdoms cannot be obtained unless they are passed on by the guru himself. The concept represented by "the five wisdoms" is a spiritual requirement, essential to anyone seeking Buddhahood. It is a concept which promises mystical transforming power.

13. The Satyadevatā of Tibetan Esoteric Buddhism in the Sera Monastery. This strange-looking deity is awe-inspiring and mystical.

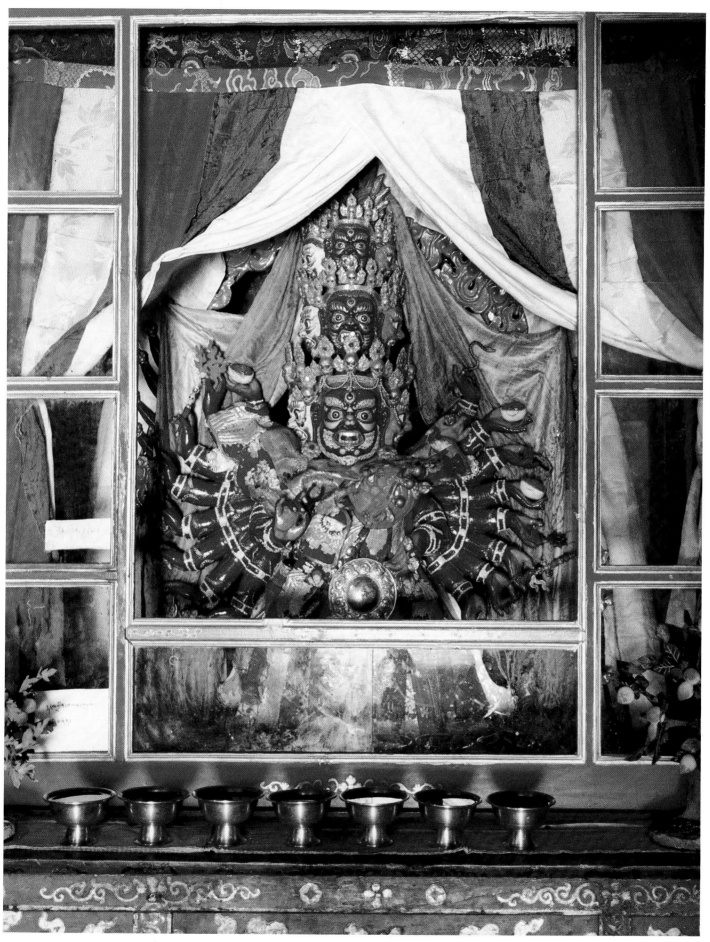

The "cause, base and final means" is the condensed version of the three lines in the *Mahāvairocana-sūtra:*

The mind of bodhi is the cause.

The great compassion is the base.

The upāya (path, method) is the final means.

The first line means that followers of the Esoteric doctrine must first achieve the mind of bodhi. Such mind will grow like a seed and eventually lead one to Buddhahood. Without this mind, no one can hope to be accepted by the Buddha, and therefore is not qualified for the practice of the Esoteric doctrine. The second line means that the follower must also be a person of great compassion. This compassion will enable him to liberate all beings by encouraging them to practise virtuous deeds in much the same way as the root and trunk of a tree give the tree its leaves, blossoms and fruit; hence the term "the base". The third line means the path a follower takes and the flexibility he is given. "The final means" may be interpreted as "thoroughness" and "the end", representing the objective, while "upāya" can be taken to mean "flexibility" and "ingenuity" in pursuing the final means. In other words, the follower in his pursuit of Buddhahood, may, when condition warrants it, be excused from the observance of some rules of Buddhist discipline. For example, Buddhism forbids sex, but followers of Esoteric Buddhism may have female companions for meditation.

The practice of having female companions for meditation is called "the union of voidness and happiness" or the union of the two polarities. This practice, based on the theory of the *Mahāvairocana-sūtra* and the *Vajrasekhara-sūtra*, is a distinctive feature of Esoteric Buddhism. Sex is strictly forbidden by Exoteric Buddhism, but it is part of the meditation practice in Esoteric Buddhism. As the *Vajrasekhara-sūtra* says, "How pure is man's nature! It's only natural that lust should change him. Keeping away from lust will restore purity in him, and keeping away from lust means conquering it with another form of lust." Sex is thus shrouded in mysticism and given the role of "conquering lust". It becomes a means by which the follower of Esoteric Buddhism can achieve the self-purification of his own nature. According to Esoteric Buddhism, "the attraction of lust will draw one into the realm of the wisdom of the Buddha," that is, by means of carnal love the Bodhisattva leads one to liberation. This accounts for the fact that Esoteric Buddhism treats women as offerings. What *The Collected Works of Buddhis Literature* terms as "love for offerings" refers to the offering of women. This theme is repeated in the *Mahāvairocana-sūtra,* which says, "Satisfy the desire for sex so that all beings will be happy." According to Esoteric Buddhism, the Mahāvairocana lives in Heaven like an earthly being — accompanied by the Marīci (Queen of Heaven) and surrounded by female attendants. As a result, the rājas (devas and vajras), instructed by the Mahāvairocana to subdue demons, are in their "wrathful forms" accompanied by devīs, their female counterparts.

Esoteric Buddhism preaches the idea of "taking upāya (compassion) as father and prajñā (wisdom) as mother" and takes the union of the rājas and the devīs

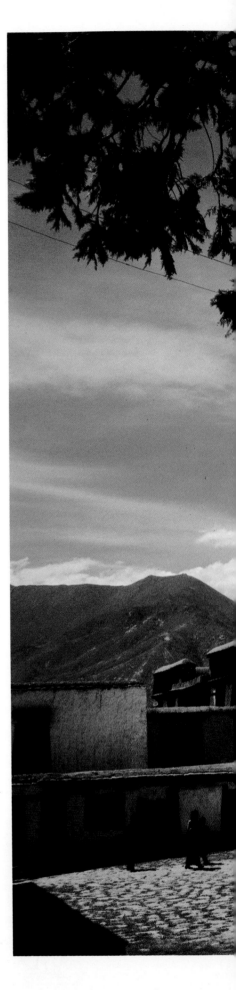

14. The grva-tshan is an institution for monastic study. The picture shows the "Tantra Apartment" in the Sera Monastery — the Mansion of the Snags-pa (Mantra) Department.

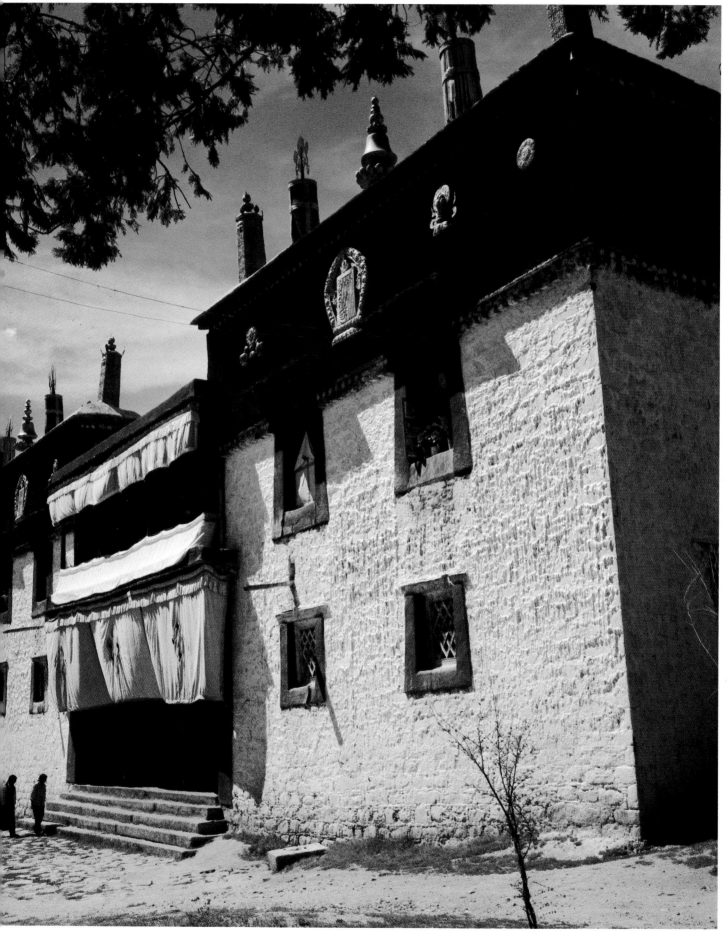

in each other's embrace as the symbol of "the union of compassion and wisdom". Therefore, to a follower of Esoteric Buddhism, his spiritual teacher is his father, and the teacher's female companion his mother (ḍākinī), and the great union of happiness of man and woman is the path which will lead to the "acquisition of supernatural powers (siddhi)". This explains why the yab-yum is also called "the path of women". The yab-yum, together with its practice that the teaching of the disciple by his teacher is done only privately, has produced a symbolic and arcane language used during meditation. For example, the phallus is called "vajra", the vulva becomes "the lotus flower" (padma), and copulation is described as "entering into the realm of samaya".

Yab-yum and the concept of great happiness originated in Saktism (Shaktism). According to this sect, all cosmic beings were created by the sexuality of goddesses. Copulation, therefore, was regarded as a form of worship of the goddesses and an expression of reverence for them. These notions were borrowed by Esoteric Buddhism and, combined with Buddhist doctrines, produced the theory of "the union of voidness and happiness".

In addition to Queen of Heaven and the devīs, among the deities revered by Esoteric Buddhists are, the Rdo-rje gro-lod (the Wrathful Guardian Deity) and the Bhairava Vajra (the Fearful Guardian Deity), who are the two deities repre-senting the doctrine of "wrath" and "fear". Rdo-rje gro-lod and Bhairava Vajra are names for all wrathful and fearful-looking vajras. According to tradition, the Buddha may appear in two forms: sometimes in his real form of Kindness and at other times in his wrathful manifestation. The Mahābhairava Vajra, the principal deity of the Dge-lugs-pa Sect, for example, is the wrathful manifestation of the Amitāyus. The Mahābhairava Vajra, whose duty is to subdue flaming demons, has six faces, six arms, six feet and three eyes. He holds in his hands various kinds of sceptres. He rides a green water-buffalo, wears a helmet studded with human skulls, and has a tiger's skin for a kilt. With flames emitting from his body, he looks extremely wrathful and fear-striking. This fearful look is intended to demonstrate to all beings that to deliver themselves from avidyā (ignorance) they must break down all spiritual barriers with the power of wisdom, and overwhelm demons with all the power they possess. In Buddhist terms, all spiritual and material obstacles to Buddhahood are demons which must be tamed, resisted or brought under control with one's innate strength.

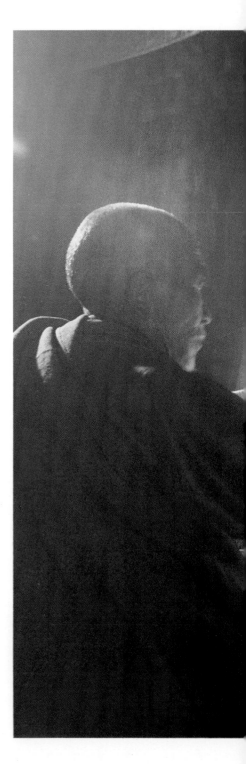

15. Student monks are required to worship the Buddha in total devotion in the Buddha Hall of the grva-tshan. The picture shows the Hall of the Mahābhairava Vajra in the grva-tshan in the Drepung Monastery.

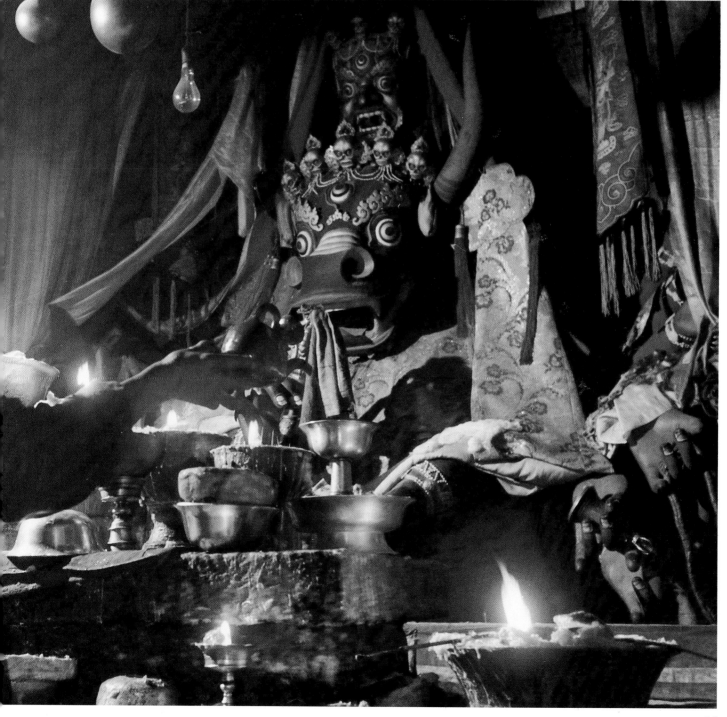

15

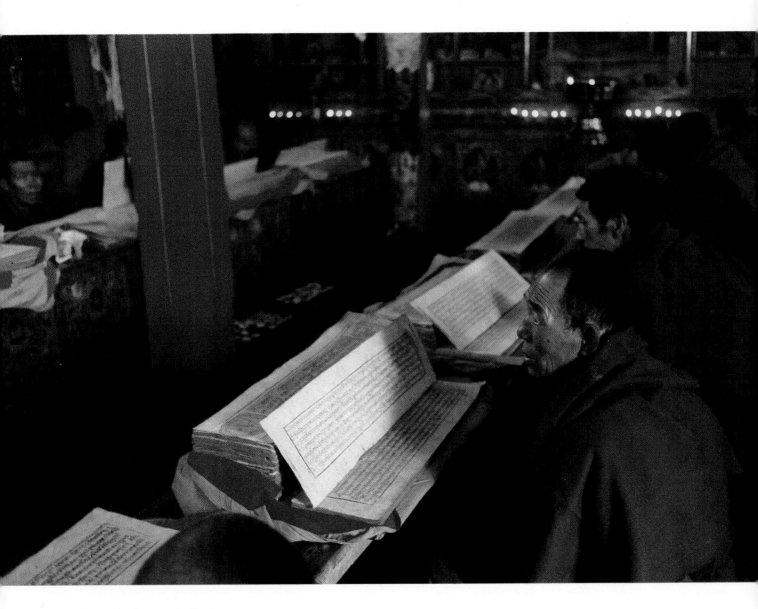

16. Monks praying in concentration.

THE ORGANIZATION,
SYSTEM AND GRADATION
OF THE MONASTIC STUDY OF
TIBETAN ESOTERIC BUDDHISM

THE ORGANIZATION, SYSTEM AND GRADATION OF THE MONASTIC STUDY OF TIBETAN ESOTERIC BUDDHISM

All the sects of Tibetan Buddhism follow roughly the same pattern in the study of Esoteric Buddhism. Therefore, a brief account of the system followed by the Dge-lugs-pa Sect will suffice.

As already mentioned, the approach adopted by the Dge-lugs-pa Sect combines the two doctrines: Exoteric Buddhism is to be studied first and Esoteric Buddhism is regarded as advanced study. Monks who wish to go through the entire course of study are sent, upon their arrival at the monasteries, to the preparatory class in the grva-tshan (school) of Exoteric Buddhism. There, they study the elementary knowledge of Buddhism under specially hired tutors. As the preparatory class has no fixed length of time for study, and no tests are demanded by the monastic authorities, the disciples move up to the regular class only as on the recommendation of their tutors. The regular class consists of a number of grades; no disciple is allowed to enter the highest grade unless he has finished the study of all the required Buddhist scriptures. Upon graduation from the regular class, the disciple, with the recommendation of his tutor and the approval of the monastic authorities granted him upon his application, will be allowed to take the qualifying examinations for the degree of Dge-bces. Dge-bces, meaning "refined knowledge", offers four grades: Lha-rams-pa, Tshogs-rams-pa, Rdo-rams-pa and Rigs-rams-pa. The qualifying examinations for the first two are administered by the Tibetan local government. Those who have passed them are regarded as the top disciples. The examinations for the next two grades are handled by monasteries or grva-tshans and are less demanding than those for the first two. The candidates who have passed the Dge-bces examination will be given the

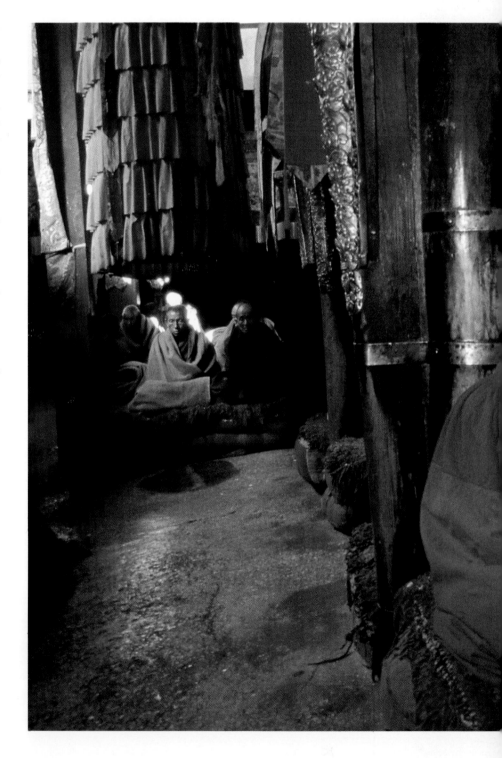

17

17. Attending sermons and praying, and cultivating total devotion to the Buddha is among the basic practices of monks.

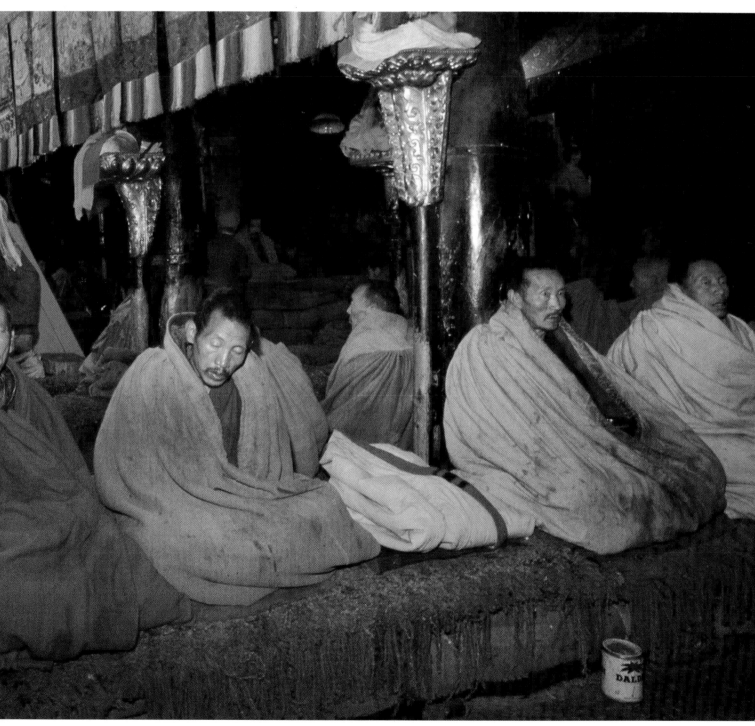

honour of riding through the streets on horseback, wearing red ribbons and flowers and they will be greatly admired by the public.

The degree Dge-bces is an indication that the candidate has completed the study of Exoteric Buddhism. Monks with this degree may then enter the Tantra Apartments in the Dgah-ldan Monastery for specialized study. There are two such apartments, one located in the west, the other in the east. As Tibetans regard the west as the upper position and the east the lower position, the two apartments are thus called the Upper Tantra Apartment (Tibetan: rgyud-stot grva-tshan) and the Lower Tantra Apartment (Tibetan: rgyud smad-grva-tshan). The two apartments are of equal importance in rank. The Tantra Apartments draw their students mainly from among the monks with the degree of Dge-bces. Monks who have finished the study of Exoteric

Buddhism but are without the degree or those who have never received any such training may be admitted, but only as irregulars.

The rules set by the apartments for study are extremely severe and they emphasize physical endurance on the part of the student monks. The day begins with the first study session at 2 o'clock in the morning, which is followed by three more such sessions before the end of the day. Winter or summer, the monks are required to sit bare-foot on pebble seats during meditation. The deities for meditation exercises include the Guhyasamāja Vajra, the Śambara Vajra, the Mahābhairava Vajra and a number of lesser vajras and dharmapālas. Monks with the Dge-bces degree may work their way up in the two apartments, but promotion can be a difficult process. The following chart shows this process:

A student monk of the Dge-lugs-pa

Sect who aspires to become a Buddha has to complete the entire course of study comprising doctrines of both Exoteric and Esoteric Buddhism. He will have to work his way from the Dge-bces up to the Dgah-ldam Khri-pa. Once he has achieved that, he is a Living Buddha and may even be given the opportunity to become a candidate for the position of an interim Dalai.

The study of Esoteric Buddhism lays much emphasis on ceremonies. A student monk begins by selecting a guru whose work is to initiate the monk into Esoteric beliefs. The initiation is repeated at the beginning of the introduction of each subsequent Esoteric theory. The ceremony is performed in the following manner: the guru bathes his disciple's head with water from a holy vessel, while his disciple drinks wine from a bowl made from a human skull, as instructed by the guru. This ceremony, as the guru tells his disciple, will cleanse him of all impurities from his heart. After this is done, serious teaching begins. Only after this ceremonial initiation is a monk allowed to begin the study of Esoteric Buddhism. The first stage in the course of study is what is known as "introductory by nature", which involves "the four practices". They are:

1. Total devotion to cittolpāda (aspiration to Buddhahood), namely devotion to Lamaism, to the Buddha, to the dharma (doctrine) and to monkhood. Of the four, devotion to Lamaism is the most important. The monk studying Esoteric Buddhism must regard his teacher as the Buddha, and the lama guru as an indispensable assistant in the pursuit of Buddhahood. As the Tibetan saying goes, "How can one approach the Buddha without a lama guru?"

2. The study of the prostration rituals.

3. The worship of maṇḍalas.

4. The recitation of the 100-Word Incantation of Vajrasattva or Bodhisattva Āpatti-pratideśanā.

A monk must finish repeating the

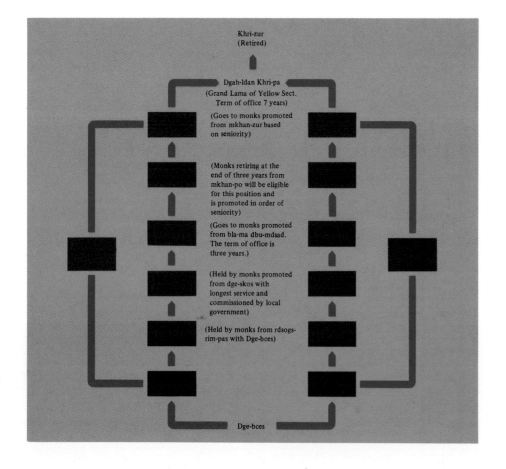

Khri-zur
(Retired)

Dgah-ldan Khri-pa
(Grand Lama of Yellow Sect. Term of office 7 years)

(Goes to monks promoted from mkhan-zur based on seniority)

(Monks retiring at the end of three years from mkhan-po will be eligible for this position and is promoted in order of seniority)

(Goes to monks promoted from bla-ma dbu-mdsad. The term of office is three years.)

(Held by monks promoted from dge-skos with longest service and commissioned by local government)

(Held by monks from rdsogs-rim-pas with Dge-bces)

Dge-bces

four practices 100,000 times before he can be qualified for the study of the dharma of the Satyadevatā. The monk regarded to be outstanding by the guru will have one of the five vajras of the *Anuttarayoga* selected for him as his Satyadevatā for concentrated study, but before this stage begins, the monk will have to be initiated again.

Monks studying the doctrines of their Satyadevatās are expected to follow two distinctly separate stages: the stage of utpattikrama and that of utpannakrama. Briefly, during the stage of utpattikrama, the meditator studies closely the image of the deity in order to engrave it on his mind so that he will eventually, by conditional reflex, be able to see his vision in his dream, and the illusion of meeting the deity is thus created. The utpannakrama represents the final and highest stage in the study of Esoteric Buddhism, Appropriately, the term means "completion" or "conclusion". During this stage the meditator practises first a series of breathing exercises designed to manipulate the pulse beat and breath, and then the yab-yum with the aim of achieving "a long life" and "Buddhahood in the present body".

It is extremely difficult for a Tibetan Buddhist monk to graduate from the study of Tibetan Esoteric Buddhism. Many monks have been known to drop out and, sadly, die in oblivion.

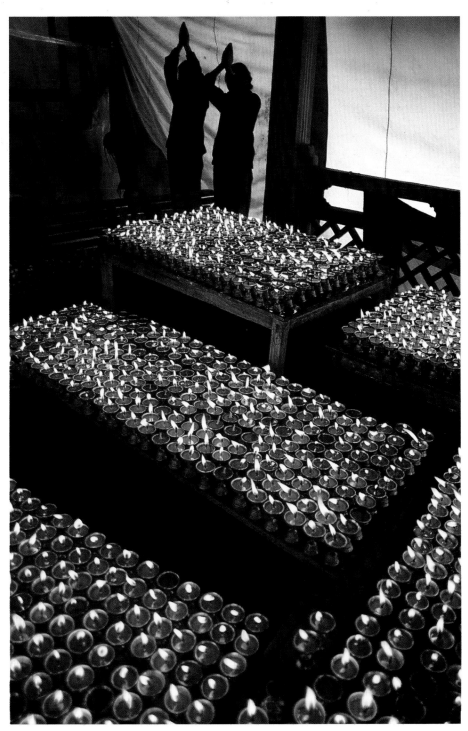

18.19.   Buddhist followers lighting the "one thousand lamps". Donating butter to the monasteries and lighting these lamps is an expression of devotion to the Buddha. Devotees of Buddhism believe that the more lamps they light the more pure their aspiration for Buddhahood becomes, and the more thoroughly they will be able to remove impurities from their hearts.

18

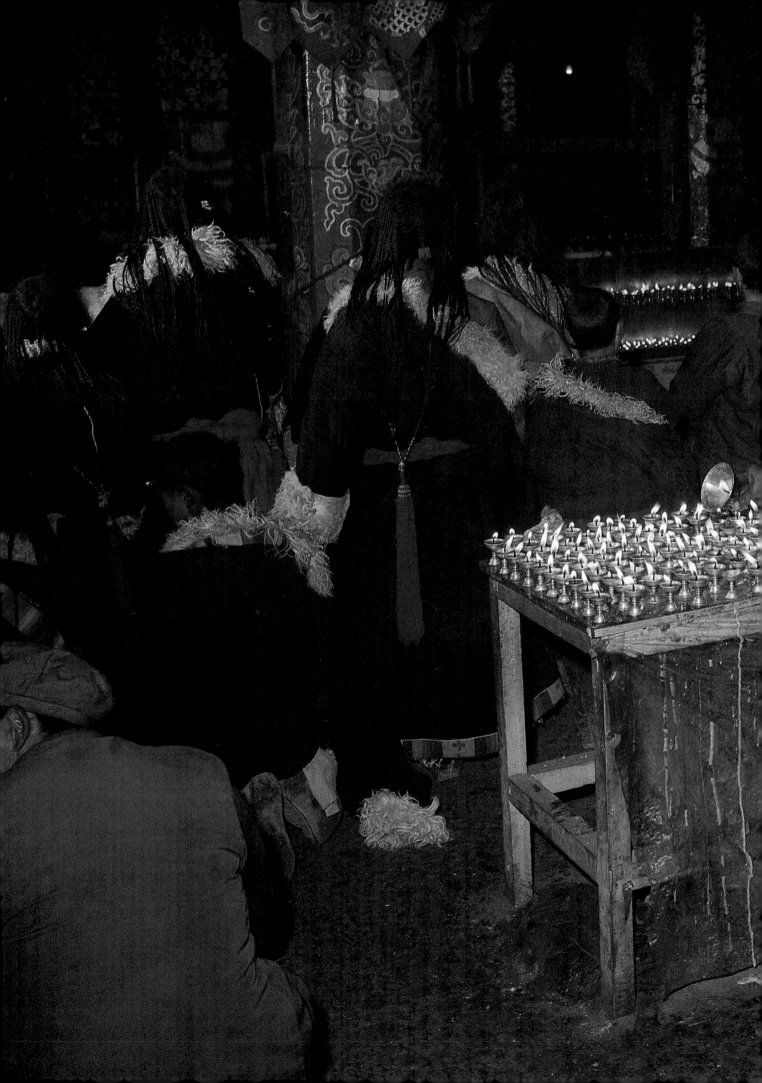

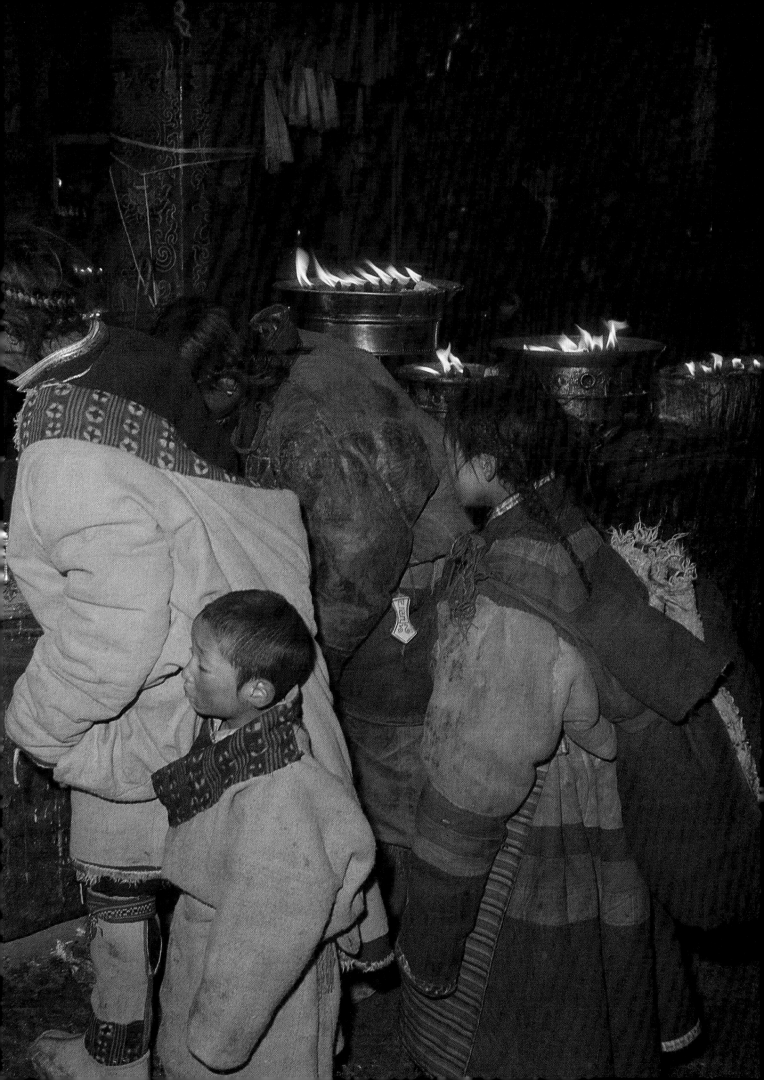

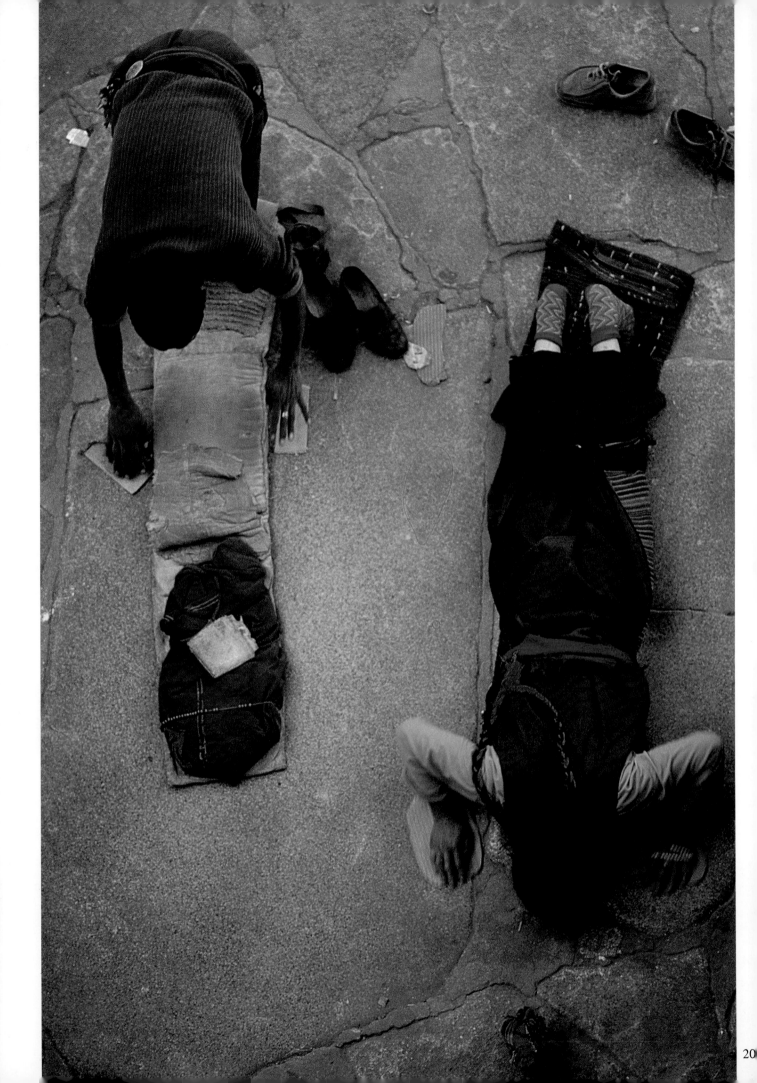

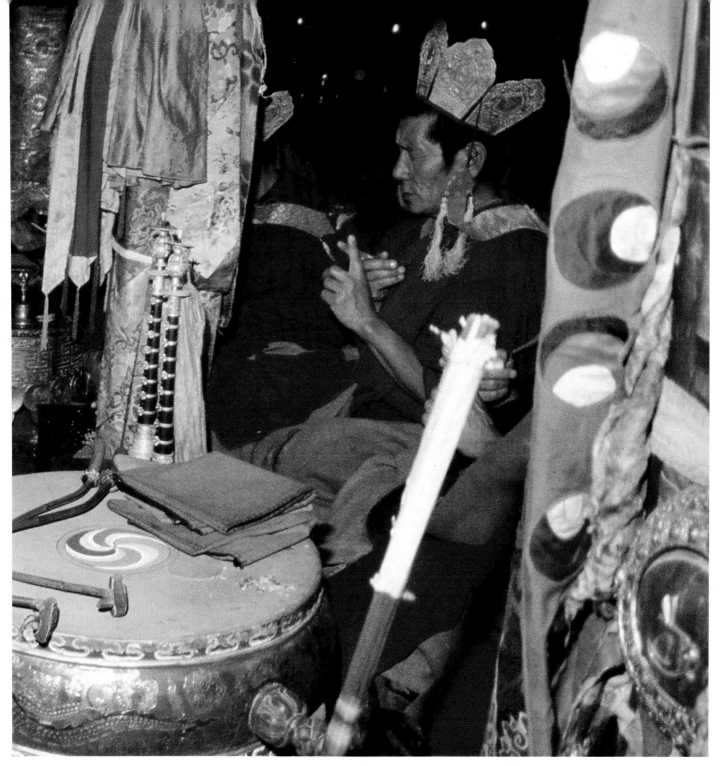

20. A prostration ritual. A Buddhist must perform this ritual at least 10,000 times. The Buddhist, barefooted, raises his hands above his head with palms joined together, bends forward and hits the floor with his forehead incessantly and noisily.

21.22. Gurus in ritual raiments worshipping.

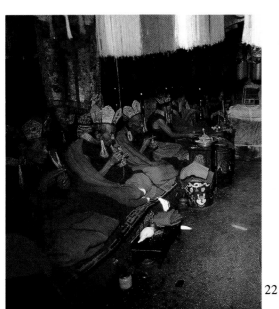

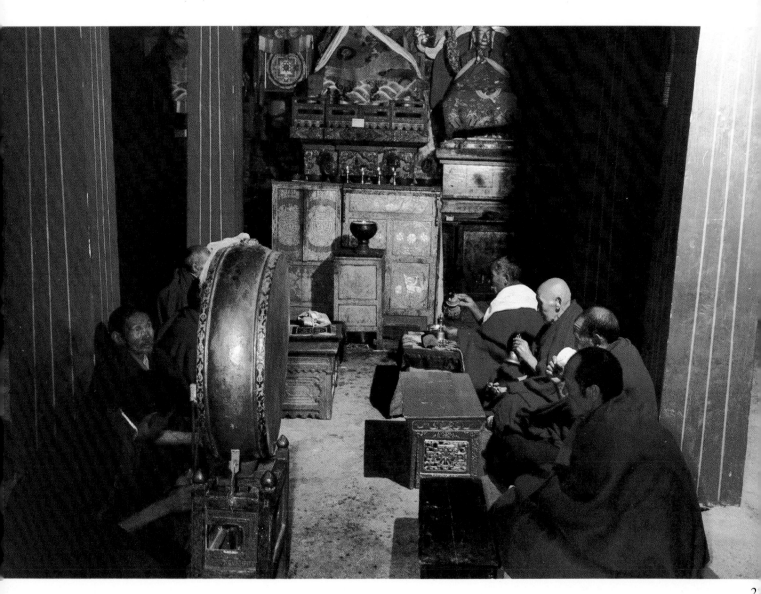

23. Sūtra-chanting sessions begin with music.

THE ART OF
TIBETAN ESOTERIC BUDDHISM

THE ART OF
TIBETAN ESOTERIC
BUDDHISM

The art of Esoteric Buddhism grew and flourished with the spread of Buddhism in Tibet. Closely linked with the doctrine of Esoteric Buddhism in theme, technique and the use of colour, it serves the purpose of religious propaganda and is believed to function with "supernatural powers". It has gone through three stages of development.

The introduction of Buddhism into Tibet in the early 7th century was followed by the building of many temples and monasteries as a result of the royal endorsement of the religion. During this period, the Qoikang and Ramoqe lamaseries, the Potala Palace and a number of lesser temples were constructed. The awareness of the potentialities of the monasteries as social institutions and the effort to create a mystic religious atmosphere eventually led to the production in large quantity of images of the Buddha, religious frescos and paintings for use in temples and monasteries.

This period was also a time when the highly developed feudal culture of the Hans began to wake its impact on Tibetan culture, and the craftsmanship brought into Tibet by Han craftsmen played an important role in accelerating the growth of Buddhist culture in Tibet. Meanwhile, many of the Exoteric and Esoteric canonical texts in Sanskrit were translated into the Tibetan language. For example, the Tibetan version of the *Śilpakar-masthāna-vidyā*, a book on the rules and methods for the construction of temples, stupas and Buddhist images and on the techniques of making maṇḍalas, introduced new notions and techniques to the art of Tibetan Esoteric Buddhism. These were the external factors that contributed much to the shaping and development of Esoteric Buddhist art. However, in the 200 years from the 7th to the 9th

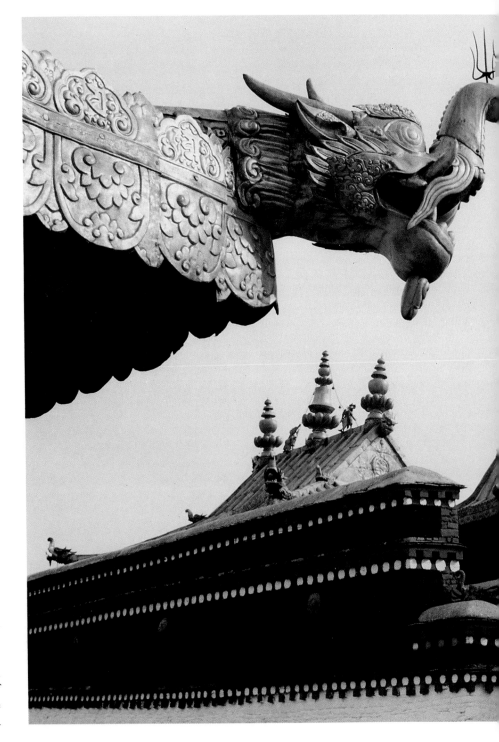

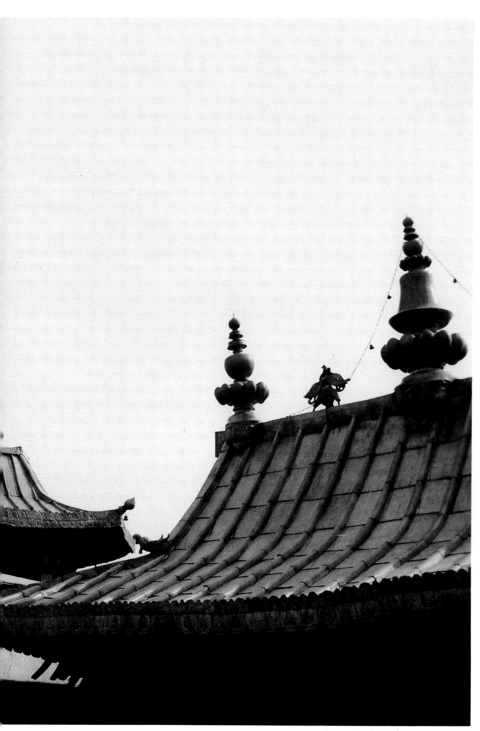

centuries, the repeated outbursts of rebellion against Buddhism by the Bonpos played havoc with Buddhist culture, and few works of art of early Tibetan Esoteric Buddhism survived these violent attacks. This was the first stage that marked the beginning of Buddhist art in Tibet.

The years from 978 on saw a vigorous revival of Buddhism in Tibet and as a feudal economy had by then emerged, Buddhist art made an impressive progress as was shown in the building of more temples and monasteries. It was a time when all Buddhist sects in Tibet and their sub-sects founded monasteries of their own. For instance, the Sagya, Drepung and Zhaxilhunbo monasteries were built – all imposing and magnificent structures with a warehouse of finely-made objects of Buddhist art. Incomplete statistics show that no fewer than 60 huge main halls and 200 prayer halls were built in the lamaseries. Frescoes and *thang-kas* (cloth painting) were created by the thousand in addition to innumerable images of Buddhist deities and carved objects of art. This period also saw the emergence of the distinguished style of painting known in the history of Tibetan Buddhist art as "the Gyangze School", so called because Gyangze was the birthplace of most of its artists, whose style was heavily influenced by Nepalese art of painting. This was the second stage of development, a period that produced far-reaching influence with its remarkable achievement in Tibetan Buddhist culture and art.

24. Gilded roofs of the Stūpa Hall in the Potala Palace and the dragon-head cornice ornament which shows the influence of Han, Indian and Nepalese art.

24

Tibetan Buddhist art entered its third stage of development at the end of the 17th century. During this period, ancient monasteries were extended or renovated. The Potala Palace after extension soared to a majestic height of 117.19 metres with its main building, a sight that inspired awe and admiration. The palace at the time already had up to 1,000 rooms, and its criss-crossing and covered walkways made it look like a labyrinth. The entire palace was decorated with frescoes, coloured paintings, wood and stone carvings and gold and silver ornaments, all of which reached an extremely high level in artistic execution. The stūpa of the Fifth Dalai is 14.85 metres in height. Nearly 6,000 kilogrammes of pure gold were used to paint it from top to bottom, and inlaid in this layer of gold were a total of about 18,000 pearls, precious stones and coral, amber and agate beads. It is a rare object of art superbly executed with a combination of skills of many different crafts. A number of gardens of a new design (for example, the Lubulyṅka) and temples of Bhaisajyarāja (the Bodhisattva of Medicine) were also built in this period.

The works of art related to Tibetan Esoteric Buddhism, which absorb the influences of Han, Indian and Nepalese art, maintain their own characteristic style, which is discernible in all their forms of artistic expression. Take, for example, the roofs of temples. There, decorating the flying cornices are not only finely carved miniature gods, recumbent deer, the Wheel of the Law, golden banners, dragons, phoenixes and lions that show the influences of ancient architecture of the Tang and Song dynasties, but also pagodas, inverted bells and lotus bases that might have been sitting on the roofs of Indian or Nepalese temples. No artist will begin his work on any image of the Buddha, or on any picture, clay figure, wood or stone block without first selecting an auspicious day. He will then bathe himself, burn incense sticks, pray and meditate. Such rituals become even more important, more complicated and more mystic in the case of the construction or renovation of temples. That religious seriousness lies behind all the art works of Tibetan Buddhism, particularly those of Tibetan Esoteric Buddhism.

25. The stūpa of the Fifth Dalai in the Stūpa Hall of the Potala Palace.

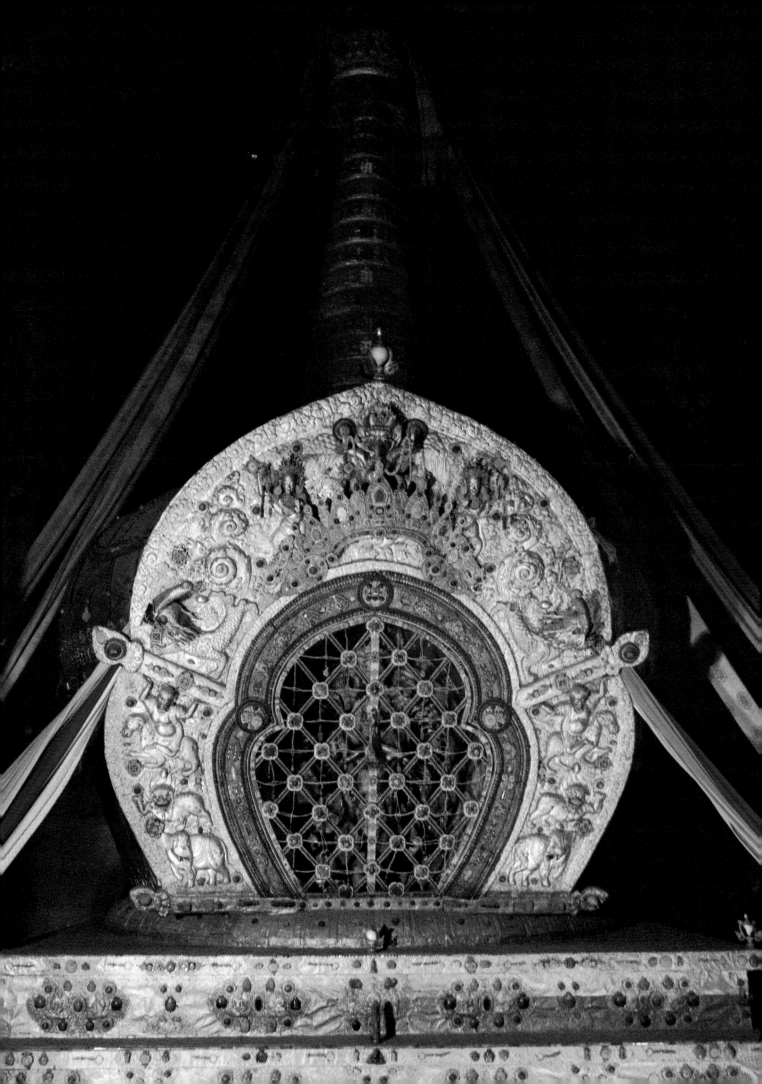

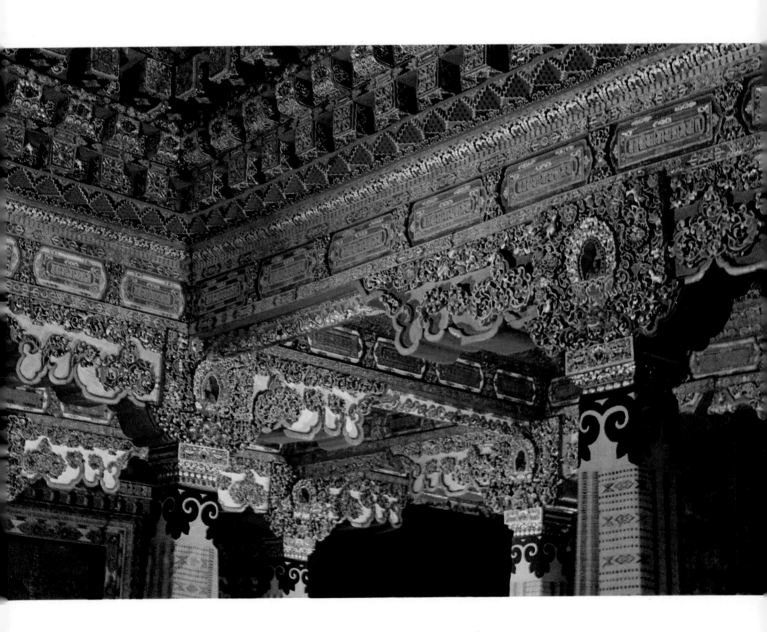

26. The carved beams of the Potala Palace are
excellent examples of the exquisite craftsmanship of Tibetan wood carvers.

ILLUSTRATIONS

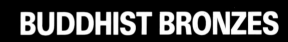

BUDDHIST BRONZES

BUDDHIST BRONZES

Mining of copper, gold, silver and iron, and the making of tools with these metals date far back in Tibetan history. With the spread and development of Buddhism in Tibet since the 7th century, more and more Buddhist bronzes were made. The smelting and casting techniques and the art of metal carving gradually improved. At the same time, the technique of silver-plating of copper had also been developed.

As Buddhism believes in the worship of idols, the production of images of Buddhas and other deities must follow the strict rules prescribed in the canon of Esoteric Buddhism for their faces, gestures, the ornaments they wear and the objects they hold. The skills that the Han craftsmen brought into Tibet proved to be an impetus to the development of smelting and casting techniques and the improvment of metal carving methods. At the same time, the style of Han sculpture was also introduced into Tibet. Thus, the lama artists absorbed the influences of the art of Indian, Nepalese and Han sculpture and developed a style and craft of their own which was distinctively Tibetan.

Tibetan Buddhist bronzes are mostly made of copper and the alloy of copper and tin; iron is rarely used. Some bronzes were cast from a combination of gold, silver, copper, iron, lead, rock crystal, graphite and mercury. The process consists of smelting, casting, carving and finishing. Sometimes a bronze has jade stones and pearls inlaid in the surface, or has ornaments such as leaves, chips, threads and rings of gold, silver and copper mounted on it by hammering, hooking or girdling. This is so skillfully done that the attached parts totally merge with the bronze proper.

Buddhist bronzes in Tibet range in size from giant Buddha images weighing several tons to tiny Buddhas about the size of the thumb. The small, exquisitely carved ones usually excel in craftsmanship and they outnumber the large ones. The shaping of a Buddhist bronze image is a complicated process. It is so difficult and time-consuming that many lama artists spent all their lives making them but did not live to see them completed. The bronze images of Buddhist deities are not only idols for worship, but represent an important part of Tibetan Buddhist art and are among important historical relics as well.

The Smiling Vajra, also known as the Happy Vajra or Blood-drinking Vajra. Called Dgyes-pa rdo-rje in Tibetan, it is a two-image bronze on a lotus throne. The vajra has 8 faces and 16 arms with the first arms embracing Vajra-nairātmya-devī, his female counterpart. Held in his other hands are kapālas (skulls) with holy objects in them. Those in his right hands are: white elephant, green deer, scarlet donkey, red ox, grey camel, red man, green lion and red cat, all facing inside. In the left hands are: the Yellow Deva of the Earth, White Deity of Water, Red Deity of Fire, Green Deity of Wind, White Deva of the Sun, Green King of Hell and Yellow God of Wealth, all facing outside. The string of skulls that hangs from his waist and the two men lying on their backs under his feet symbolize the deity's physical power. The devī has one face and two arms. She has a curved knife in her right hand and holds a skull in her left. She wears a crown of 5 skulls, and the 50 skulls strung around her neck stand for the 50 letters of Sanskrit alphabet.

27. A craftman making a Buddhist bronze.
28. The Smiling Vajra. Bronze, 25cm in height. In the Sagya Monastery.
29. The Smiling Vajra. Bronze, 50cm in height. In the Sagya Monastery.

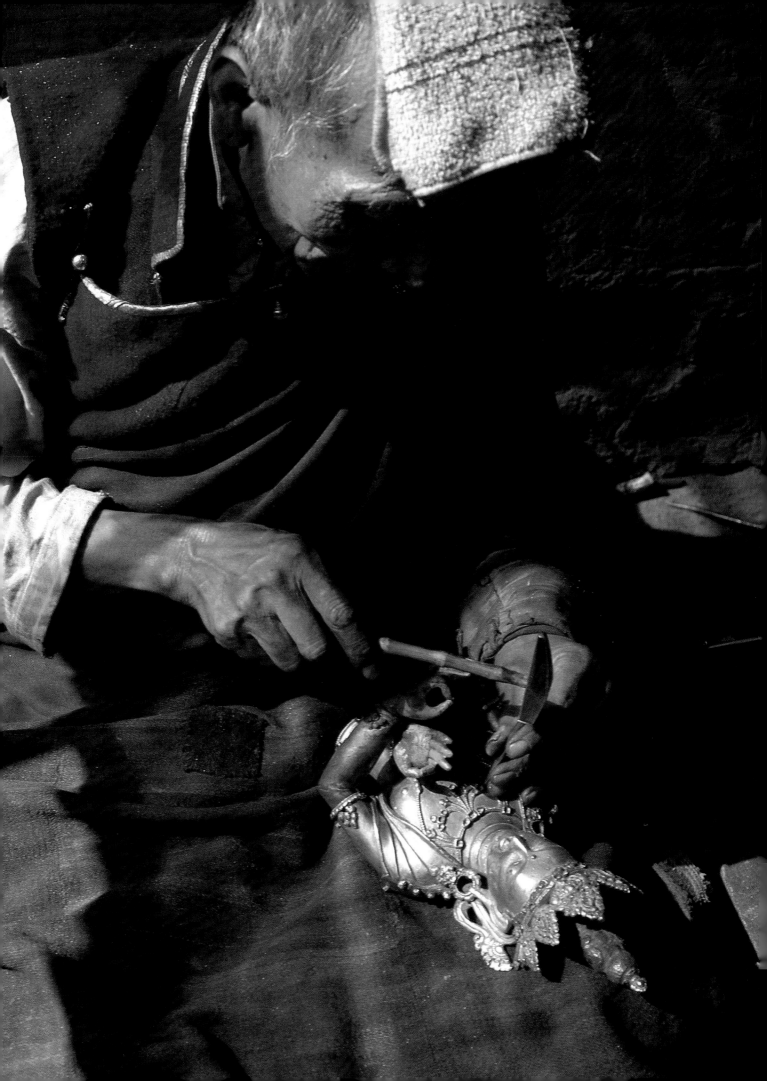

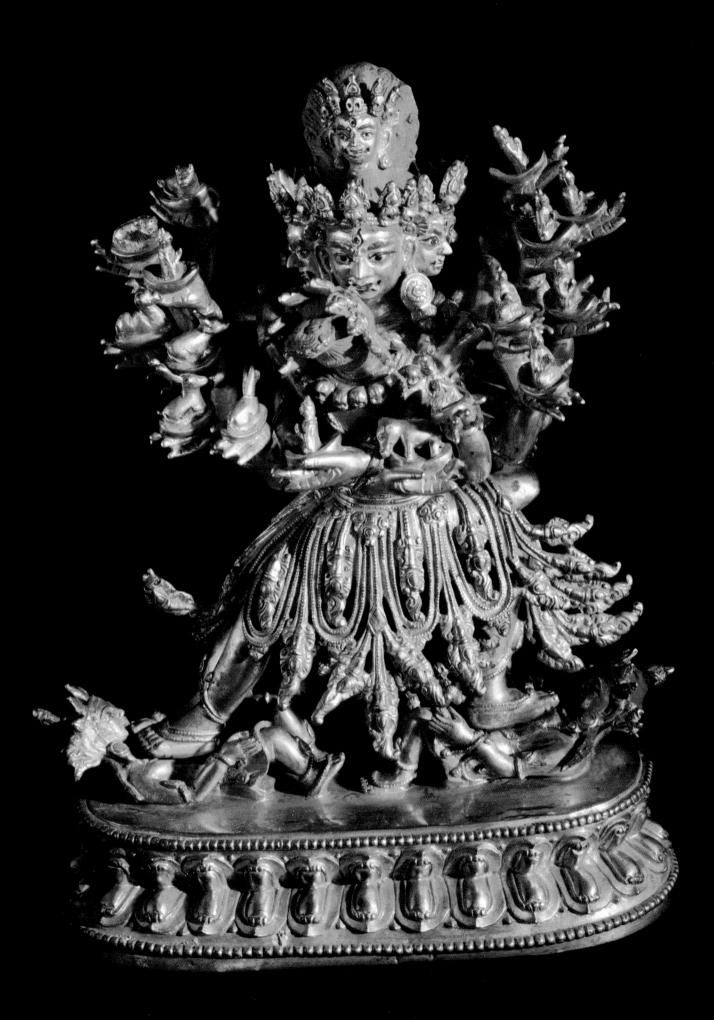

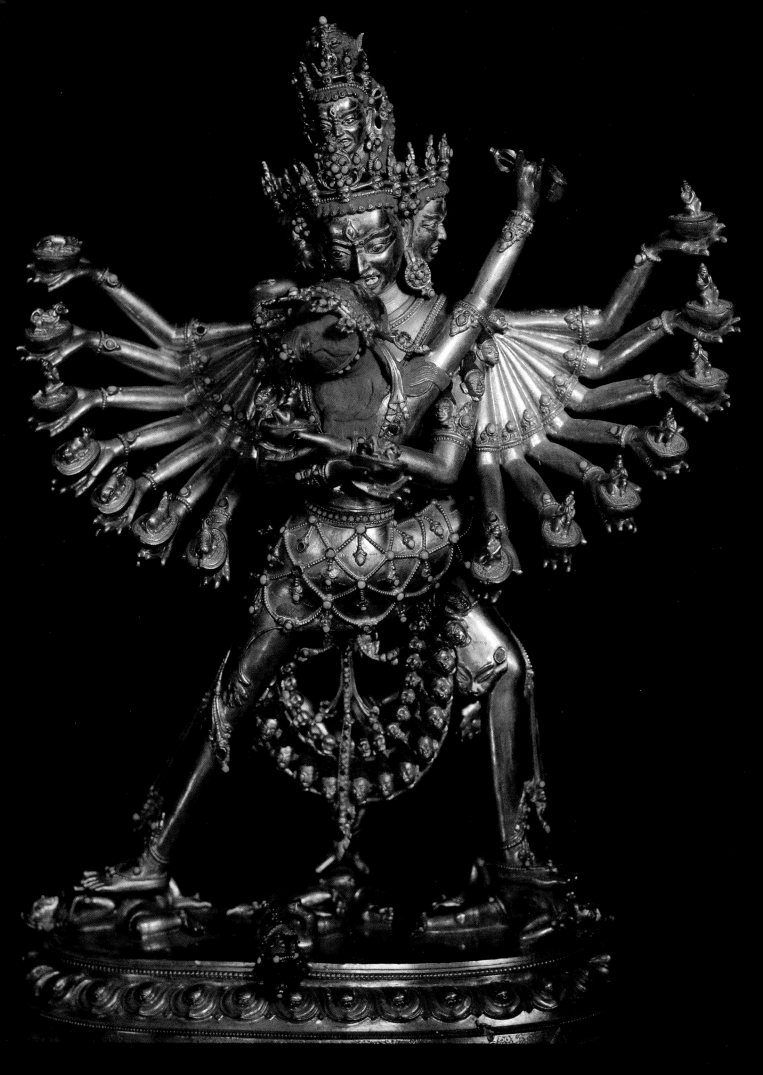

The Fearful Guardian Deity, also called the Mahābhairava Vajra (the Vajra of Power and Virtue), Six-Foot Deity, Six-Face Deity, and Six-Foot Wrathful Guardian Deity. It is commonly known as the Ox-Head Vajra. His name in Tibetan is Rdo-rje Vjigs-byed. According to Tibetan Esoteric Buddhism, the deity is the wrathful manifestation of Amitāyus (Buddha of Long Life), who in his fearful form instructs the dharmadhātu (dharma sphere) and subdues demons. His usual image is one with 9 heads (the one in the middle is an ox head), 34 arms and 16 feet. He is of dark blue colour, and in an aura of flames he embraces Vetāla, his female counterpart. He carries Amitāyus on his head, stands on a recumbent deer and holds ritual objects in his hands. The Dge-lugs-pa Sect pays particular attention to the study of the doctrine of the deity.

30. The Fearful Guardian Deity. Bronze, 30cm in height. In the Sagya Monastery.

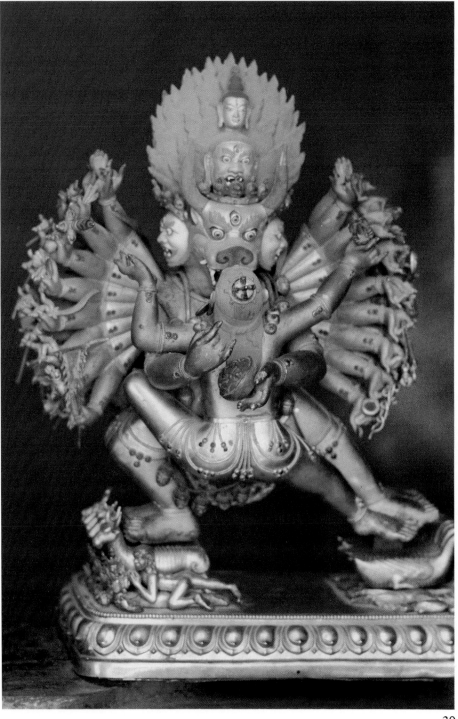

30

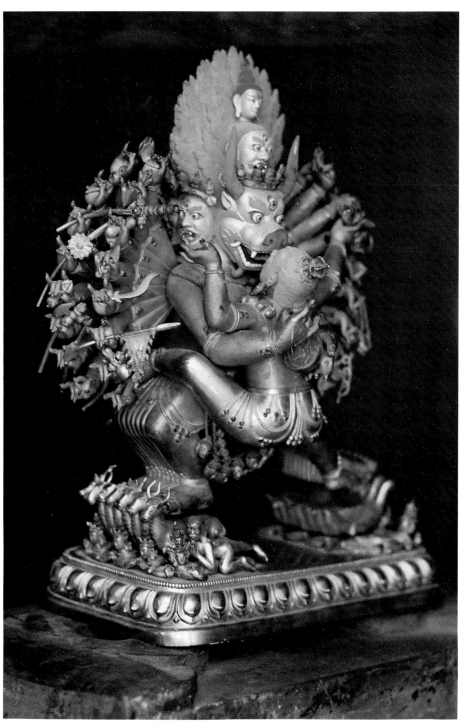

31. Side-view of the Mahābhairava Vajra.

31

65

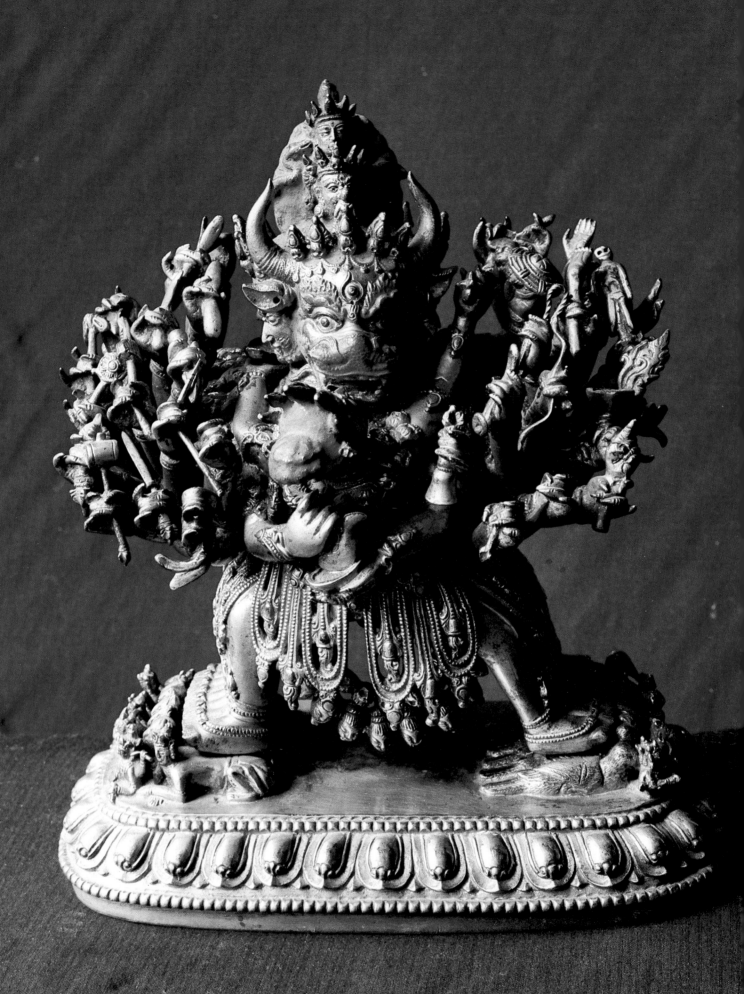

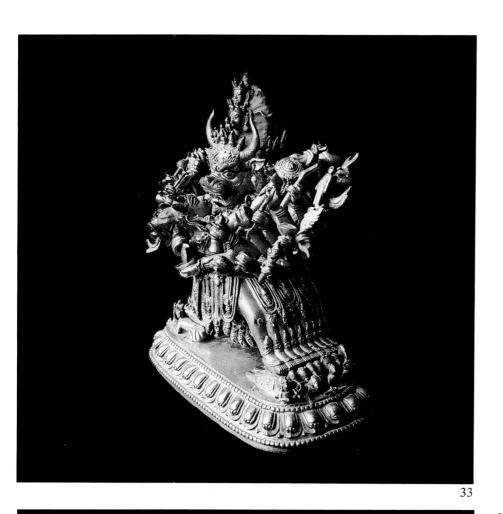

33

32. Mahābhairava Vajra, 22cm in height. In the Drepung Monastery.
33. Side-view of Mahābhairava Vajra.
34. Rear view of Mahābhairava Vajra.

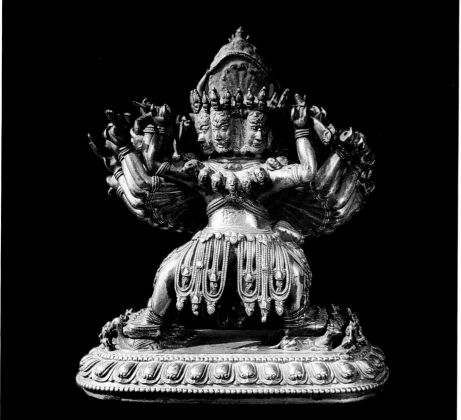

34

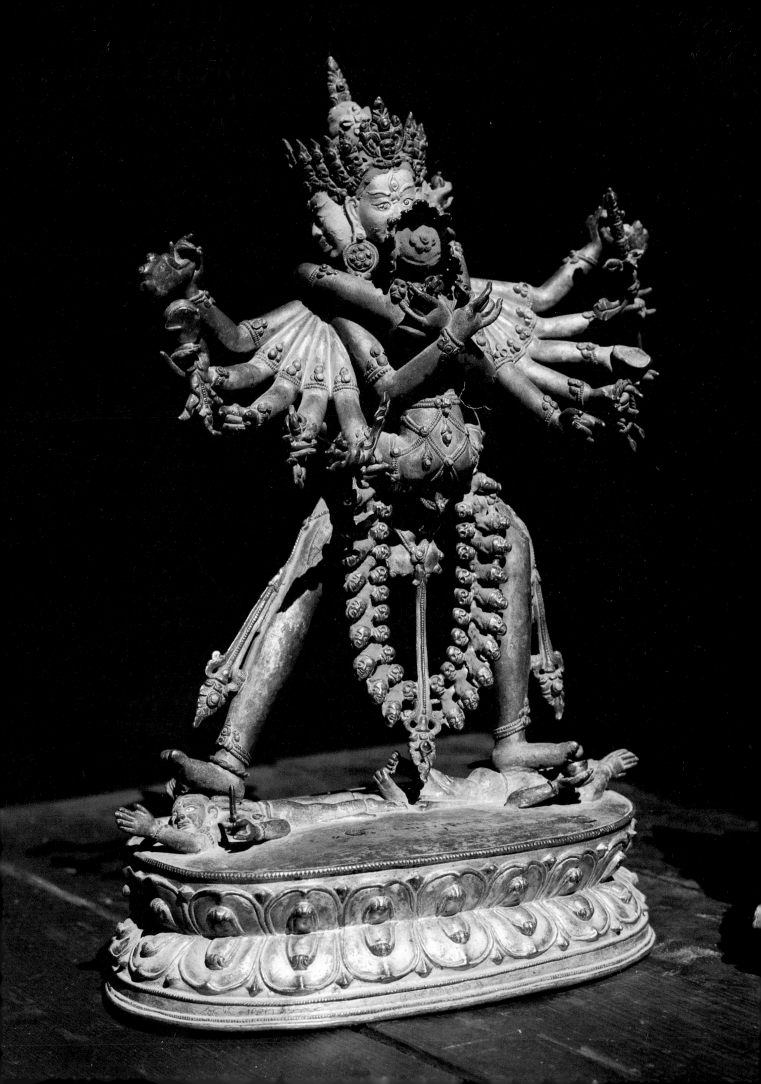

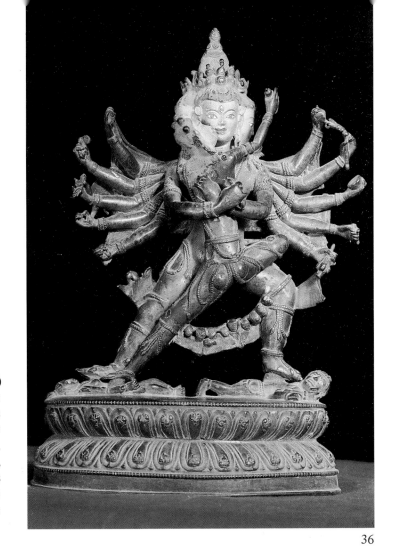

The Śambara Vajra (Tibetan: Bde-mchog) is one of the Satyadevatā of Tibetan Esoteric Buddhism. His doctrine receives particular emphasis in the monastic study at the Lower Tantra Apartment in Lhasa. The deity has four faces in white, yellow, red and blue respectively, with three eyes in each of them. This 12-armed Esoteric deity embraces the Rdo-rje Pha-mo, the devī, in his first arms.

36

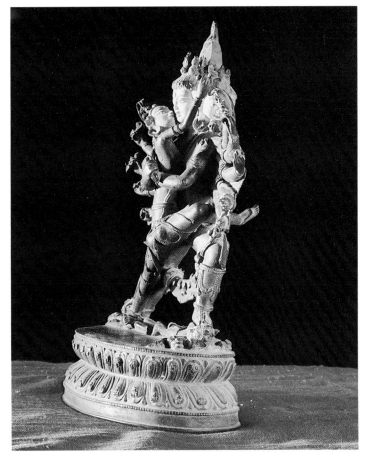

35. The Śambara Vajra. Bronze, 45cm tall. In the Sagya Monastery.
36. The Śambara Vajra. Bronze, 29cm in height. In the Potala Palace.
37. Side-view of the Śambara Vajra.

37

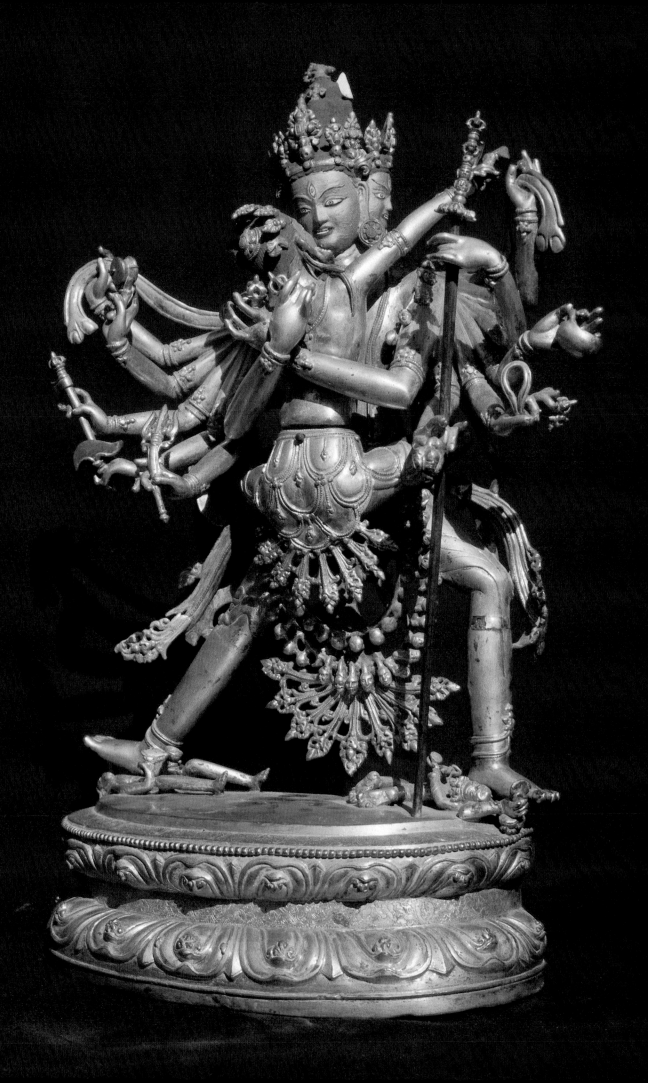

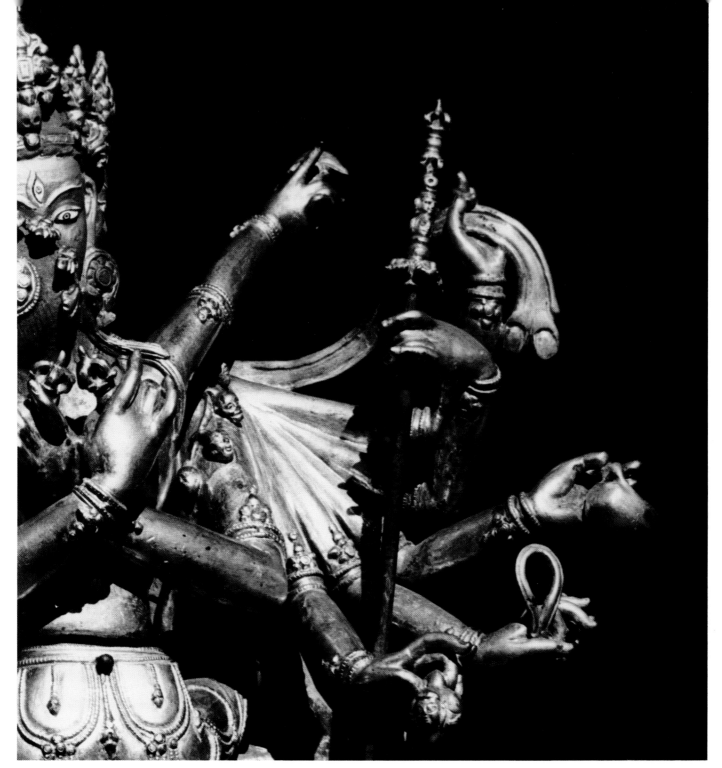

38. The Śambara Vajra. Bronze, 45cm in
height. In the Drepung Monastery.
39. The left half of the Śambara Vajra.
40. His right half.

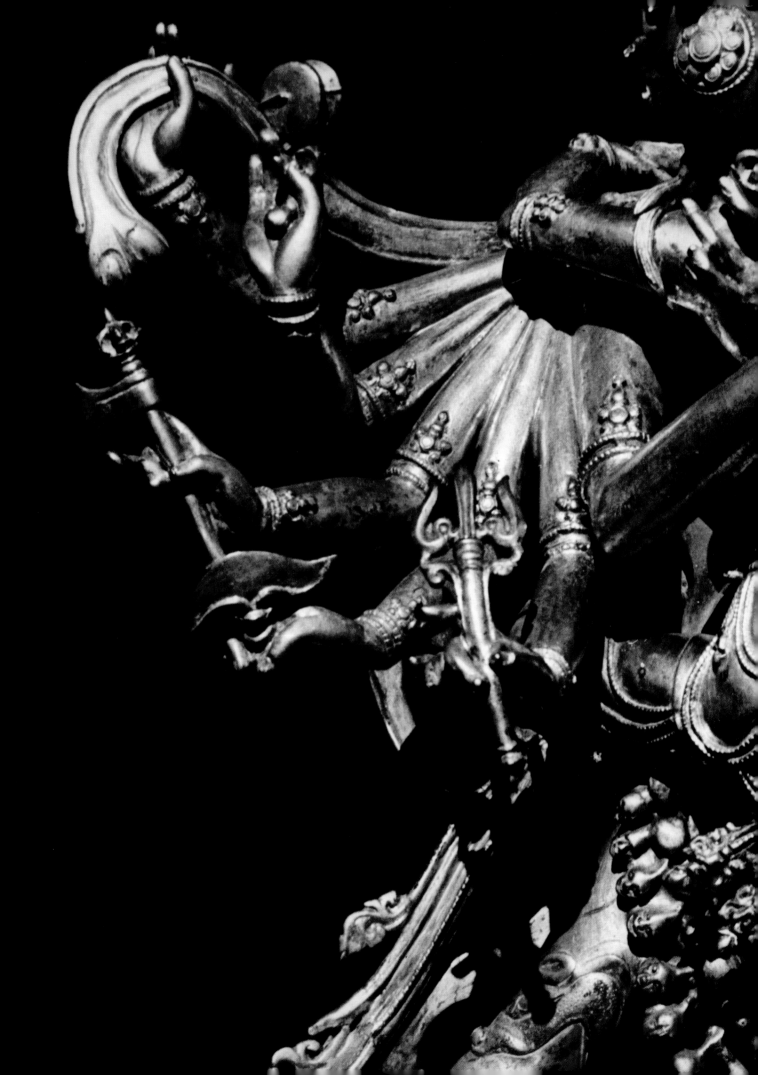

The Kālacakra Vajra, or the Vajra of the
Wheel of Ages (Tibetan: Dus vkhor), is
the Satyadevatā of the tantric doctrine of
the Kālacakra Vajra. According to
Tibetan Esoteric Buddhism, this doctrine
originated in Sambhala, a kingdom in the
north of ancient India, the equivalent of
the Land of Supreme Bliss, and was
introduced into Tibet in the 12th century.
The doctrine says that all beings live in
"the state of ignorance" in the "three
ages" of the past, present and future
which are indicated on the wheel. There
is a supreme Buddha above Śākyamuni —
the Ādibuddha, who is the origin of all
cosmic beings. The practice of the
doctrine includes the manipulation of
"the living wind" in the body to ensure a
long life, and the combination of "the
five wisdoms" with "dhyāna" ("meditation") to achieve "Buddhahood in the
present body".

41. The Kālacakra Vajra. Bronze, 15 cm tall. In
the Potala Palace.

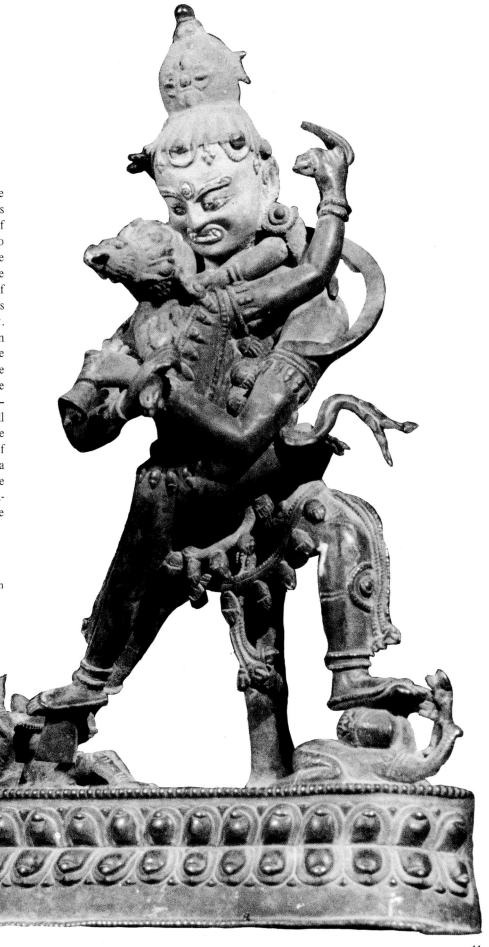

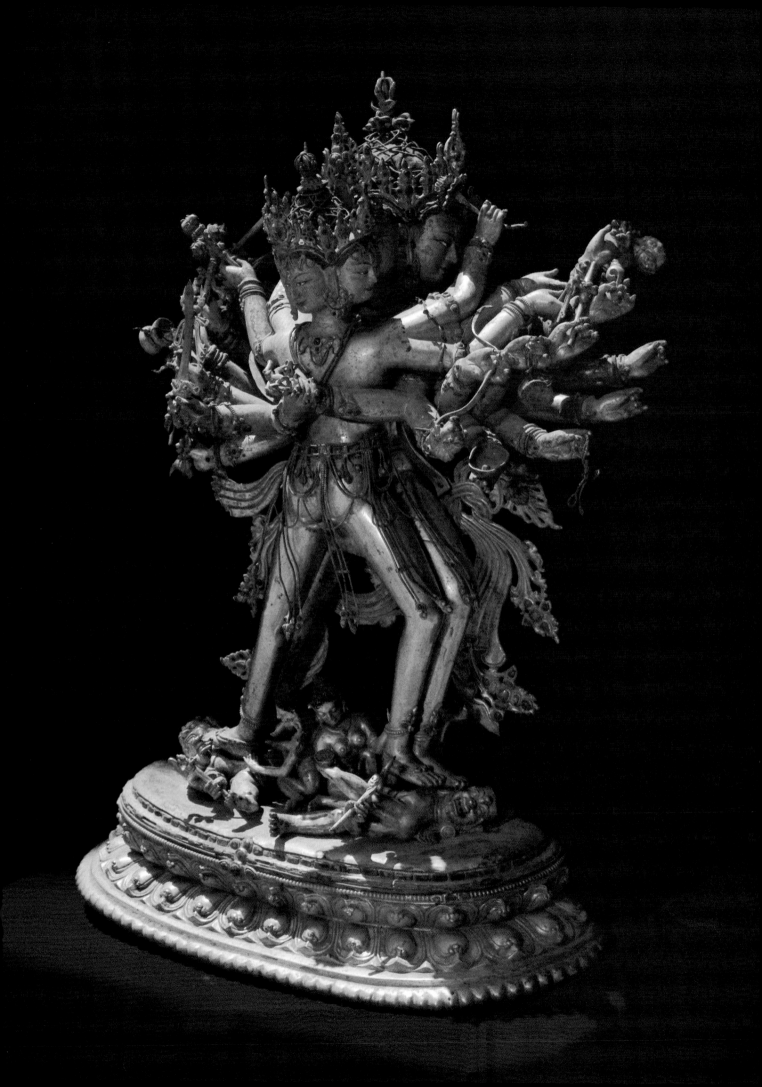

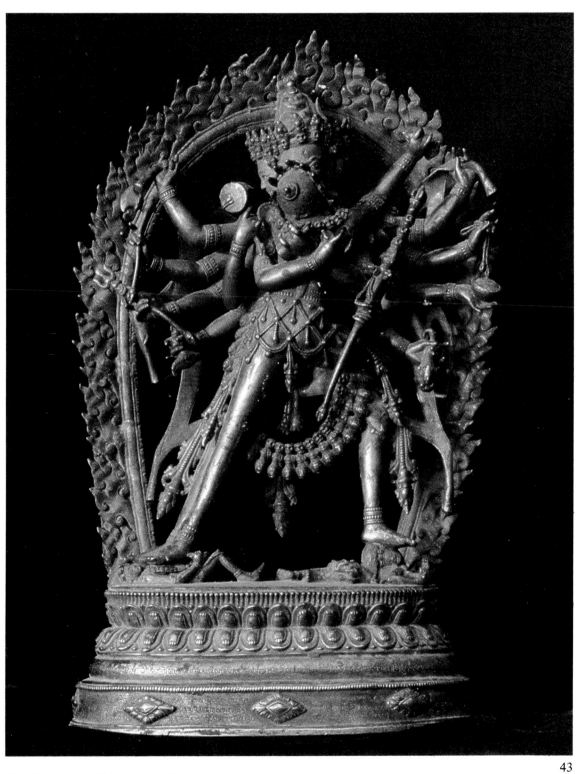

43

42. The Kālacakra Vajra. Bronze, 62cm tall. In the Xalu Monastery.
43. The Kālacakra Vajra. Bronze, 30cm tall. In the Sagya Monastery.

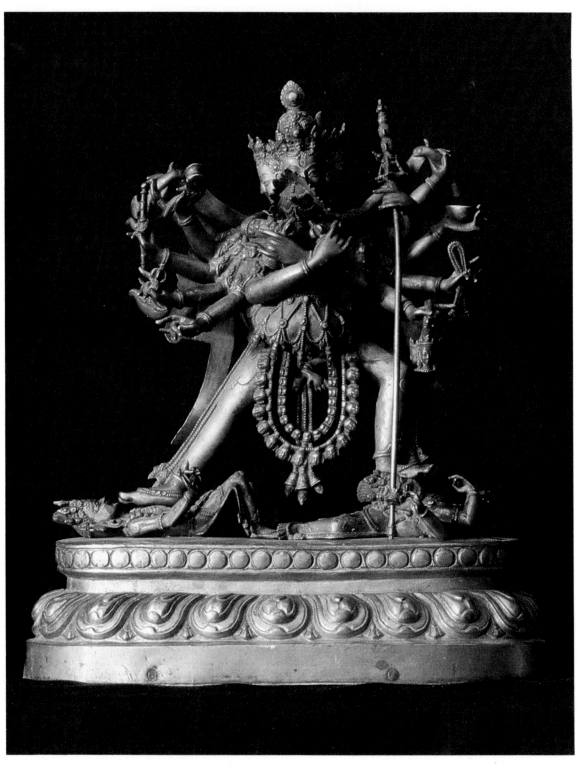

44. The Kālacakra Vajra. Bronze, 30cm tall. In
the Sagya Monastery.

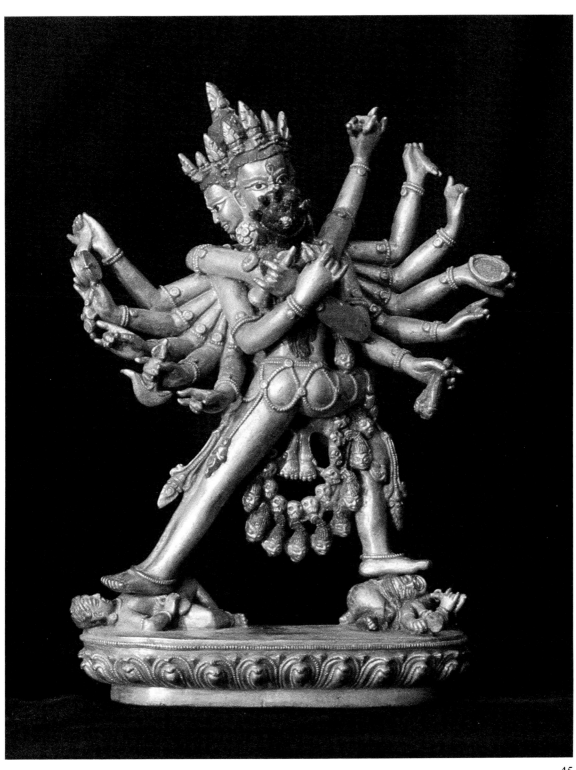

45. The Kālacakra Vajra. Bronze, 30cm tall. In
Sagya Monastery.

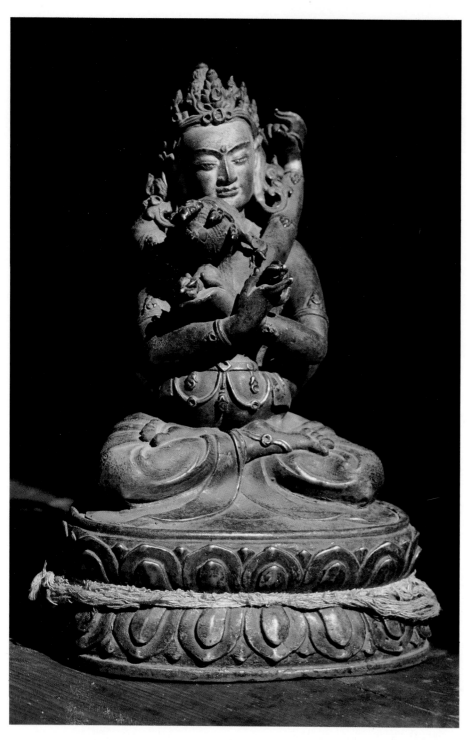

46

Vajrapāṇi, also known as Natha, or Vajradhara (Tibetan: Phyages na rdo rje).

46. This Vajrapāṇi sits cross-legged on white lotus flowers, and wears a crown with the images of five Buddhas on it. With the vajra in his right hand, and the ghantā (bell) in his left, the deity embraces his devī Sundarī. This Vajrapāṇi looks different from the one shown in Picture 47 in that he bears resemblance to Śākyamuni. Bronze, 30cm in height. In the Sagya Monastery.

47. Vajrapāṇi, also known as Vairadhara (Holder of the Vajra), Guhyapati (Master of the Esoteric Doctrine) or, in Tibetan, Phyagsna rdo-rje. According to Tibetan Esoteric Buddhism, the deity is the manifestation of Śākyamuni when he preached the Esoteric doctrine. With a single, three - or five-pronged vajra in his hand, the deity is the symbol of the indestructible power of wisdom. Bronze, 30cm in height. In the Zhaxilhunbo Monastery.

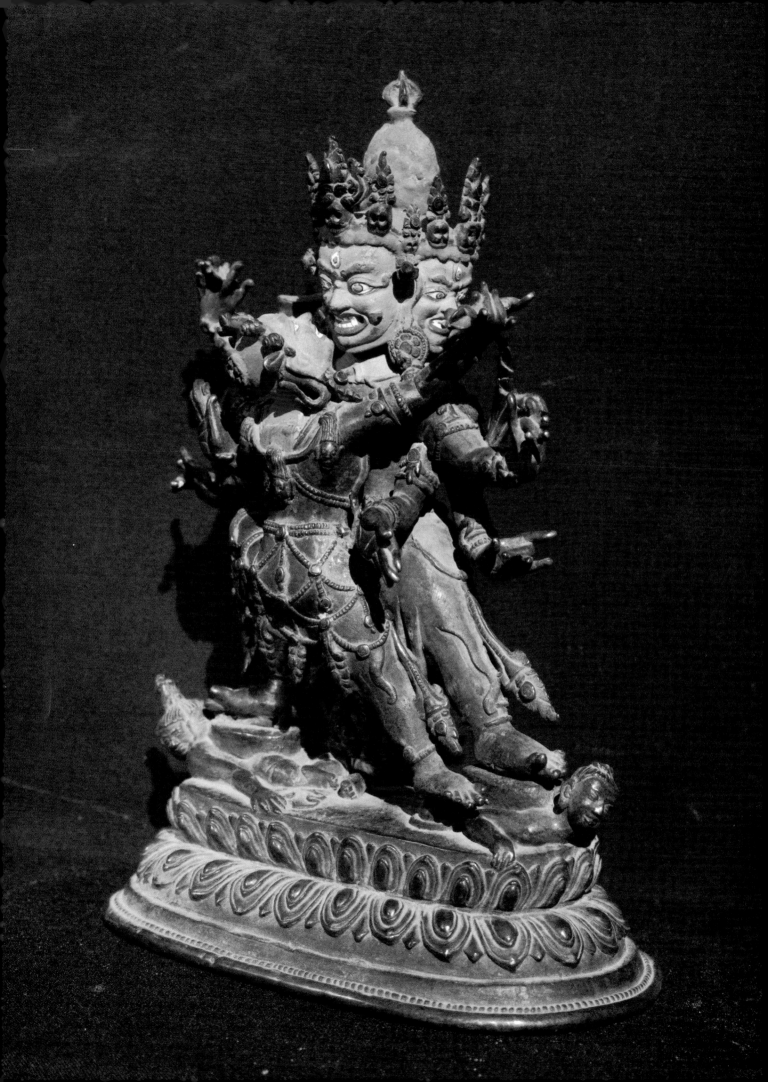

The Kila Vajra, or Phur-pa rdo-rje in Tibetan, is one of the Satyadevatās of Tibetan Esoteric Buddhism. The vajrakila in his hand is a ritual object of Esoteric Buddhism, and it has the power to subjugate demons.

48. The Kila Vajra. Bronze, 22cm tall. In the Sagya Monastery.

The Mahācakra Vajrapāṇi, or the Great Wheel Vajra (Tibetan: Phyagrdo vkhor-chen). With the Vajra in one hand and the vajrapāśa in the other, he is one of the 33 Garbhadhātu (Enlightenment) Vajras of the Vajrapāṇi's Quarters. "Mahācakra" ("The Great Wheel") symbolizes the power of wisdom which can remove ignorance.

49. The Mahācakra Vajrapāṇi. Bronze, 45cm tall. In the Potala Palace.

Natha, or Dgra-lha mgon-po in Tibetan, the war deity, is one of the dharmapālas of Tibetan Esoteric Buddhism.

50. The Natha. Bronze, 19cm tall. In the Zhaxilhunbo Monastery.

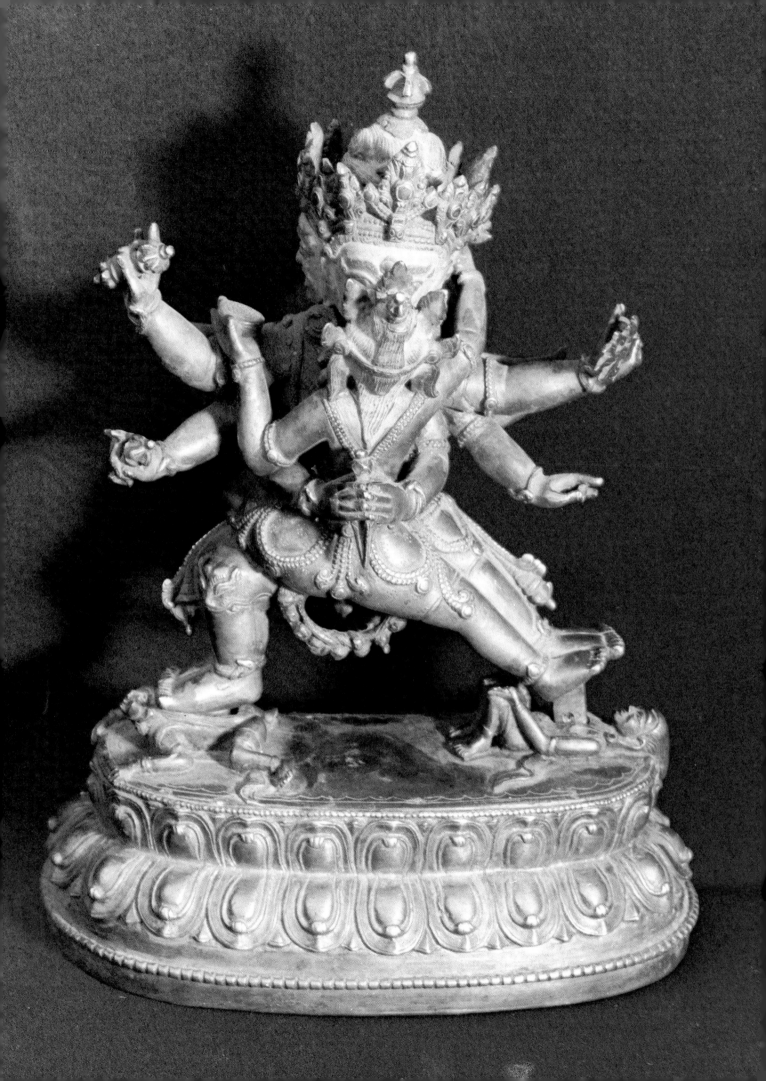

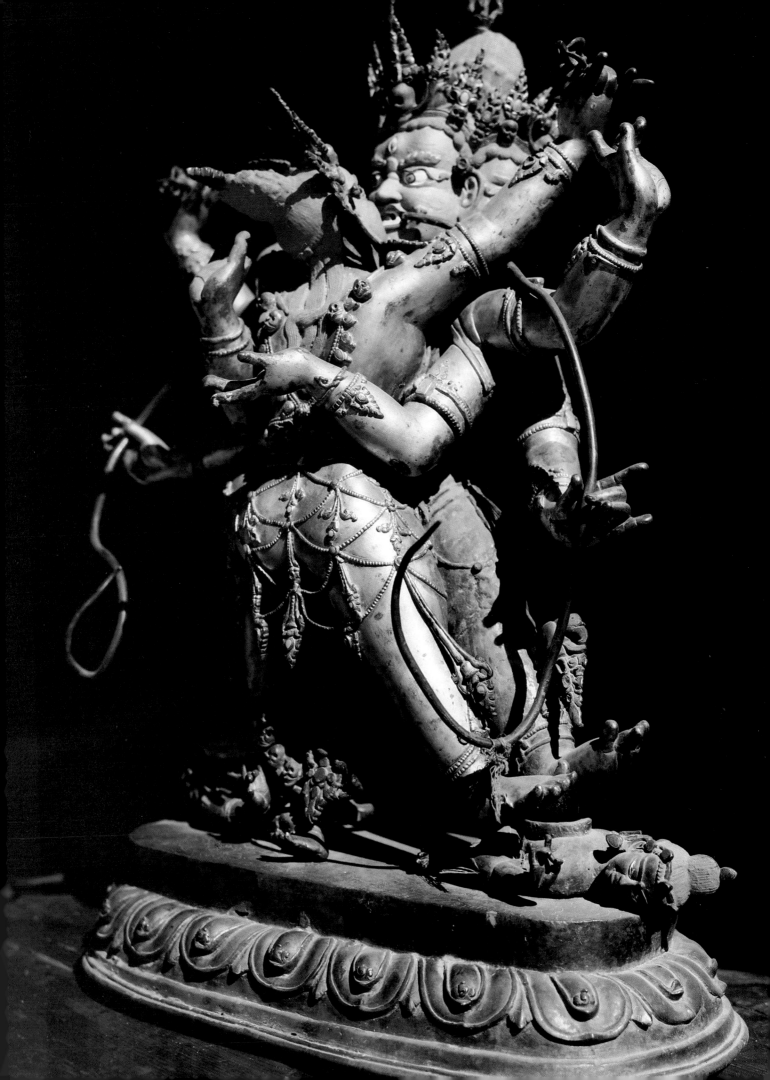

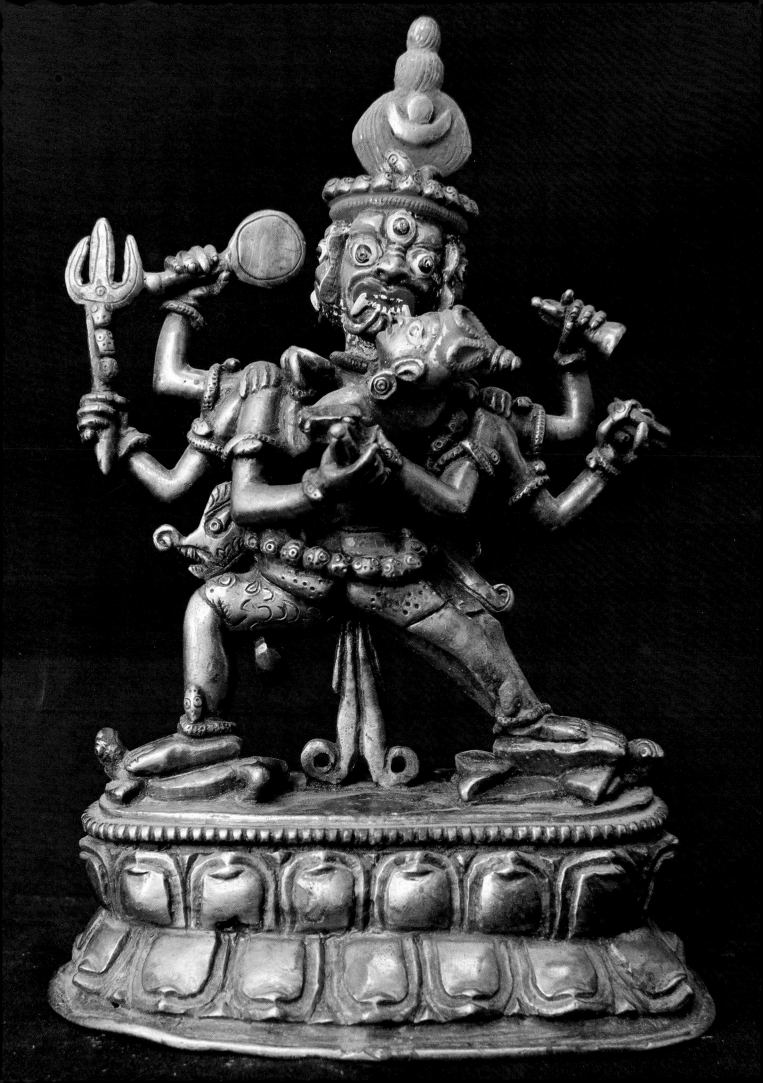

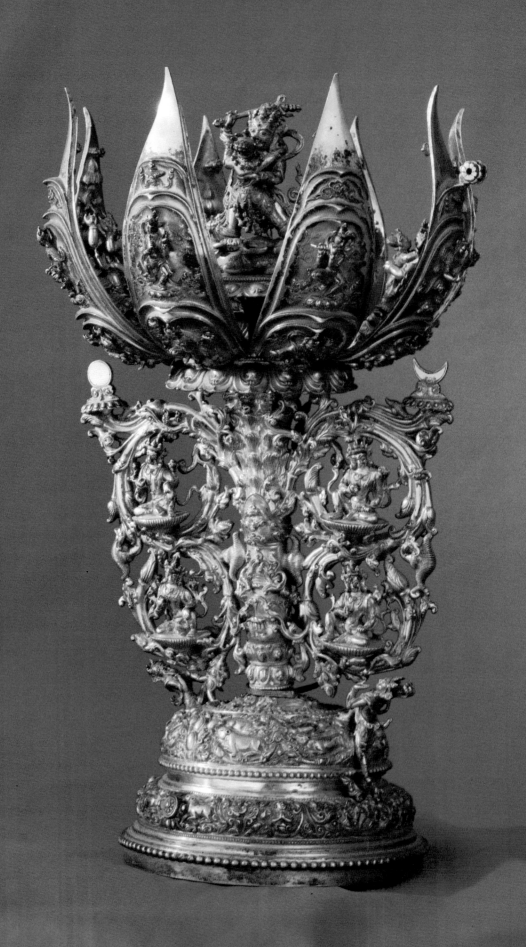

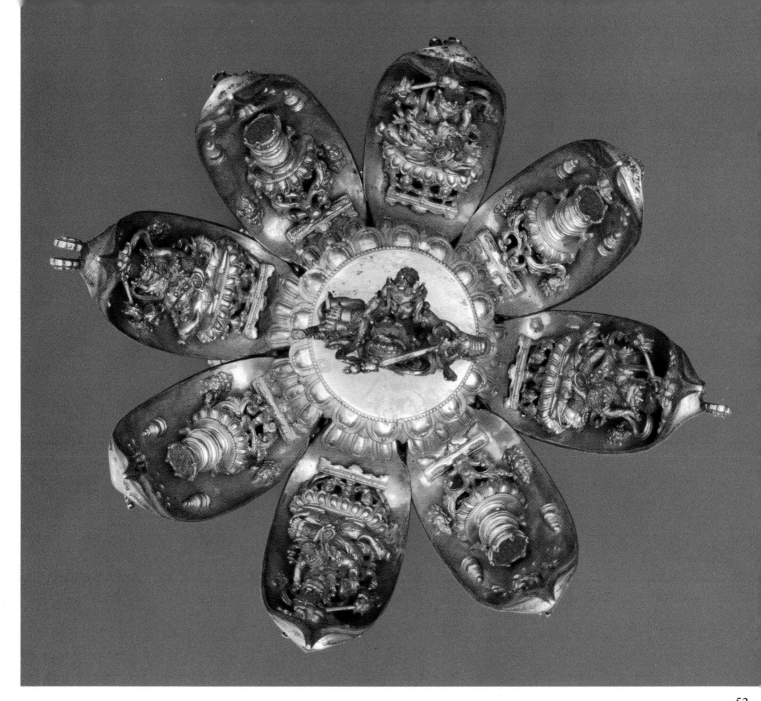

The Yamāntaka, also known as the Fear-
Striking Vajra or the God of Death
(Tibetan: Gshin-rje-gshed), is another
Satyadevatā of Tibetan Esoteric Buddhism. According to the *Mahāvairocana-
sūtra,* he is a guardian of Mañjuśrī with
enormous strength. The vajra has six
faces, six arms and six feet, and rides a
water-buffalo. The deity, of black colour
with three eyes in each of the faces, looks
extremely wrathful.

51. This exquisitely sculpted bronze is placed
inside a lotus flower whose petals may be
closed or opened. The stem of the lotus flower
and the supporting base are gracefully shaped.
Bronze, 54cm in height. In the Sagya
Monastery.
52. Top view of the bronze in Picture 51.

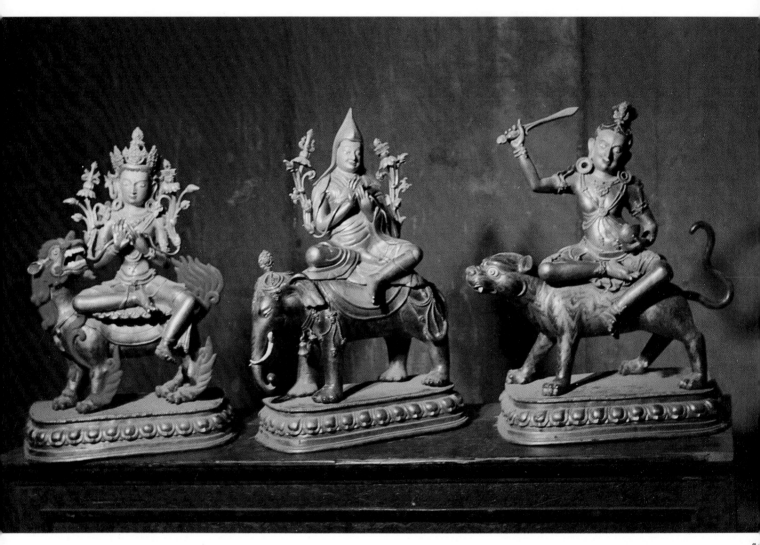

53. Tsong-kha-pa, founder of the Dge-lugs-pa
Sect. Bronze, 30cm tall. In the Drepung
Monastery.

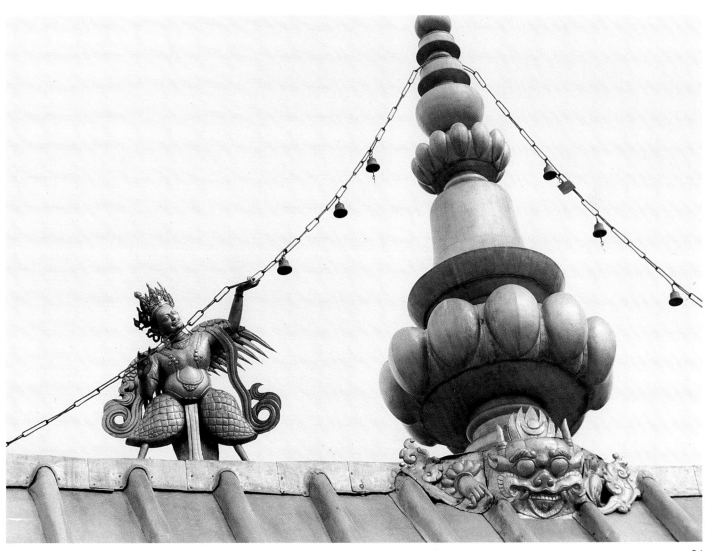

54. Metal carvings and copper bells atop a monastery.

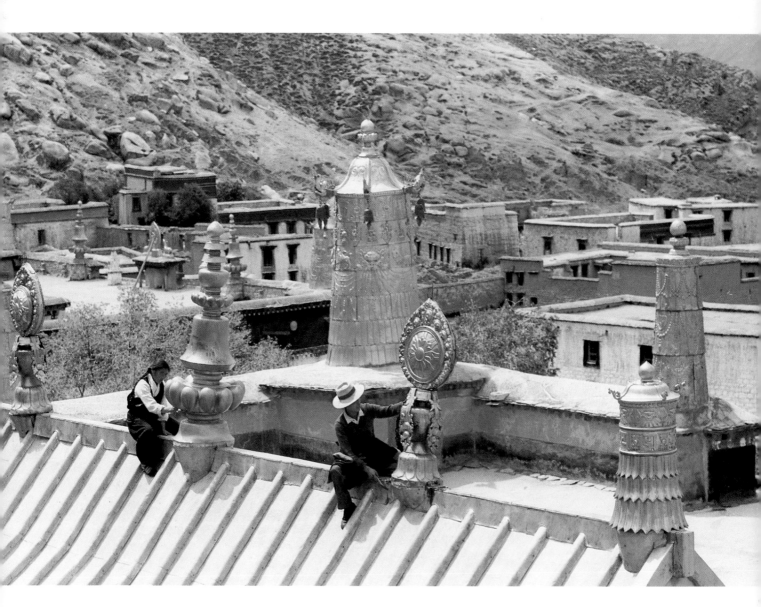

55. Tibetan workmen polishing the metal carvings atop a monastery.

THANG-KA

THANG-KA

The *thang-ka*, or cloth painting, is a special product of Tibetan Buddhism. It also shows influences of Han and Indian Buddhist art. In ancient India, for instance, there was the Paṭa, Buddhist portraiture, which was executed on the kasāya (the monk's outer garment) cloth, and the Hans sometimes used silk fabric as material for paintings.

The material used for *thang-kas* is linen cloth or coarse woolen fabric; silk cloth is reserved for important subjects. Before painting begins, the material is stitched along the edges with flax thread and stretched on a specially made wooden frame. Then a paste made of animal glue mixed with talcum powder is spread over its surface to block up the holes in it. When the paste is scraped off and the cloth gets thoroughly dried, the material is ready for painting. To begin, the artist works out the sketches of the portraits with charcoal sticks. The drawing usually begins with the portrait in the centre and then goes to the surrounding deities or landscape. Colouring comes last. The pigments used come from non-transparent minerals and plants such as malachite and cinnabar. They are mixed with animal glue and ox bile to make the lustre stay. When the painting is done, it is mounted on a brocaded silk border. A roller is put at the top and another at the bottom so that it may be displayed, a technique similar to that of picture-mounting of the Hans. Important *thang-kas* are embroidered on transferred outlines; some of them use a great variety of stitch patterns such as flat and piled stitches to give them a three-dimensional effect.

The pictorial subjects of *thang-kas* include portraits of Buddhas, stories from the lives of saints and great masters. A few *thang-kas* reveal the everyday life of the ordinary people; one of such paintings is *The Home of a Herdsman,* made in the Qing Dynasty. *Thang-kas* are usually rectangular in shape, and the square ones are reserved for maṇḍalas. *Thang-ka* paintings vary in size, ranging from a little over one square foot to several dozen square feet. A large *thang-ka* often takes a large team of artists months, even years, to make.

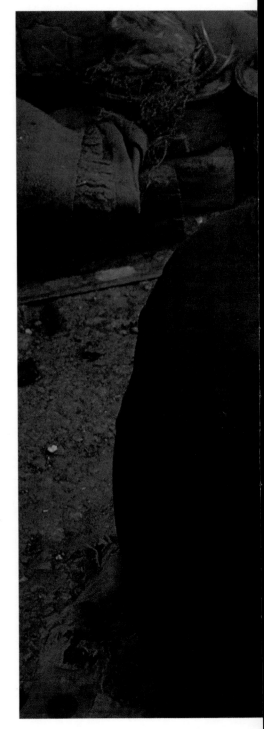

56. The artist working on a *thang-ka.*
57. The Smiling Vajra. *Thang-ka,* 98 × 67cm. In the Sagya Monastery.
58. The Smiling Vajra. *Thang-ka,* 98 × 67cm. In the Sagya Monastery.
59. The Smiling Vajra. *Thang-ka,* 98 × 67cm. In the Sagya Monastery.
60. The Smiling Vajra. *Thang-ka,* 58 × 43cm. In the Sagya Monastery.
61. Part of the Smiling Vajra in picture 60.

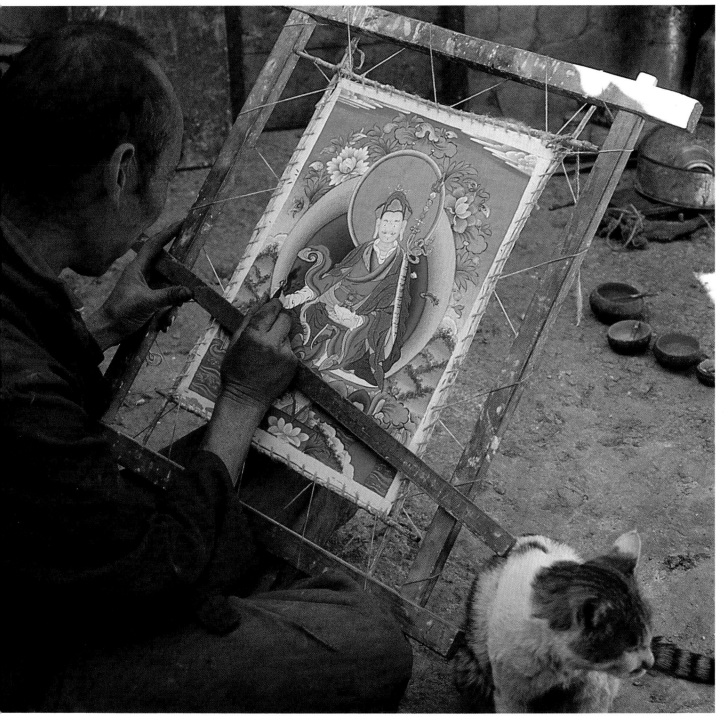

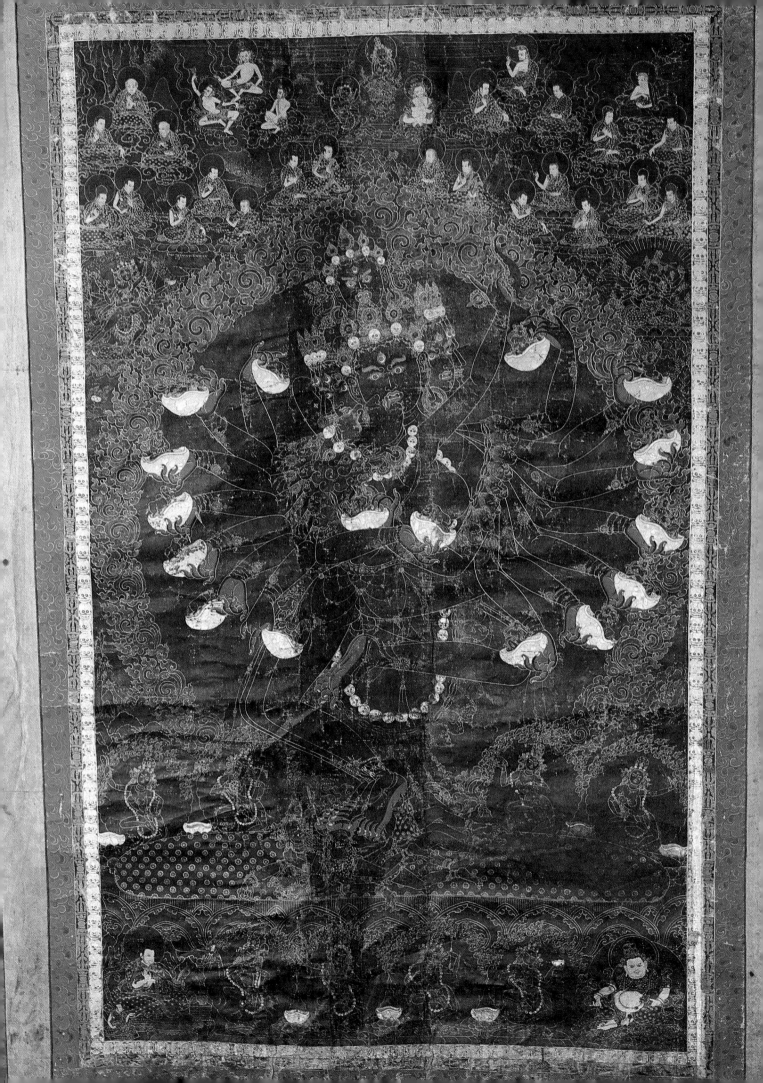

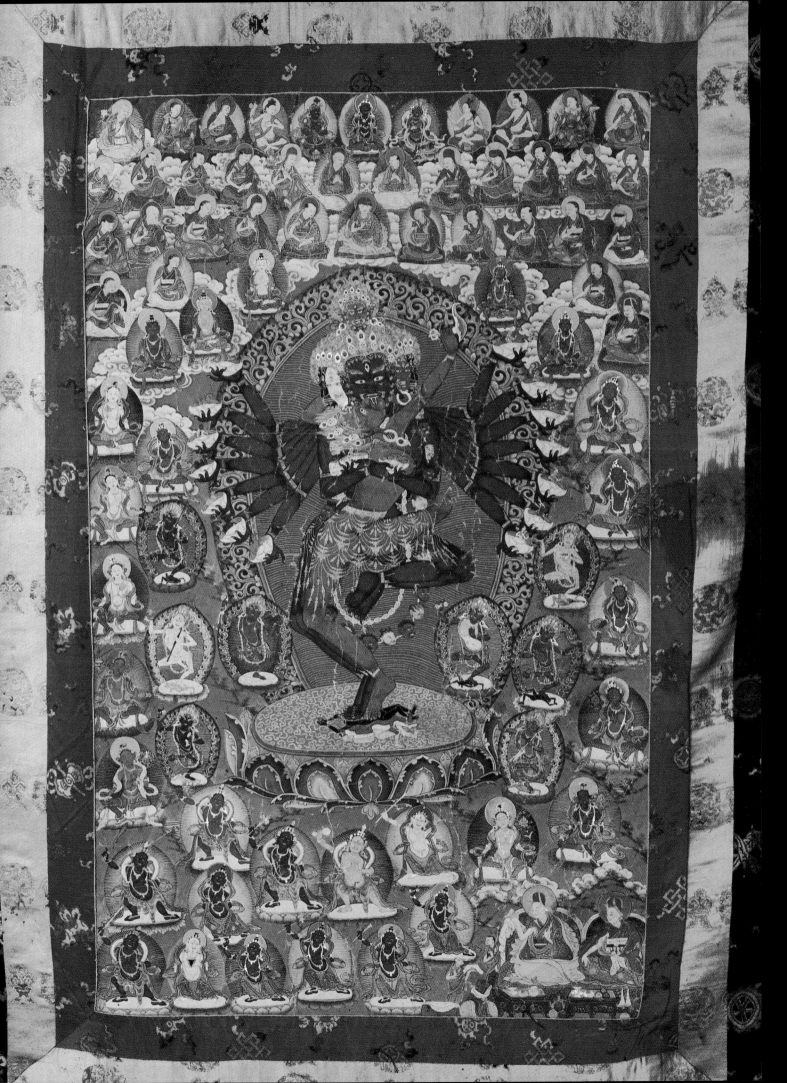

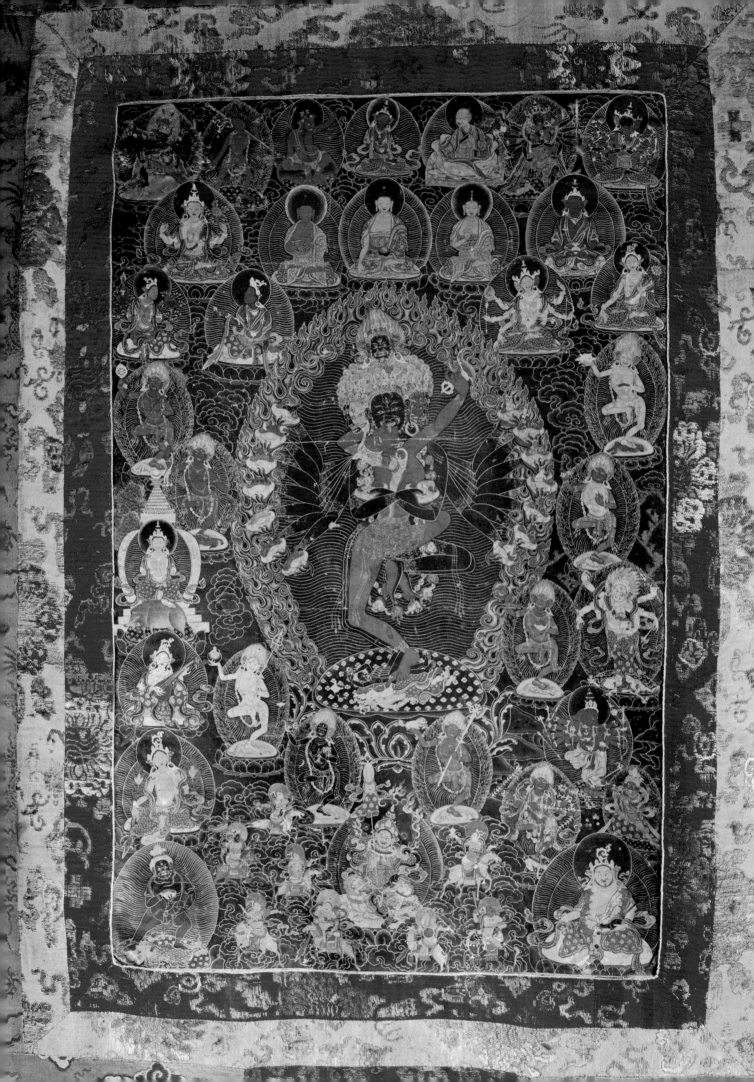

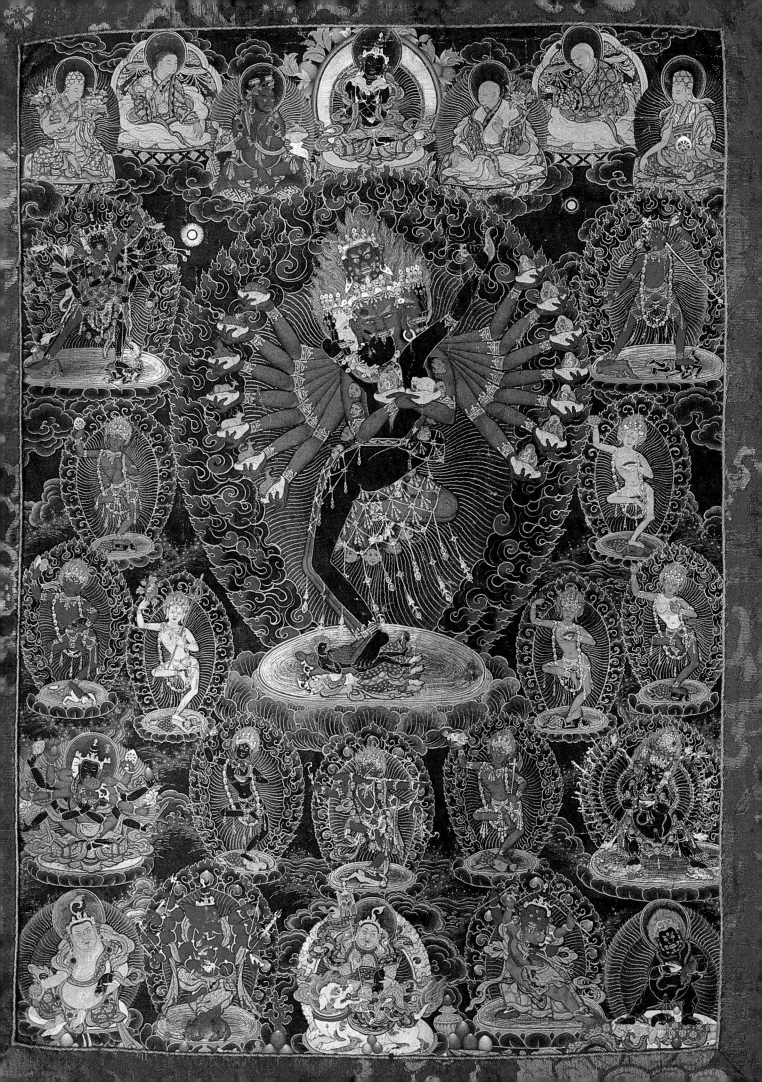

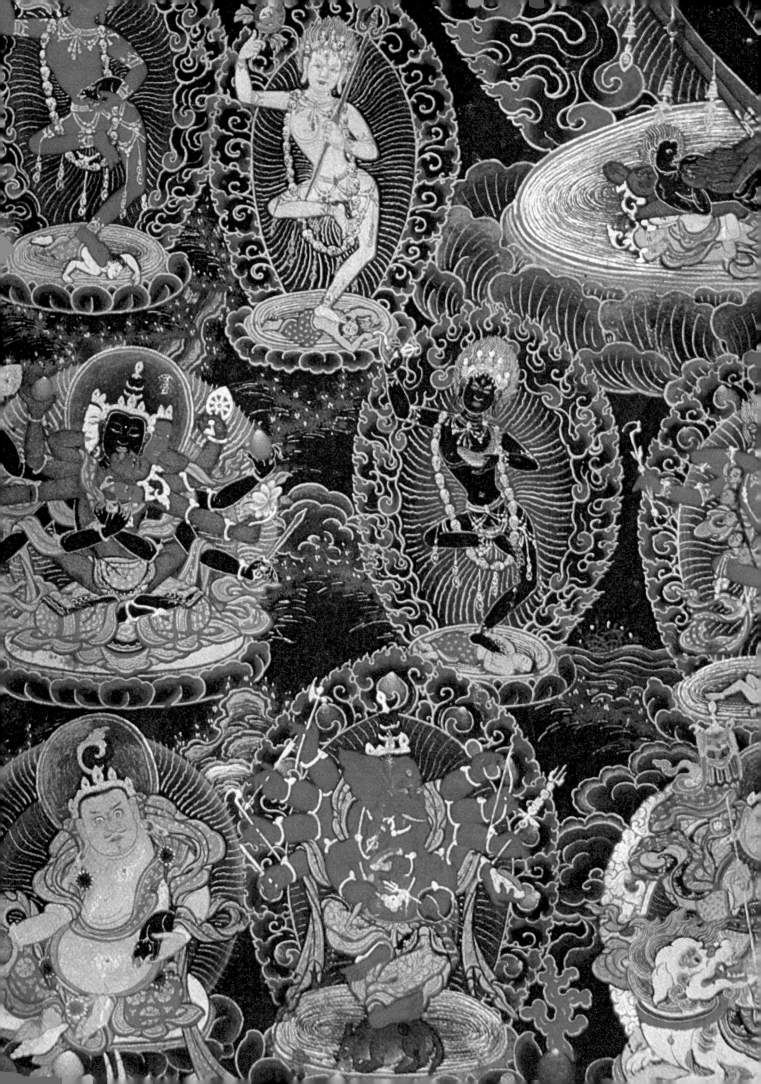

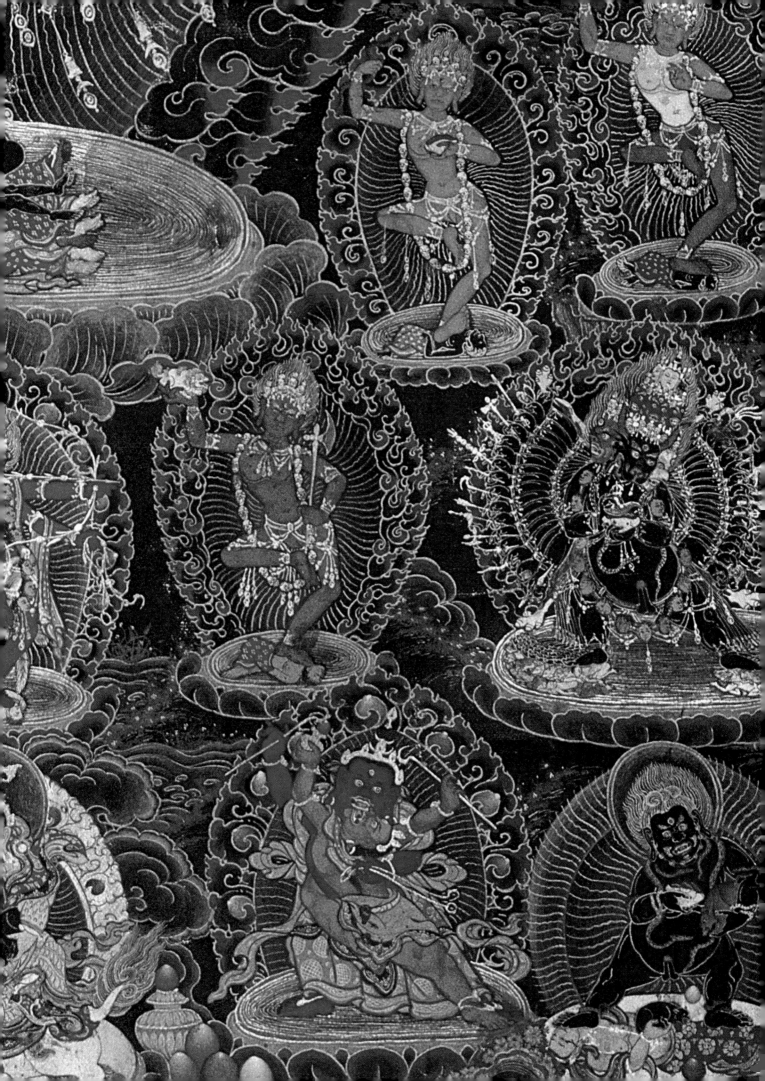

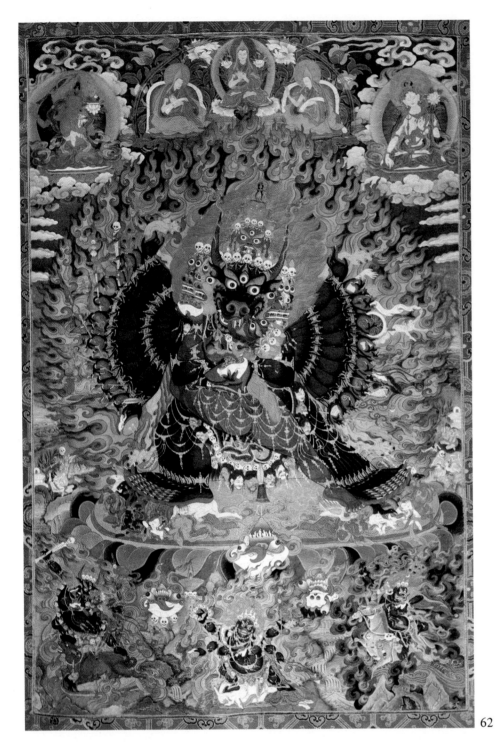

62

62. The Fearful Vajra. *Thang-ka,* 98 × 65cm. In the Drepung Monastery.
63. The Fearful Guardian Deity. This one is the Blue Mahābhairava, also called the Blue Yamāntaka. *Thang-ka,* 58 × 40cm. In the Drepung Monastery.
64. The Fearful Guardian Deity, one of the Thirteen Bhairavas. *Thang-ka* in detail, 58 × 40cm. In the Drepung Monastery.

65. The Fearful Guardian Deity, the Green Mahābhairava Vajra or the Green Yamāntaka. *Thang-ka,* 98 × 65cm. In the Sagya Monastery.
66. The Red Yamāntaka, also known as the Fearful Guardian Deity or Mahābhairava Vajra. According to Tibetan Esoteric doctrine, there are 13 of them such as the Red Mahābhairava, Black Mahābhairava, and Blue Mahābhairava. Thang-ka, 99 × 67cm. In the Sera Monastery.

98

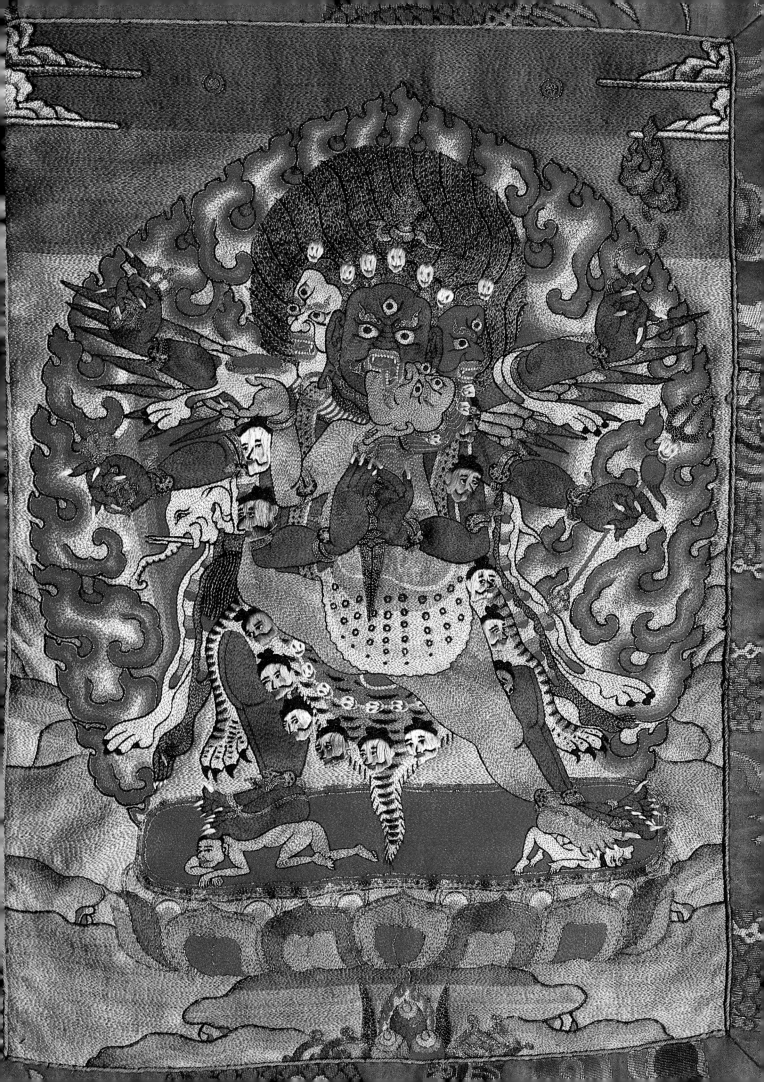

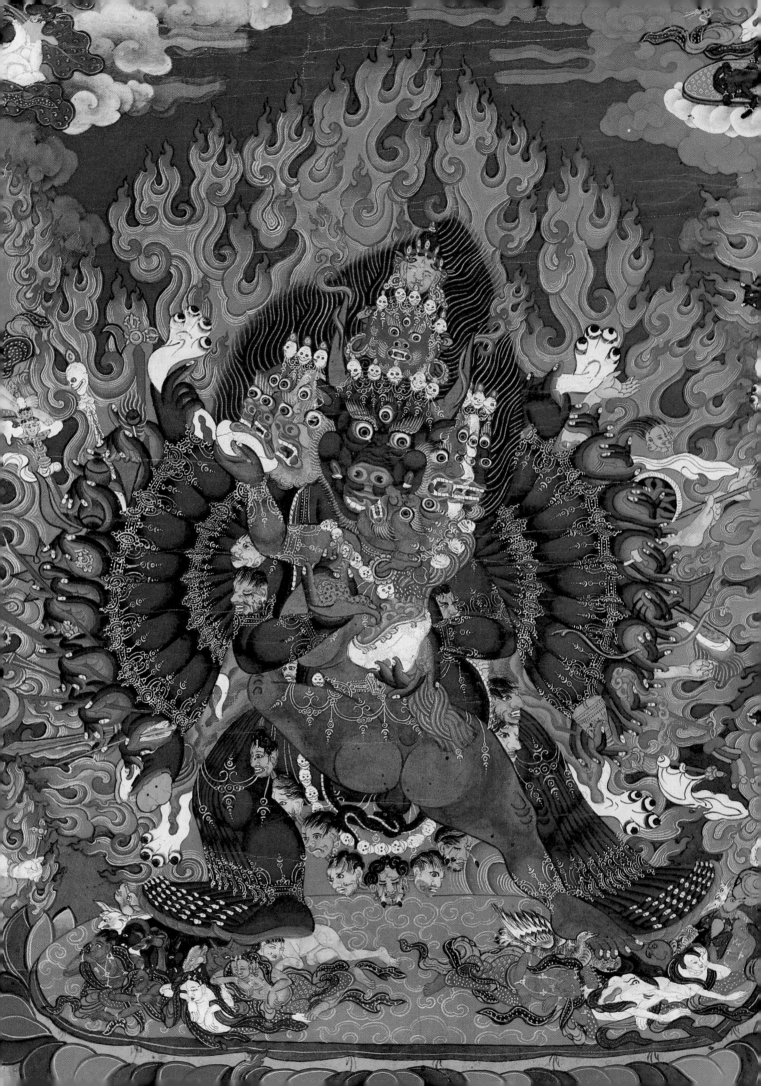

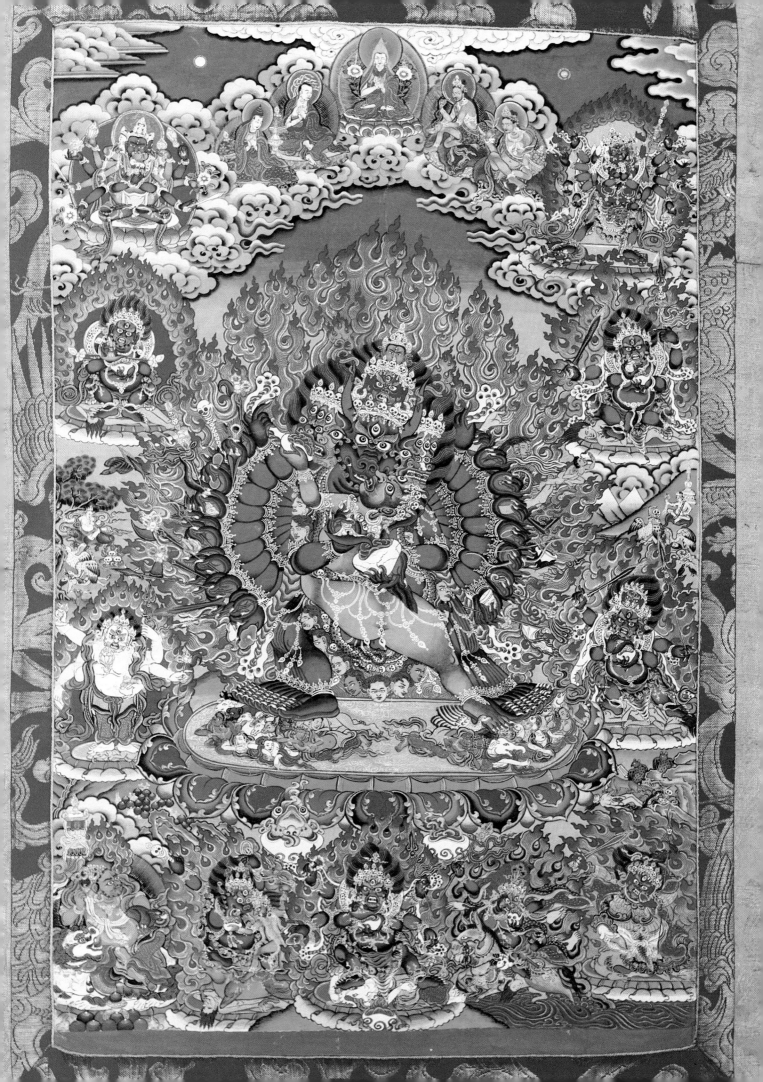

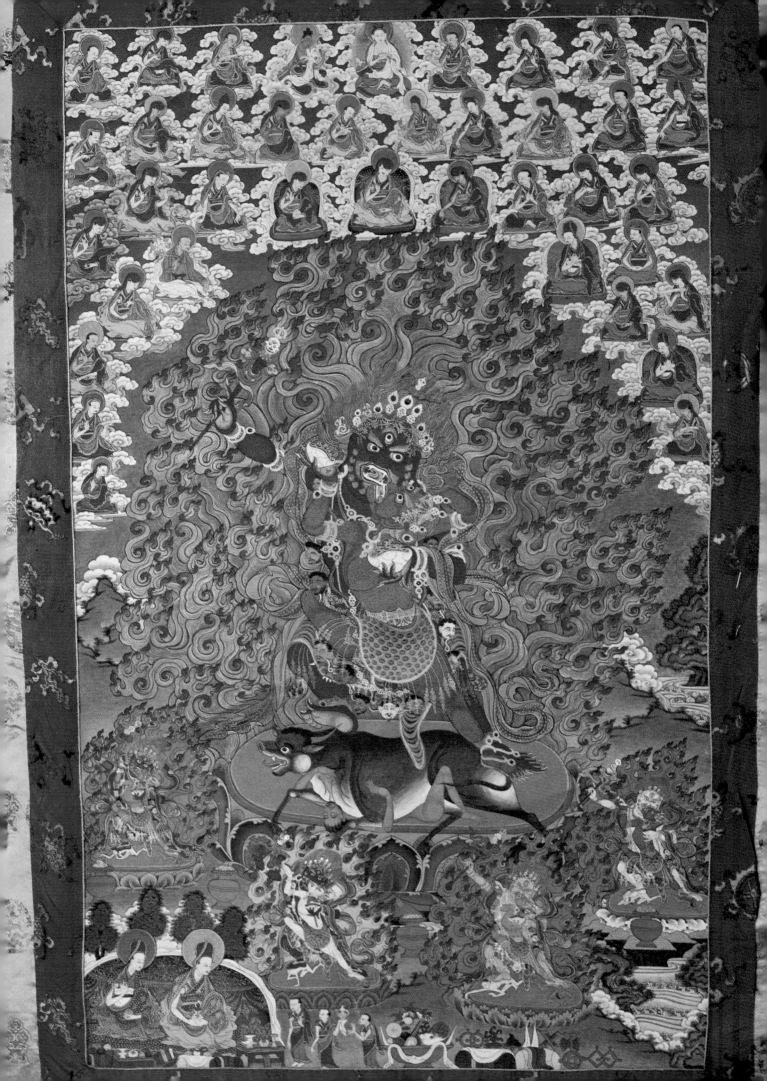

7. The Śambara Vajra. *Thang-ka*, 70 × 35cm. This is an embroidered *thang-ka*, and is therefore more valuable than painted *thang-kas*. In the Drepung Monastery.

68. The Śambara Vajra. *Thang-ka*, 10 × 7cm. In the Sagya Monastery.

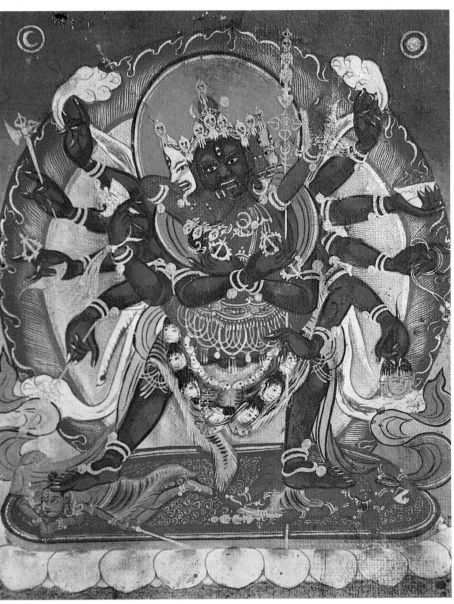

68

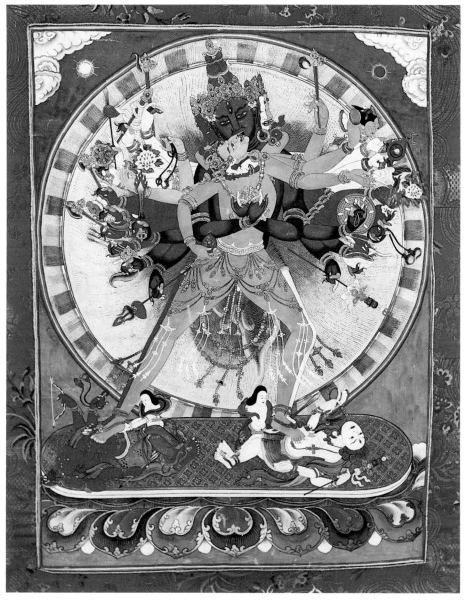

69

69. The Kālacakra Vajra. *Thang-ka*, 58 × 48cm. In the Drepung Monastery.
70. The left upper section of Picture 69.
71. The right upper section.
72. The Kālacakra Vajra. *Thang-ka*, 98 × 60cm. In the Sagya Monastery.

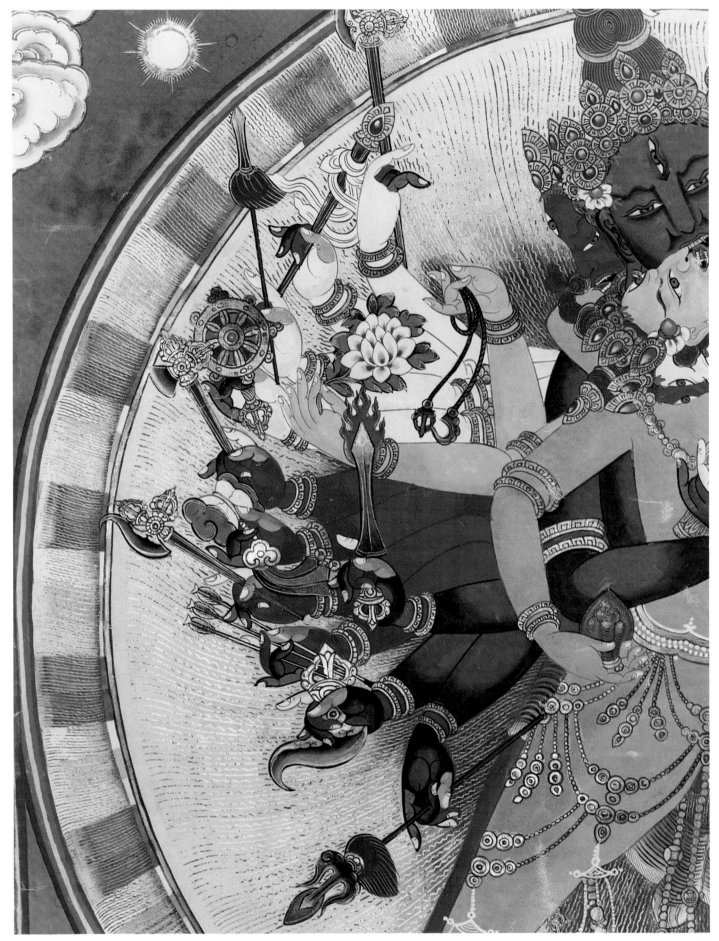

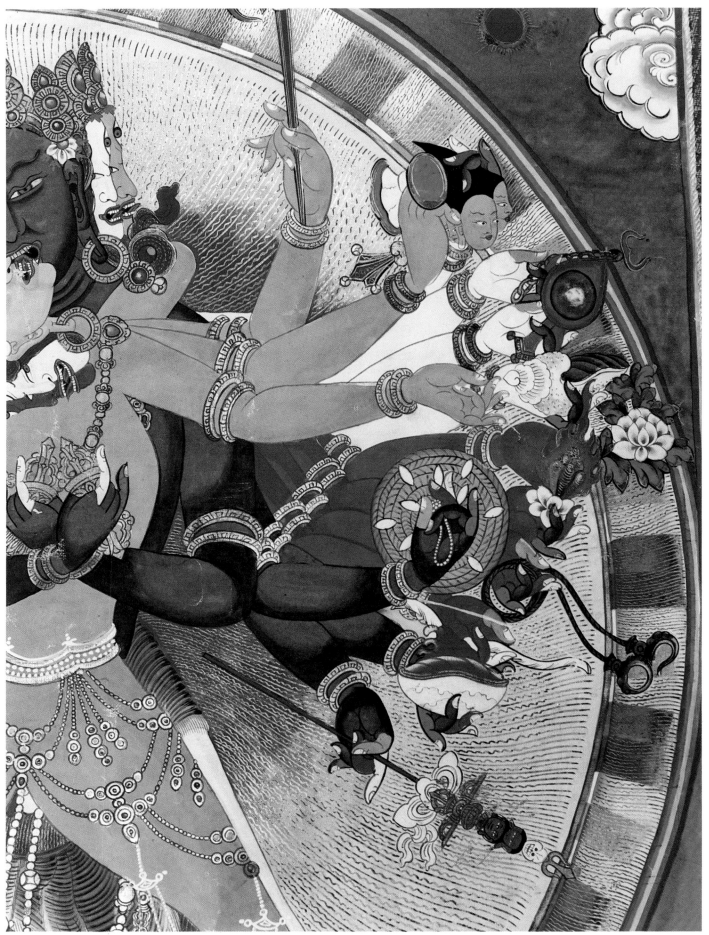

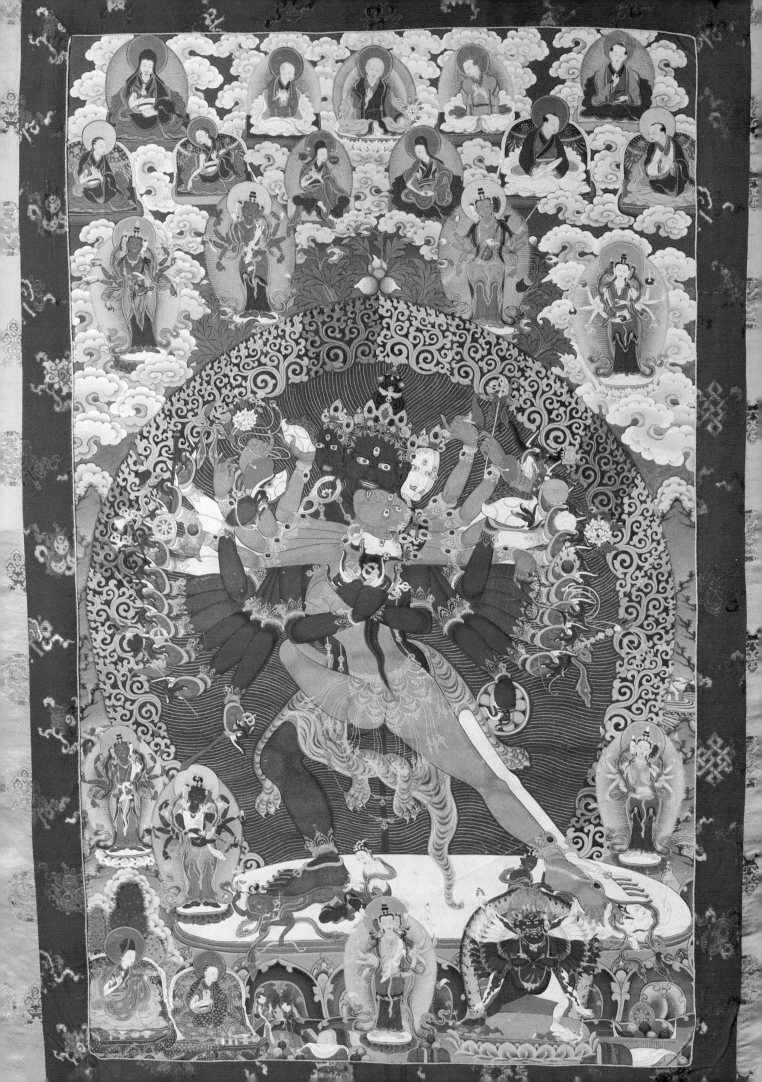

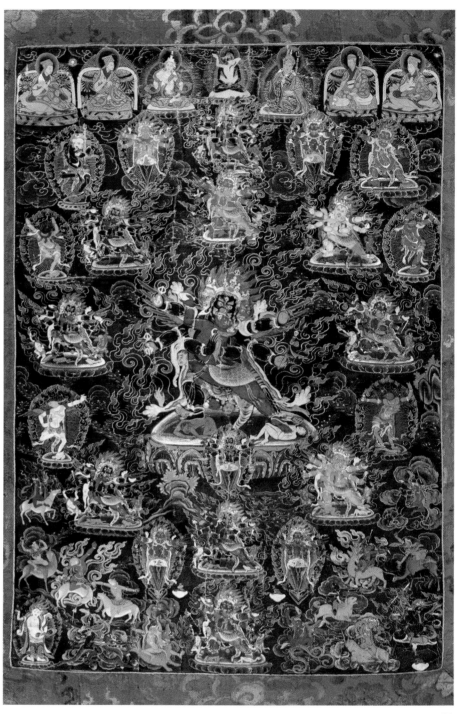

73. The Kila Vajra. *Thang-ka,* 61 × 43cm. In
the Sagya Monastery.
74. Part of the Kila Vajra in picture 73.
75. The Kila Vajra. *Thang-ka,* 96 × 65cm. In
the Sagya Monastery.
76. The Kila Vajra. Embroidered *thang-ka,*
36 × 29cm. In the Sagya Monastery.
77. The Kila Vajra. *Thang-ka,* 15 × 15cm. In
the Sagya Monastery.

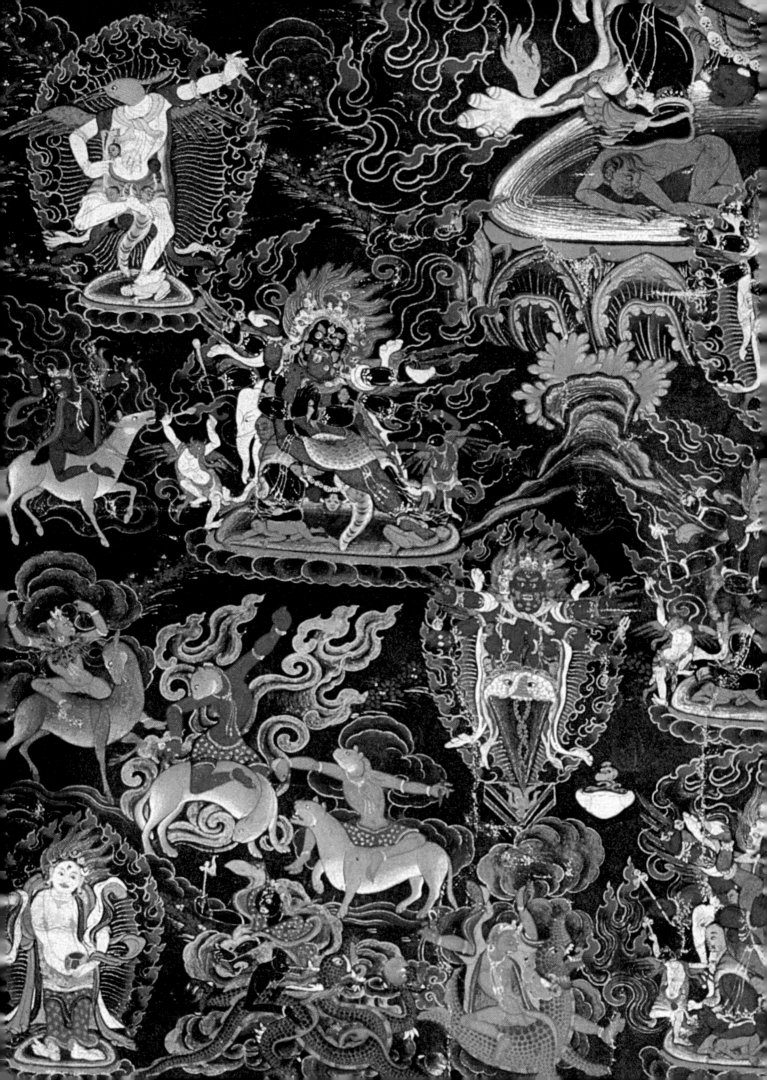

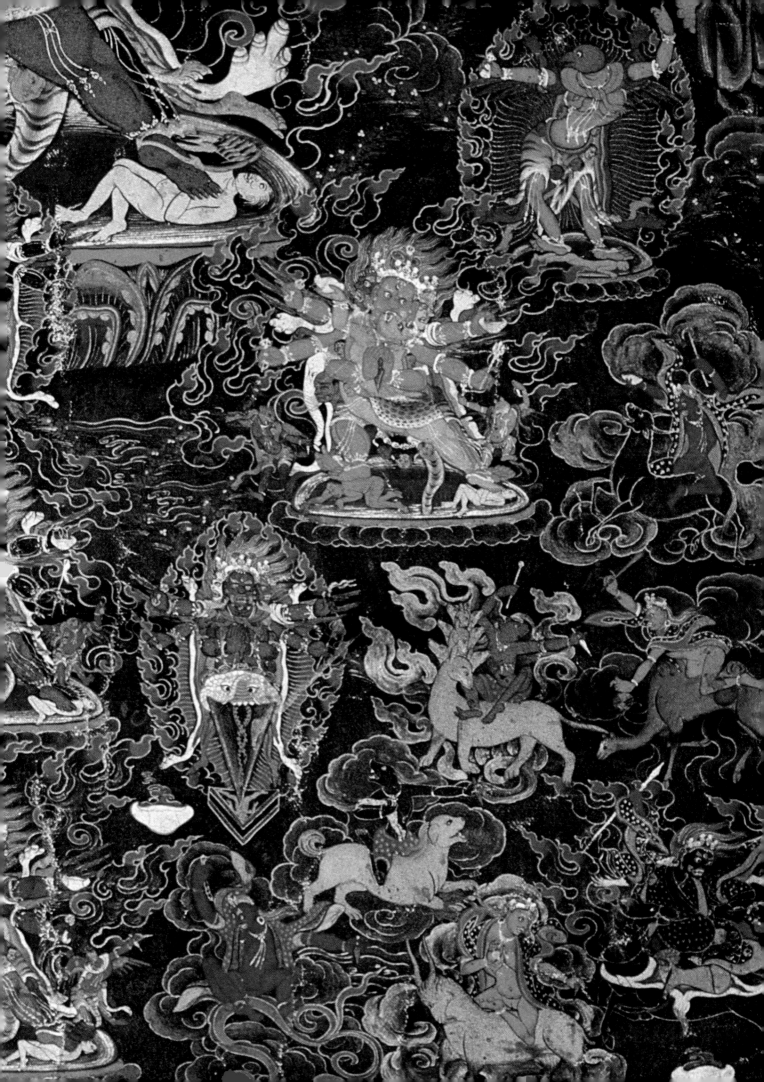

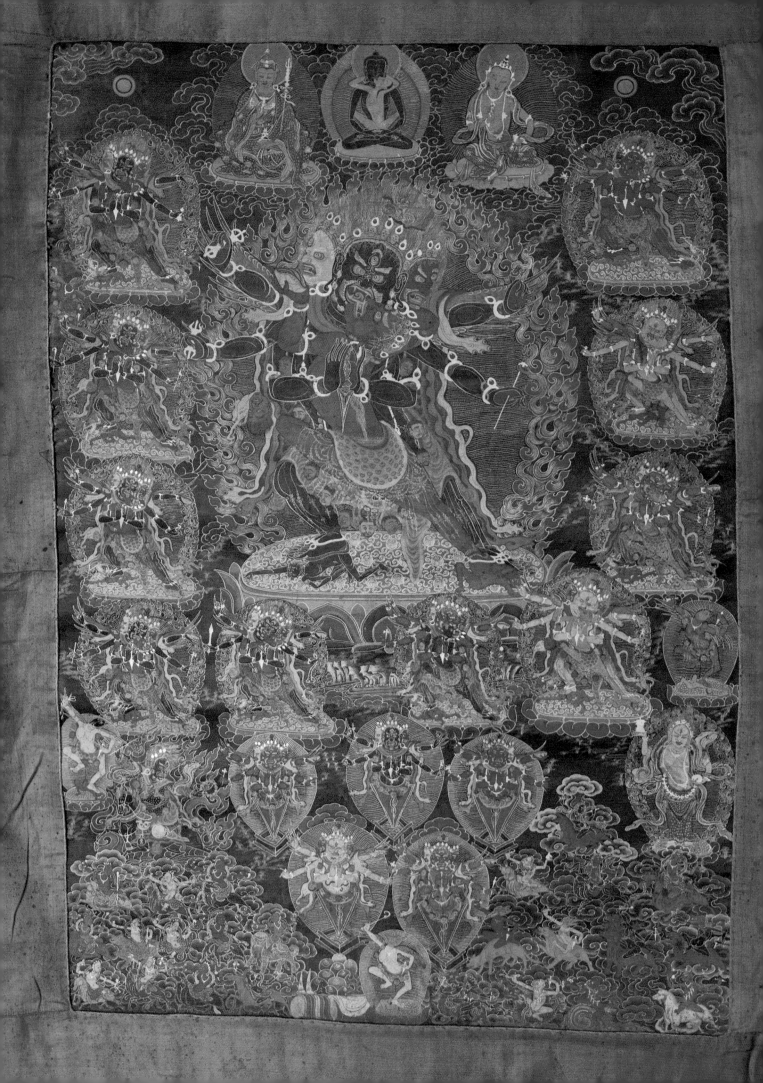

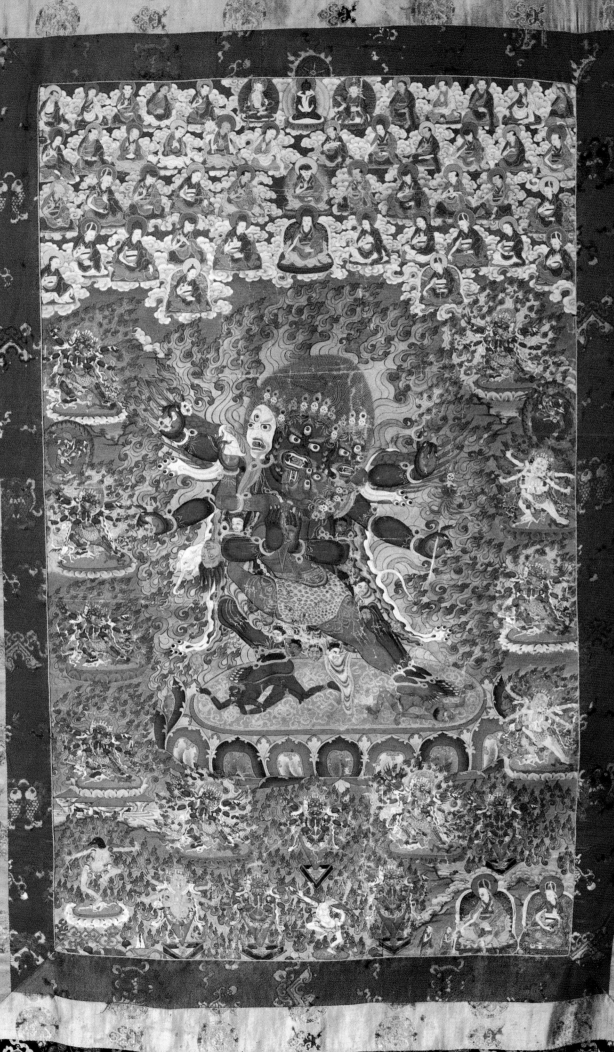

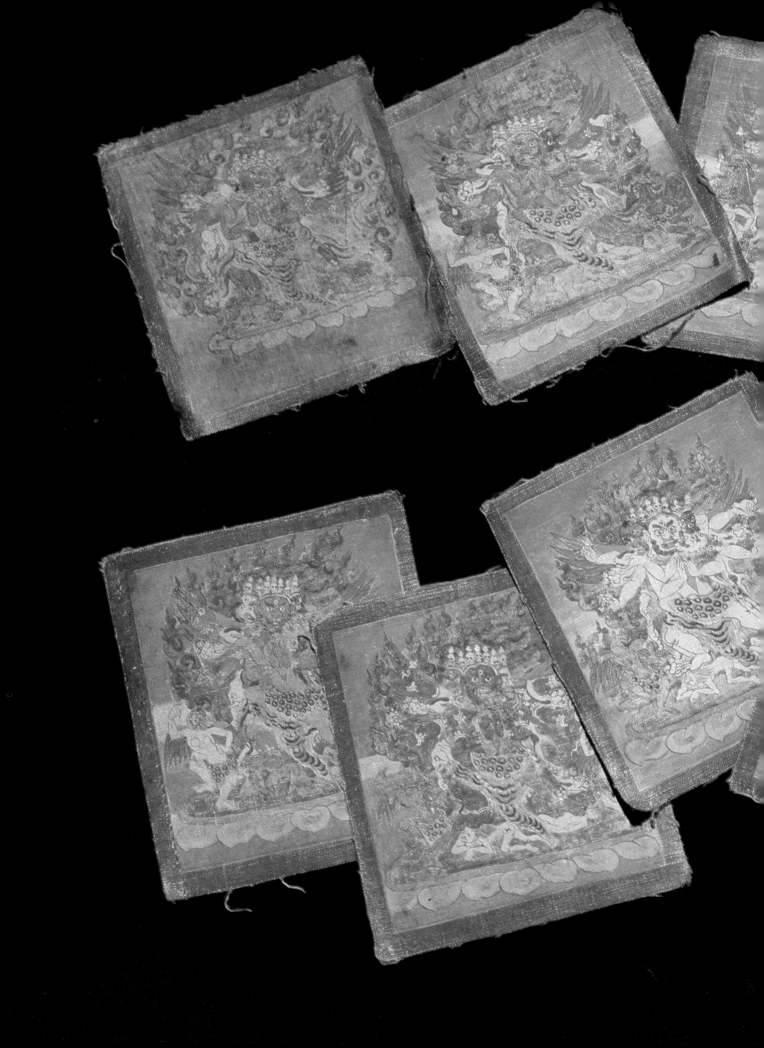

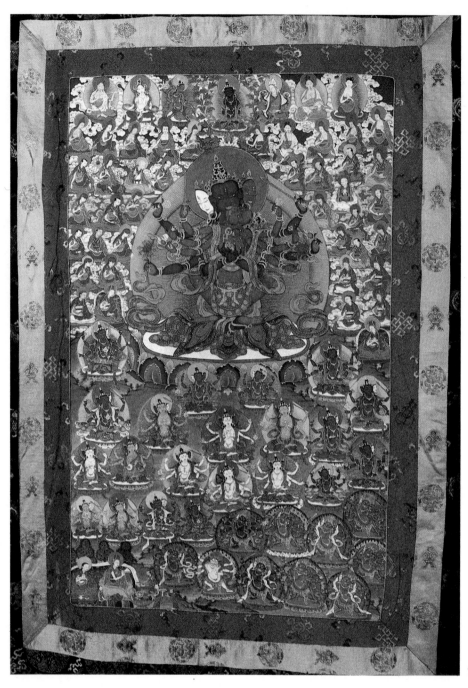

The Guhyasamāja, or Guhyasamāja Vajra (Tibetan: Dsang-vdus), is one of the five Satyadevatās of the vajra dharmas. The five Satyadevatās are the Mahābhairava Vajra, the Śambara Vajra, the Kālacakra Vajra, the Guhyasamāja Vajra and the Smiling Vajra. This one has three faces, each with three eyes, and six arms. The devī in his embrace also has six arms. The Dge-lugs-pa Sect pays particular attention to the study of the doctrine of this vajra.

78. The Guhyasamāja. *Thang-ka,* 98 × 67cm. In the Sagya Monastery.
79. Part of the Guhyasamāja.

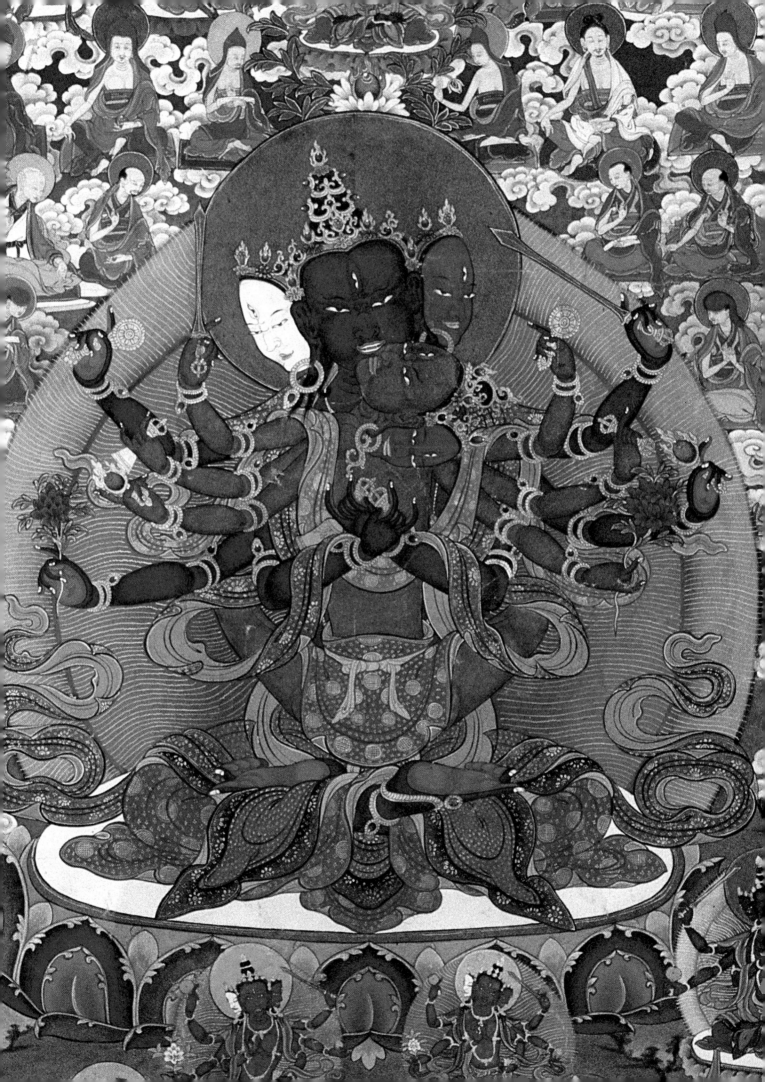

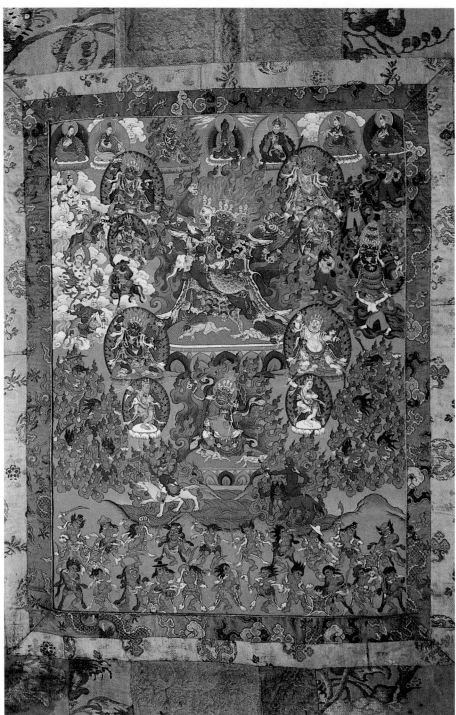

80

The Hayagrīva (Horse-headed Vajra), also known as the Horse-headed Avalokiteśvara (Tibetan: Rta-mgrin). He is the Garbhadhātu Satyadevatā of the Avalokiteśvara's Quarters, one of the six Avalokiteśvaras, and the god of the animal world. According to Tibetan Esoteric Buddhism, the Horse-headed Vajra is the wrathful manifestation of the Amitābha (Buddha of the Boundless Life), and the horse head symbolizes great wrath and power, which, like a heavenly horse sweeping across the land and the sea of life and death, can crush underfoot all demons and barriers of ignorance. He has a dark flesh-tinted body, three faces with two teeth bared, and a halo of angry flames over his back. The Rdo-lo is his devī. The Upper and Lower Tantra Apartments of the Dge-lugs-pa Sect regard the deity as its dharmapāla.

80. The Hayagrīva. *Thang-ka,* 65 × 49cm. In the Sagya Monastery.
81. Part of the front view of the Hayagrīva.
82. Lower part of the Hayagrīva.

118

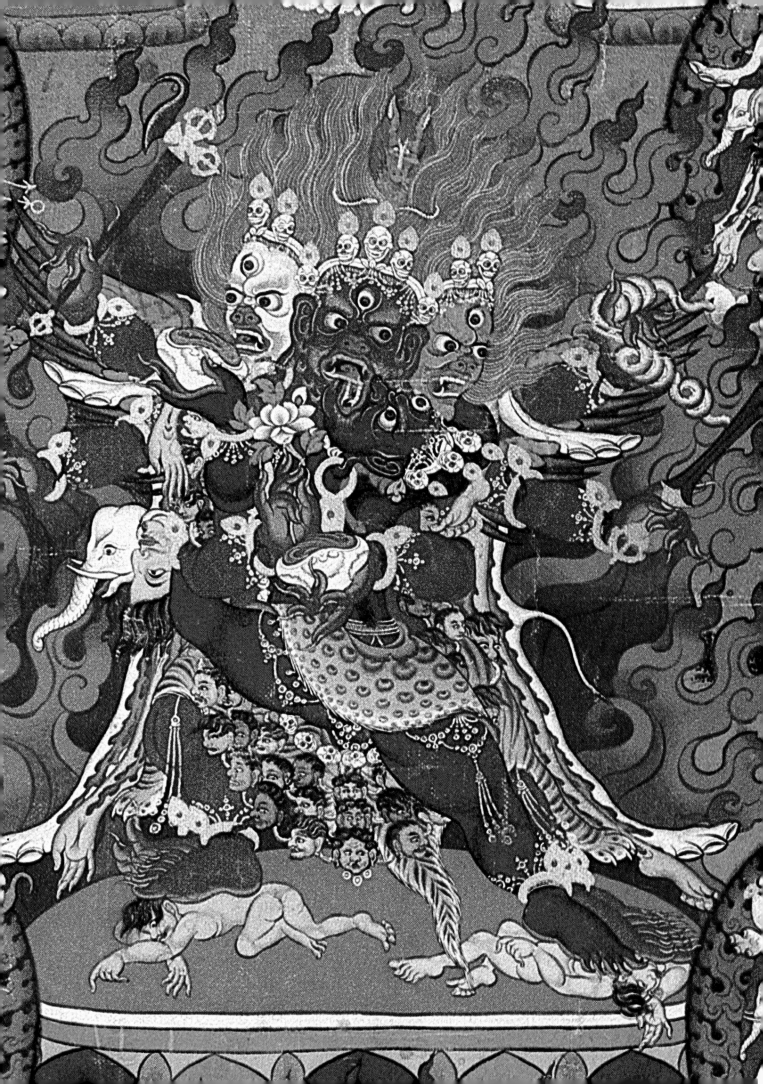

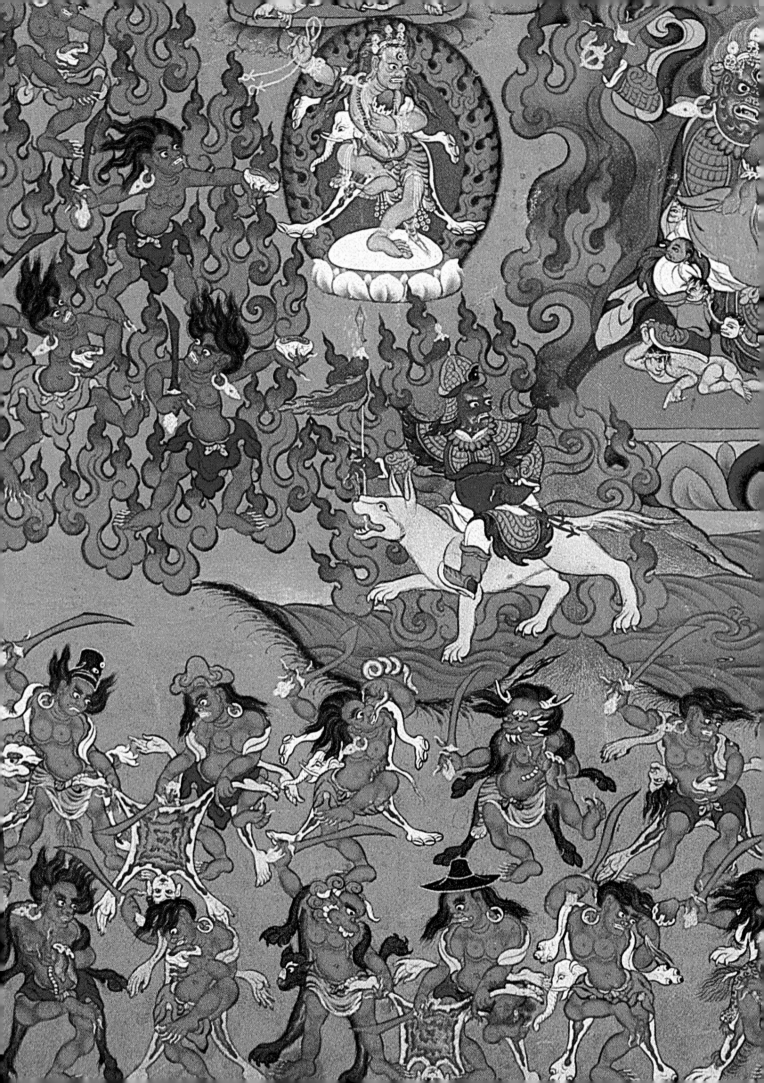

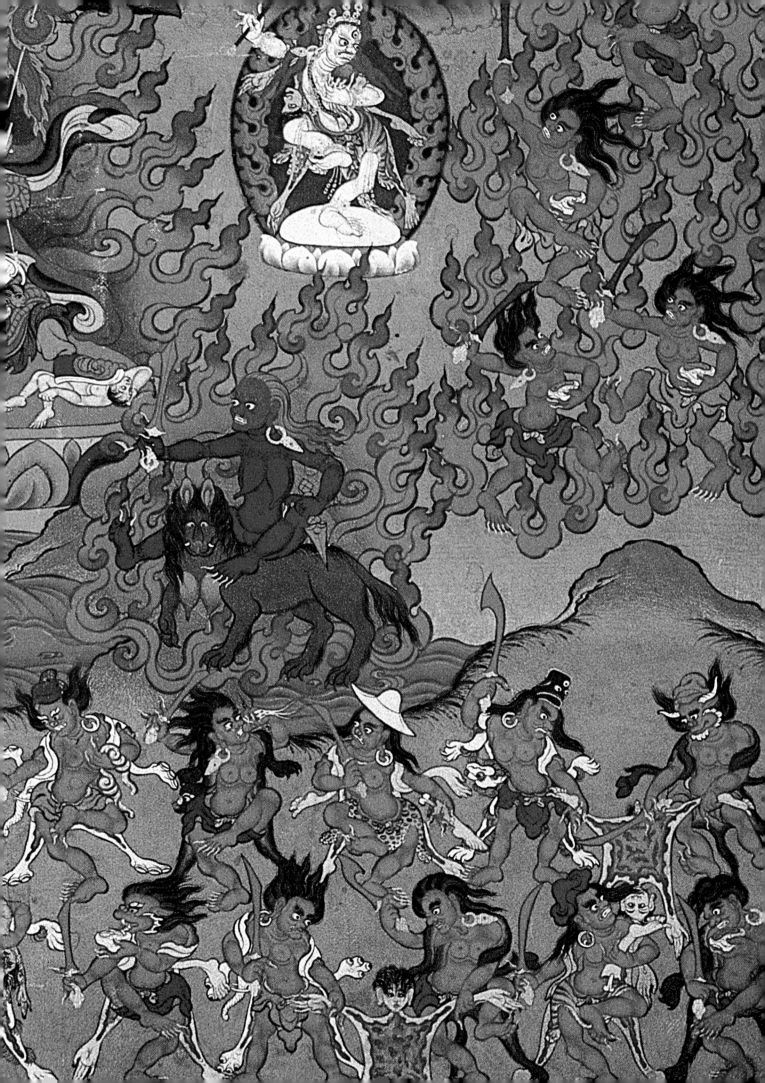

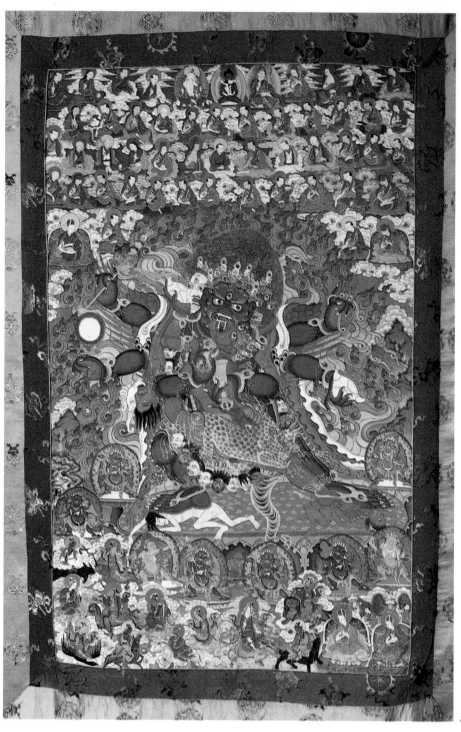

83

The Protector of Life, or Guardian Deity
of Life (Tibetan: Tshebdag mgon-po),
is a dharmapāla of Tibetan Esoteric
Buddhism. According to tradition, the
deity is the Yama, King of Hell. He has
two faces, one genial and the other
fearful, symbolizing good and bad karmas.

83. The Protector of Life. *Thang-ka,* 95 ×
60cm. In the Sagya Monastery.
84. Part of the Protector of Life.

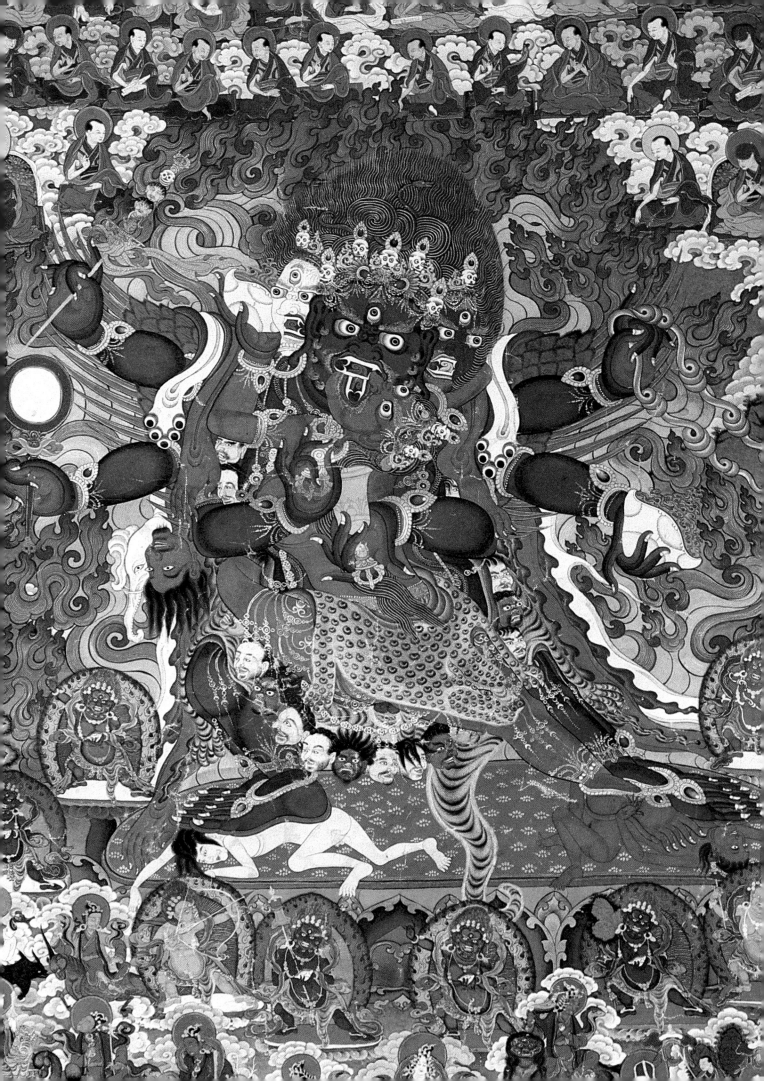

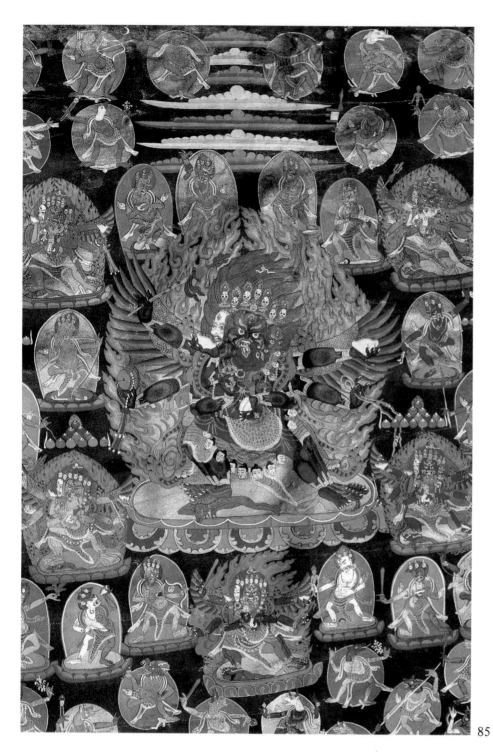

85

85. The Protector of Life. Detail of a *thang-ka*, 65 × 50cm. In the Sagya Monastery.
86. The Protector of Life. *Thang-ka*, 80 × 56cm. In the Sagya Monastery.

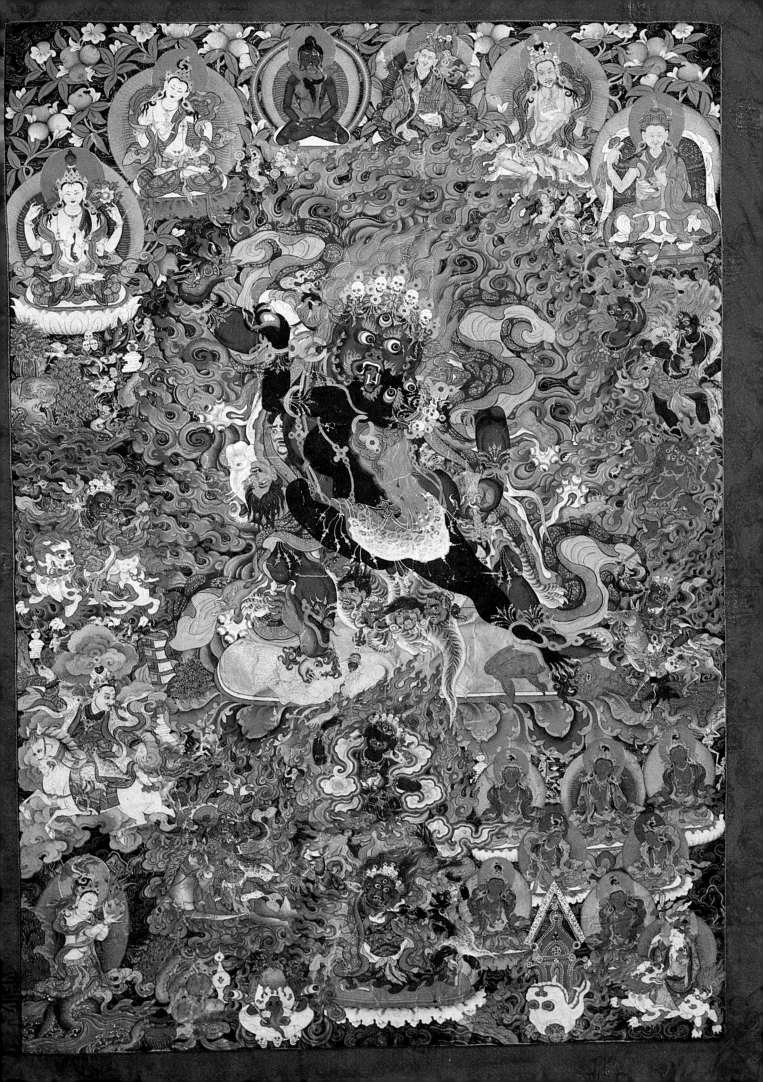

Mañjuśrī Bodhisattva, known in Tibetan as Vjam-pvi rdo-rje. This deity varies in title and shape. The one holding a sword in the right hand and riding a lion is Mañjuśrī of the Vajradhātu; the one with a green lotus flower in the left hand and seated on a white lotus throne is Mañjuśrī of the Garbhadhātu. The sword symbolizes "the severance of all earthly cares", and the lion signifies the power of wisdom, as Tibetan Esoteric Buddhism believes that "the Mañjuśrī represents the wisdoms of the Tathāgata".

87. Mañjuśrī Bodhisattva. *Thang-ka* in detail. The image is 15cm tall. In the Sagya Monastery.

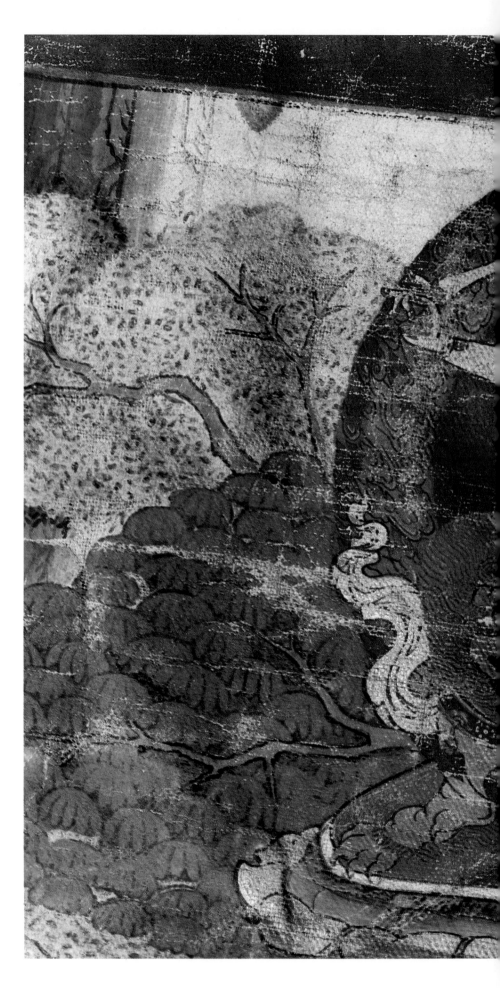

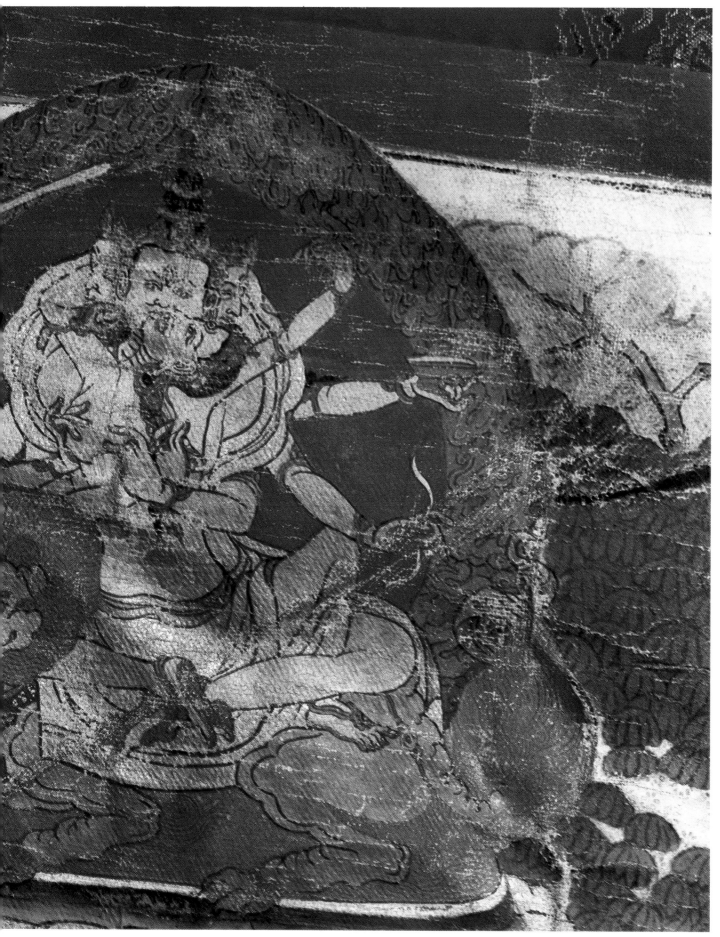

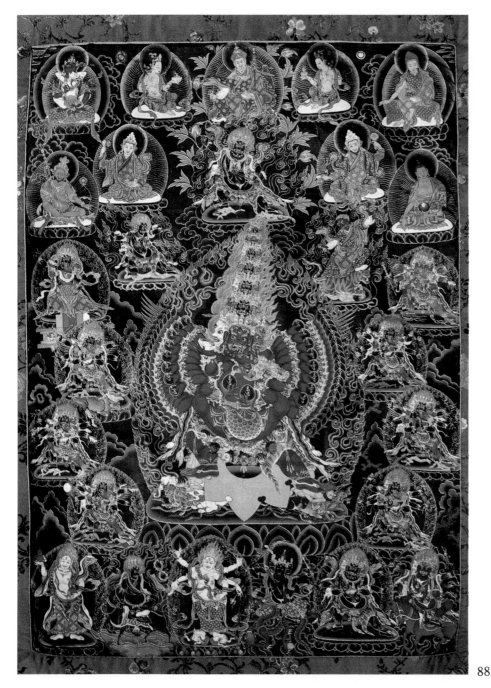

88

The Supreme Heruka (Tibetan: Bde gshegs sgrub pa bkav brgyad) or the Deva of Eight Methods of the Tathāgata. He is the Wrathful Guardian Deity of Tibetan Esoteric Buddhism and the Dharmapāla of the Eight Dharmas. This deity, of green colour and with a halo of flames and wings on his back, is multi-faced in different colours. Originally a Bon-po demonic god, he has 18 arms, 8 feet, and embraces the devī Mamo.

88. The Supreme Heruka. *Thang-ka,* 95 × 56cm. In the Sagya Monastery.
89. Part of the Supreme Heruka.
90. Upper part of the Supreme Heruka.
91. Lower part of the Supreme Heruka.

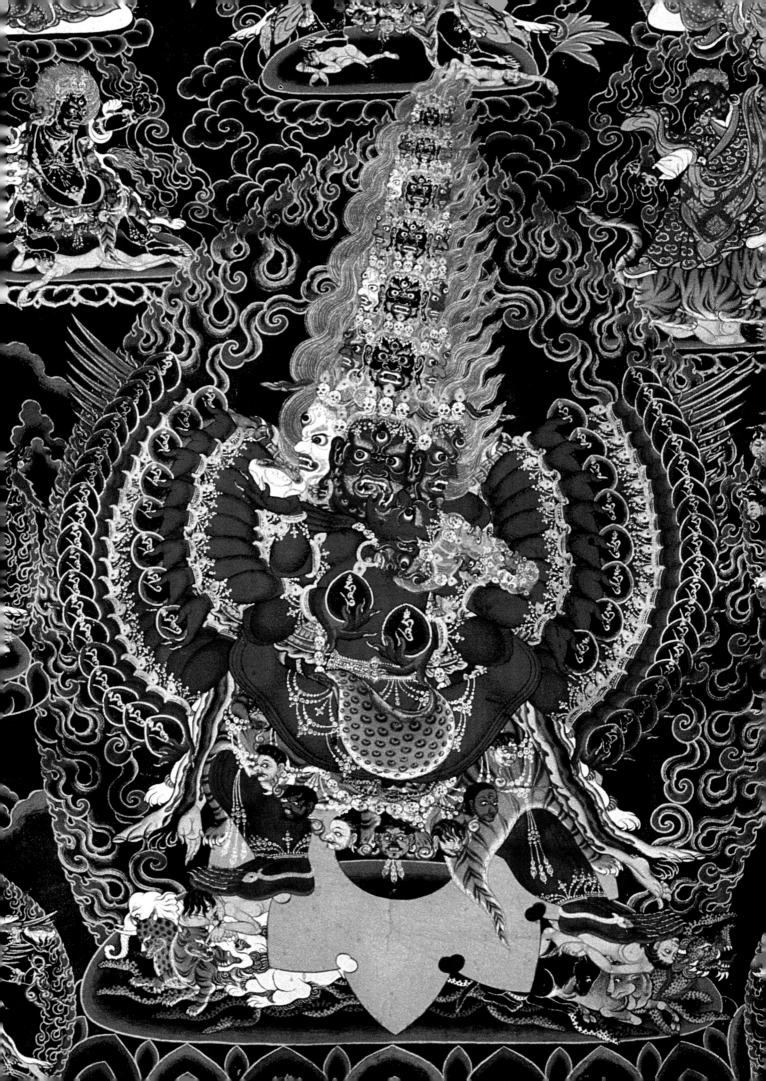

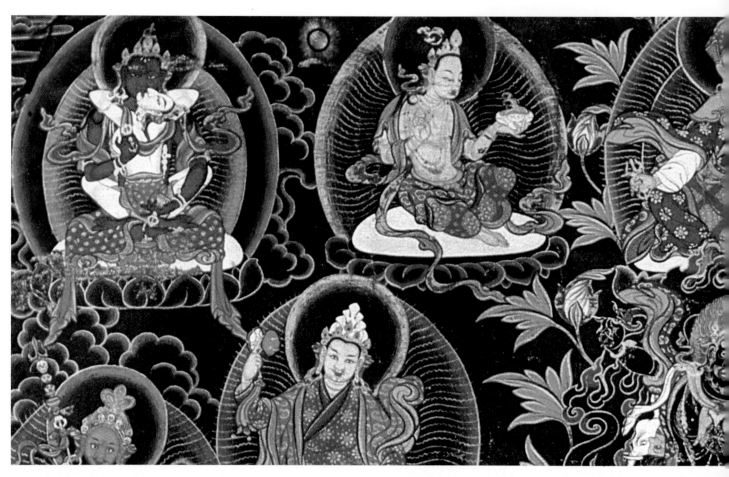

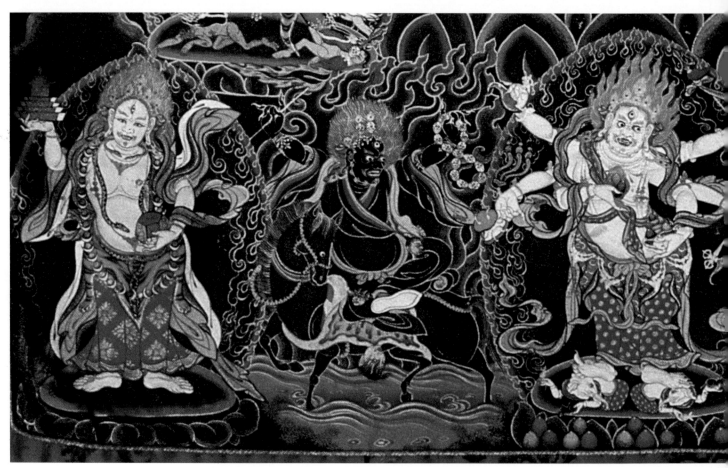

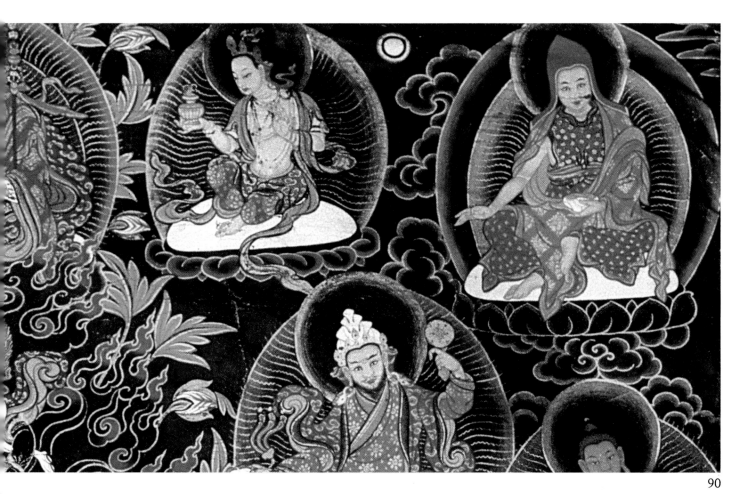

90

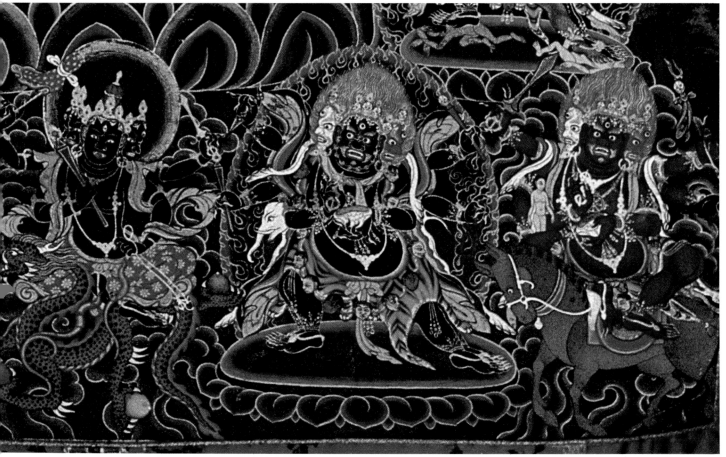

91

131

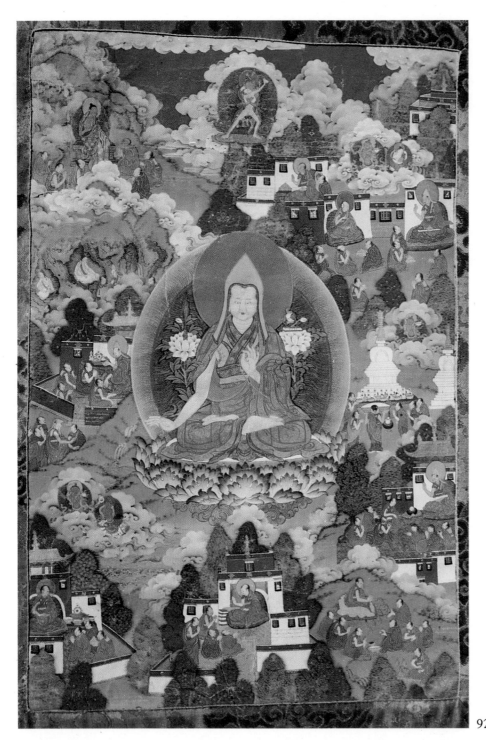

92. Tsong-kha-pa preaching. His gesture signifies that he is going to give sermons, a gesture representing the future time. The small picture at the top showing the twin-image of the Kālacakra Vajra signifies that Tsong-kha-pa is going to preach the doctrine of the Kālacakra. *Thang-ka*, 90 x 60cm. In the Drepung Monastery.

93. The Bhaiṣajya gurus (Buddhas of Medicine). This *thang-ka* shows seven of them praying. *Thang-ka*, 90 x 60cm. In the Drepung Monastery.

94. Part of the Bhaiṣajya Gurus.

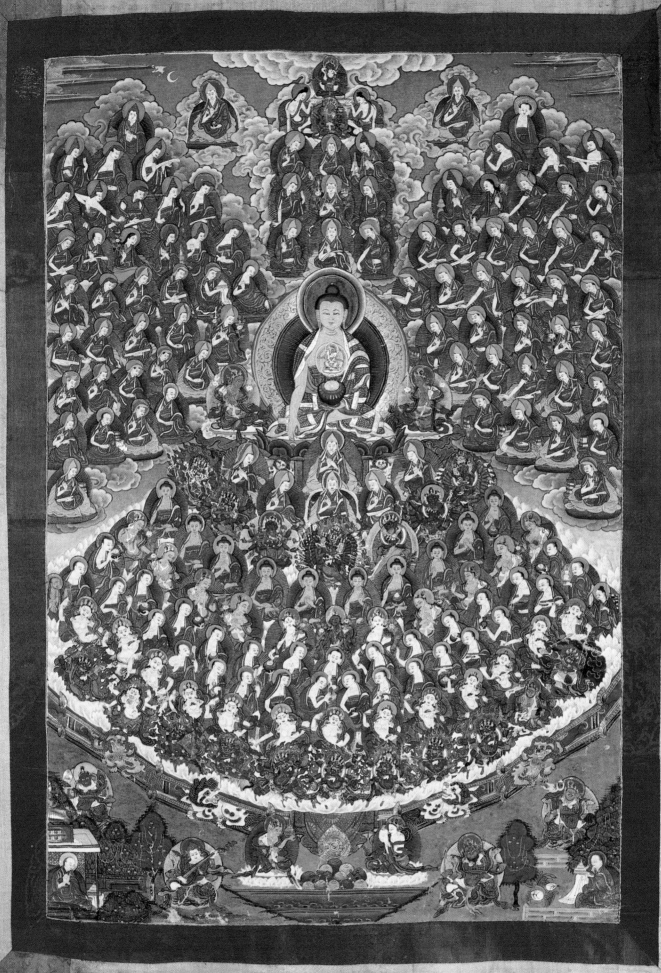

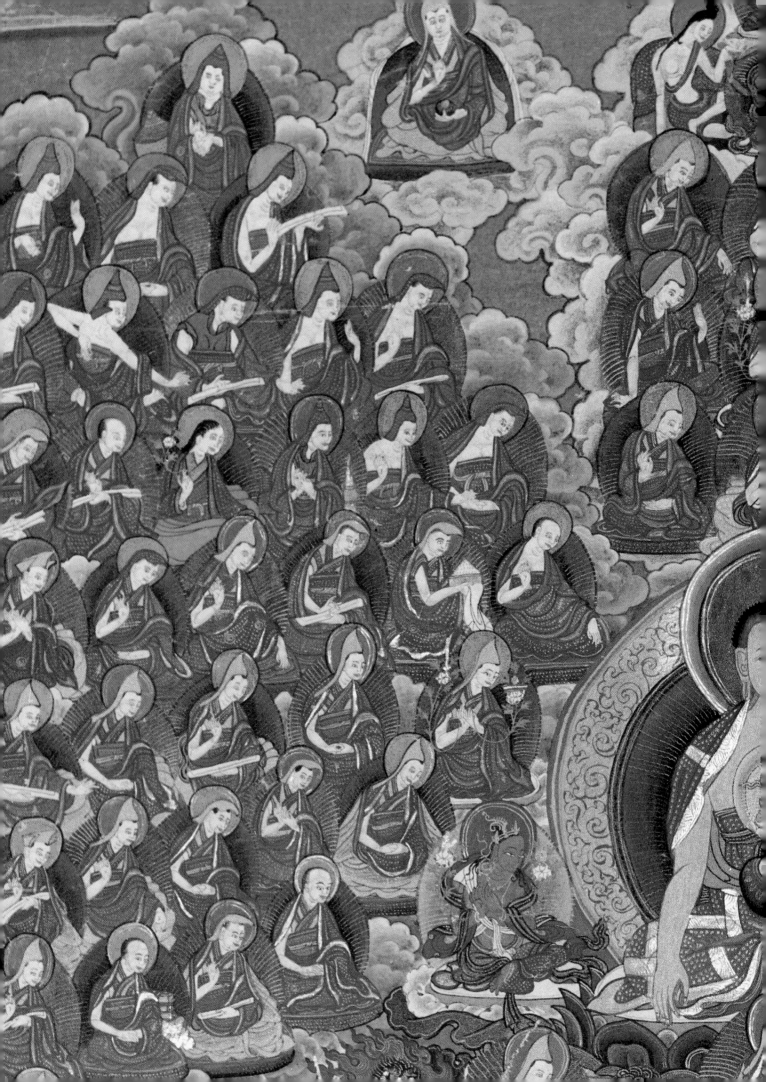

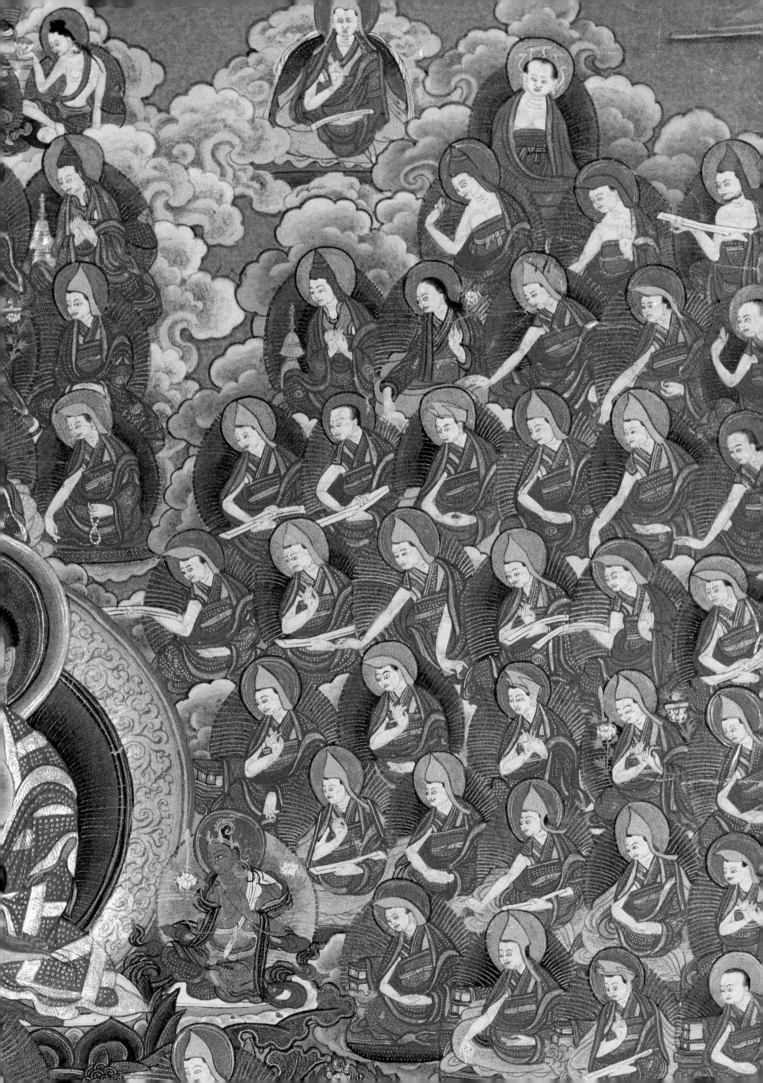

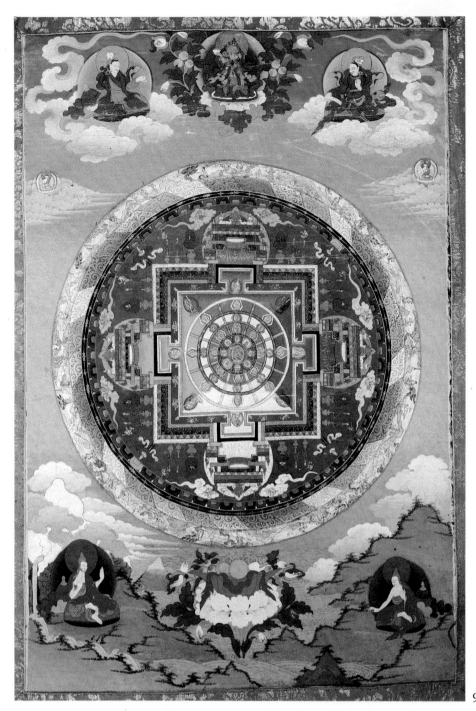

The maṇḍala of the Śambara Vajra. The
maṇḍala (Tibetan: Dkyil-vkhor), meaning
"rostrum ground", used to refer to the
round or square mud platform in the
middle of a meditation site. Esoteric
Buddhists studying the doctrine of a
Satyadevatā are required to meditate on
the maṇḍala of the Satyadevatā.

95. The maṇḍala of the Śambara Vajra. *Thang-ka*, 61 × 45cm. In the Drepung Monastery.
96. The maṇḍala of the Mahābhairava Vajra. *Thang-ka*, 58 × 45cm. In the Drepung Monastery.
97. The maṇḍala of the Kila Vajra. *Thang-ka*, 40 × 33cm. In the Sagya Monastery.
98. The maṇḍala of the Kila Vajra. (Detail). The entire *thang-ka* measures 55 × 55cm. In the Sagya Monastery.

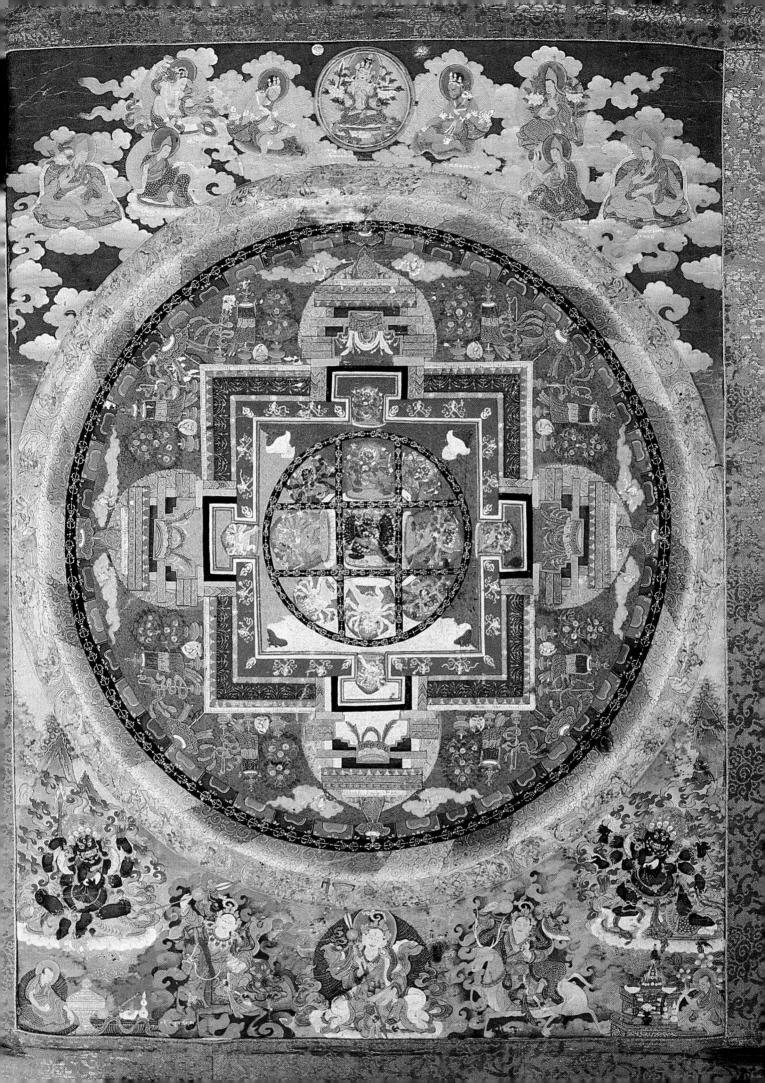

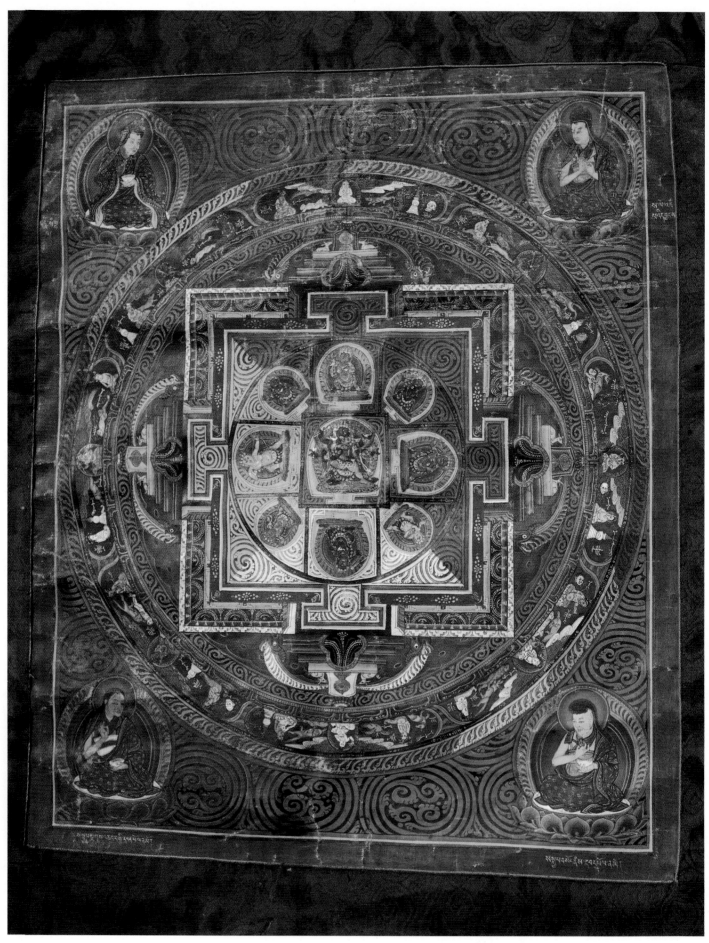

97

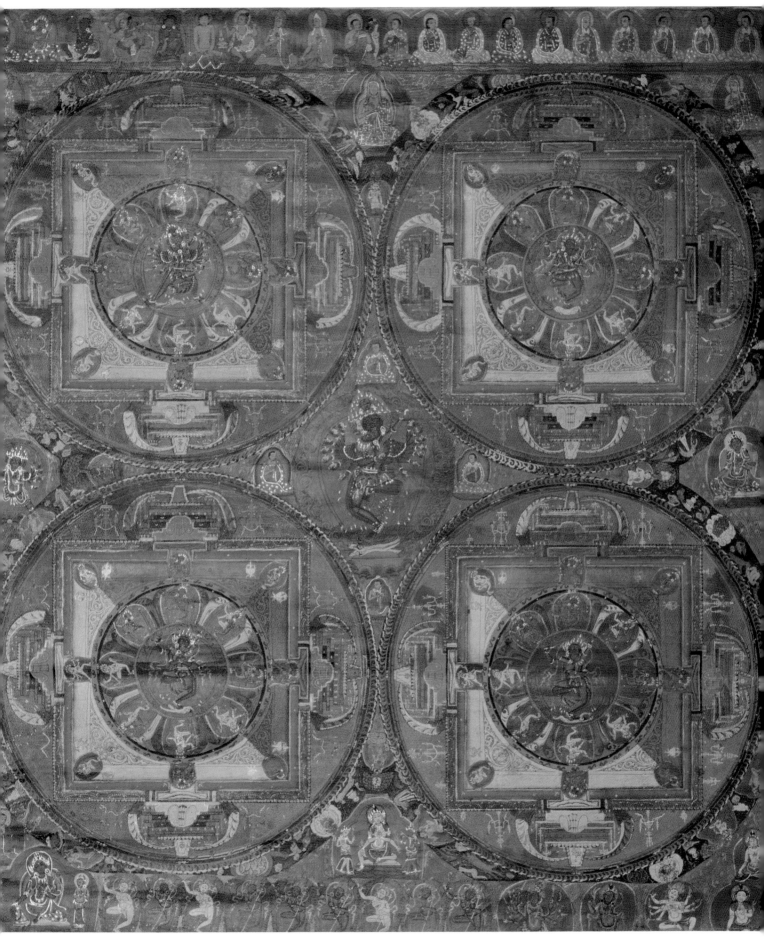

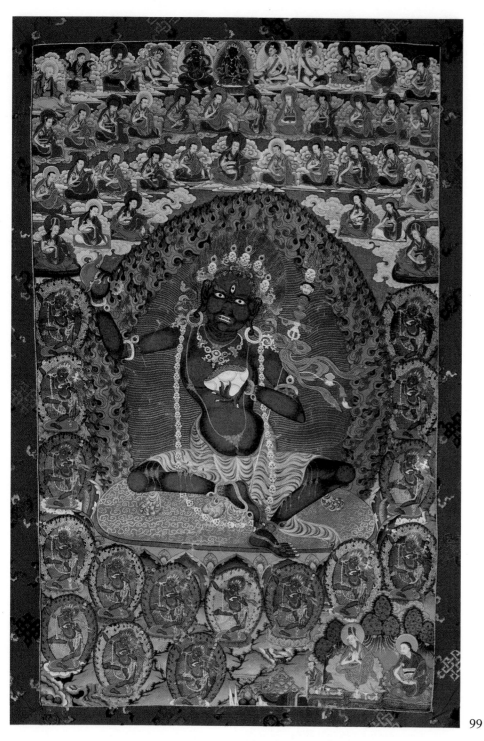

99

99. The Black Wrathful Devī. *Thang-ka*, 60 x
30cm. In the Sagya Monastery.
100. Part of the Black Wrathful Devī.

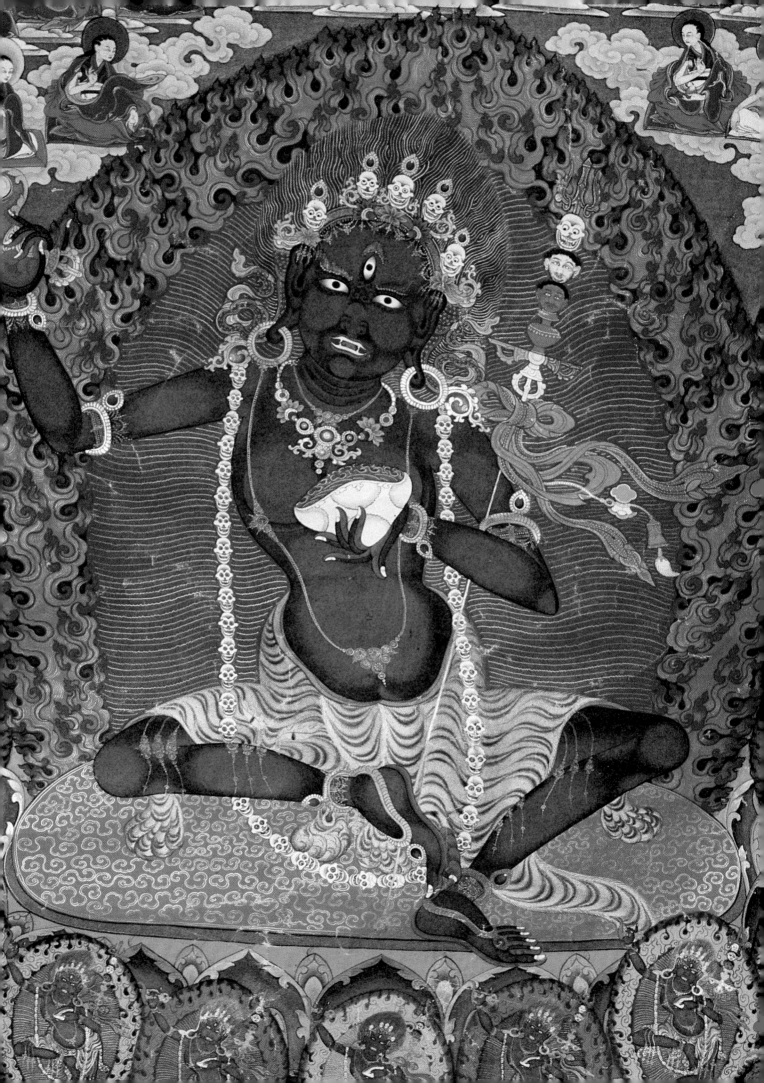

The Skeletons, or the Keepers of Graveyards, are the dharmapālas of the Śambara Vajra. They are so called because in Esoteric Buddhism the principal deities of graveyards are represented by two skeletons which guard the sky burial grounds as defenders of Buddhism. The flaming blue deities which surround the skeletons are the Mahābhairava Vajras.

101. The Skeletons. *Thang-ka*, 90 × 60cm. In the Sagya Monastery.
102. Part of the Skeletons.
103. Bhairavas. *Thang-ka*, 90 × 60cm. In the Sagya Monastery. The two principal deities of graveyards are surrounded by flaming Bhairavas. Top centre is Tsong-kha-pa who is flanked by the Green Tārā (right) and the White Tārā (left). *Thang-ka*, 90 × 60cm. In the Drepung Monastery.

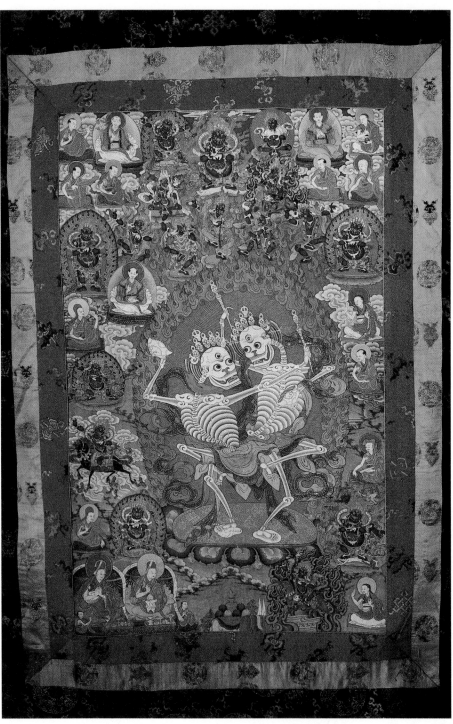

101

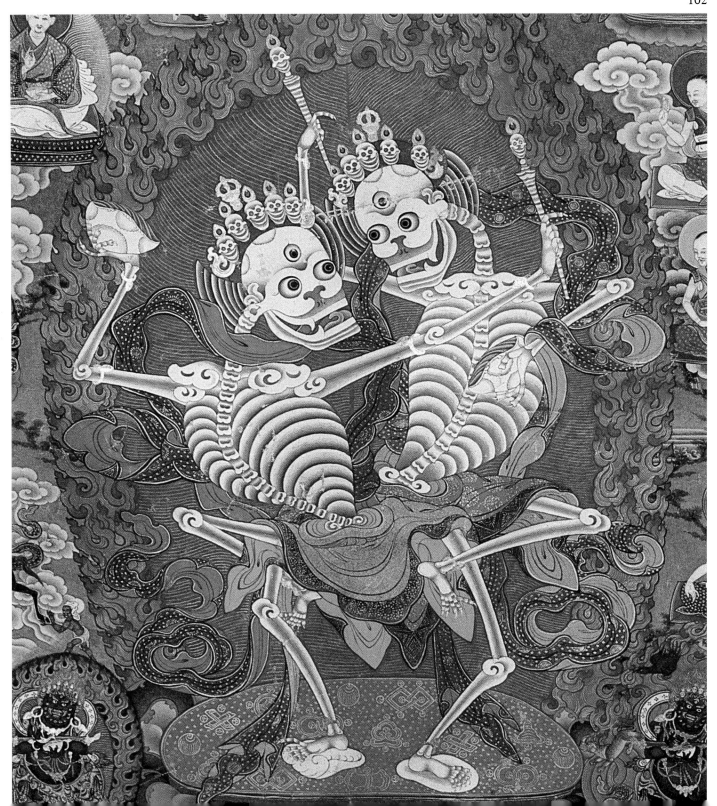

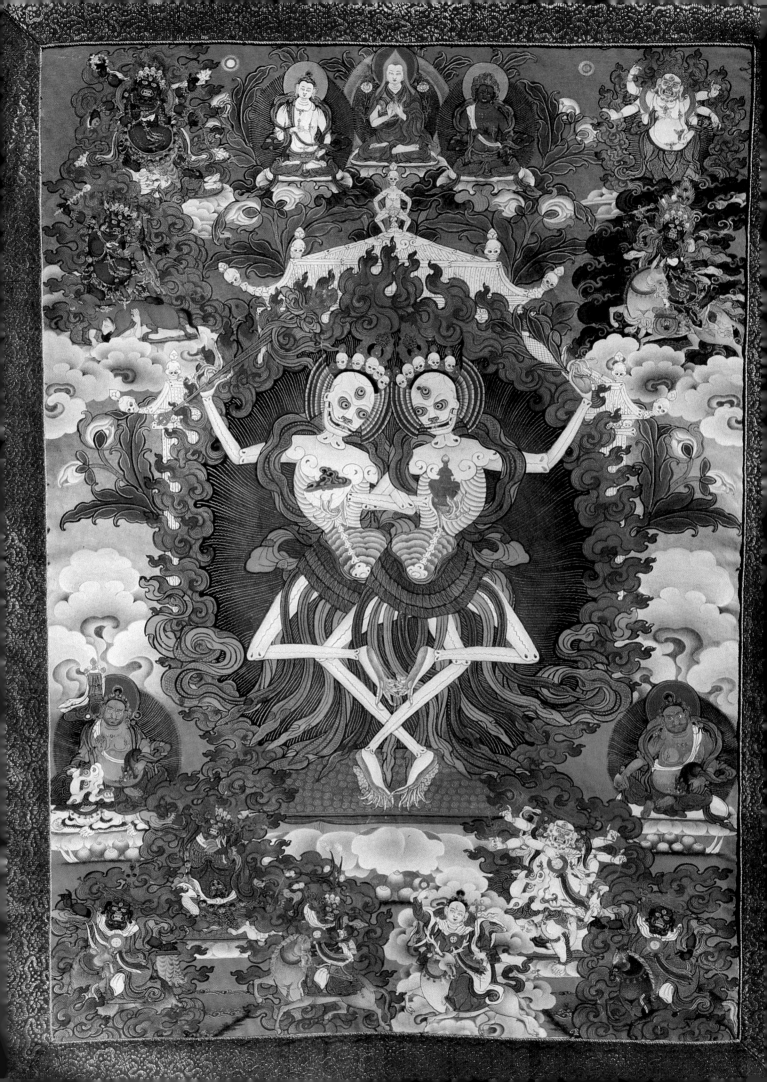

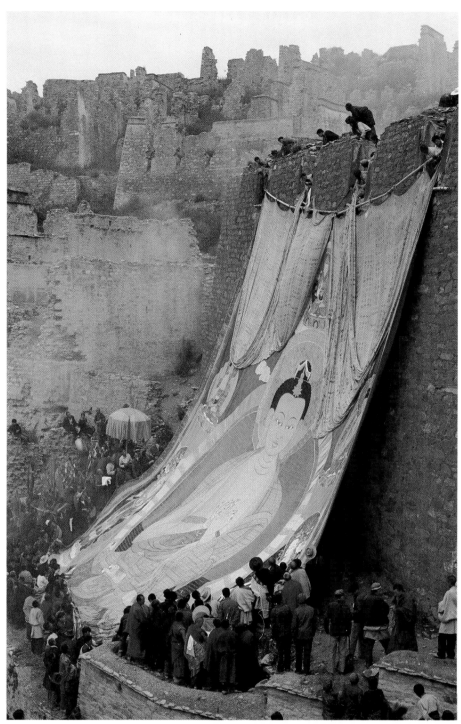

104. Each year on April 7 and June 7 of the lunar calendar huge portraits of the Buddha embroidered with piled stitches are displayed in the sun at monasteries for Buddhist followers to worship. These portraits range from several dozen square feet to over 100 square feet in size. They are either hung on high walls or spread out on hill slopes, and attract large crowds. This annual ceremony, called "sunning the huge Buddha", signifies the coming of the Buddha to the world to deliver men from suffering.

105. Images of the deities. Top row from left: the Guhyasamāja, the Guhyasamāja, the Guhyasamāja, the Bhairava, the Kālacakra Vajra, the Smiling Vajra, and the Bhūtadamara. Bottom row from left: the Kila Vajra, the Kila Vajra, the Śambara Vajra, the Śambara Vajra, the Śambara Vajra, the Ḍākinī mkhah-spuyod-ma, and the Vajrasattva. A cloth painting measuring 196cm across and 35cm tall. In the Sagya Monastery.

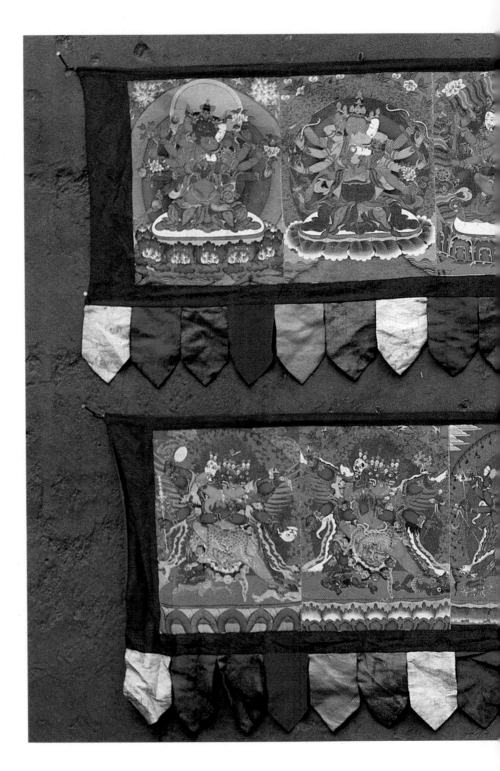

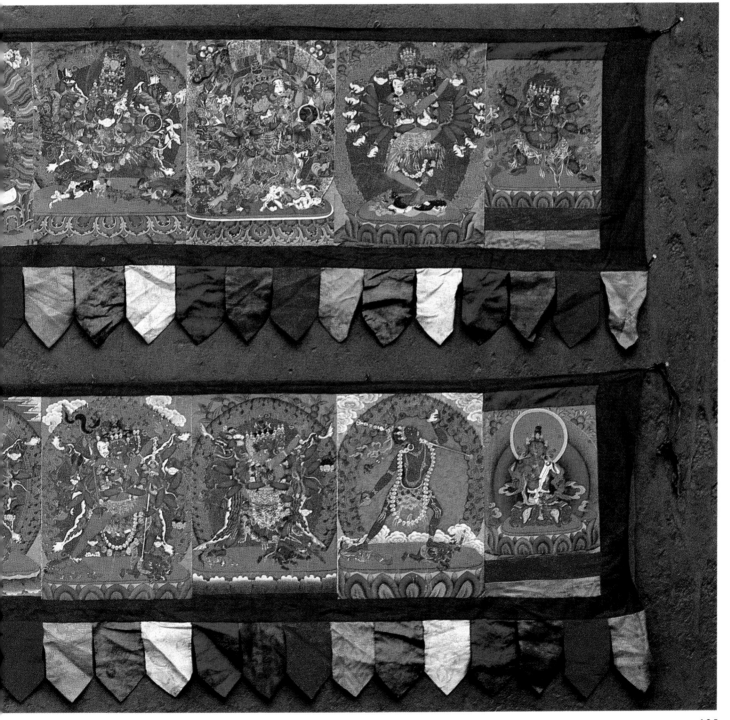

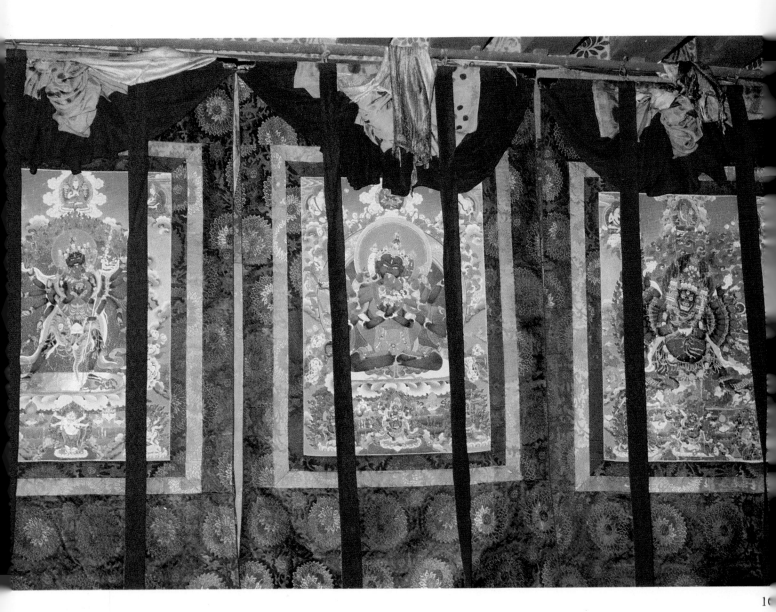

106. *Thang-kas* in the Potala Palace.

FRESCOES

FRESCOES

Frescoes are an important part of Tibetan Esoteric art. Their huge quantity would defeat any attempt at reliable statistics. They are to be found in almost every monastery. In the Qoikang Monastery alone, for example, the frescoes cover an area of well over 1,000 feet.

Tibetan fresco painting is characterized by a great variety of techniques. The painting of Buddha images must follow the rigid principles and the proportion diagrams set out in the "Pratibimba-lakṣaṇa-sūtra" ("The Textbook on Measurements for Image-Making") and the "Pratibimbamāna-lakṣaṇa" ("Measurements for Painting") in the *Śilpakarmas-thāna-vidyā*. These images are drawn in single lines with even colouring; the finished product is a well-proportioned, stately and serene-looking deity. Frescoes showing historical events and the everyday life of the people are done in bird's-eye-view perspective with the backdrops for the figures and buildings appearing in geometric patterns. The strokes are quaintly elaborate, and the general appearance of the fresco suggests a distinctive style.

Tibetan frescoes are painted in extremely bright colour and the pigments used are of non-transparent minerals. If transparent ocher is used, it is mixed with egg white and talc powder so that light will not pass through it. As with *thang-ka* painting, the pigments are mixed with animal glue and ox bile so that the colour will never lose its lustre.

Frescoes cover a wider range of subjects than *thang-kas* do. They include the images of Buddhas and deities, those of the Buddha in his many manifestations, portraits of saints, great masters, founders of various Buddhist sects and the stories of their lives, wars, scenes of manual labour, construction of monasteries and the everyday life of the people. Because of their wide range of subjects, their huge size and bright colour, the frescoes can always produce the kind of artistic effect that Buddhism demands of them, whether they show the image of a genial, peaceful Bodhisattva, or that of a wrathful, fear-striking Esoteric vajra or dharmapāla. Also, because they are housed in the monasteries, they are especially effective in creating a mystic atmosphere which will lead the viewers to believe that "this is where the Buddha resides."

Most of the Tibetan frescoes are the works of lama artists and lay craftsmen. In the 17th century, Tibet produced two schools of painting: the Mentang School and the Qenze School. Almost all the frescoes in famous monasteries, temples and palaces were done by the masters of these two schools.

107. The 62 Attendant Deities of the Śambara, or Bde mchog vkhor drug bcu re gnyis in Tibetan. Fresco (detail), 61cm tall. In the Sera Monastery.

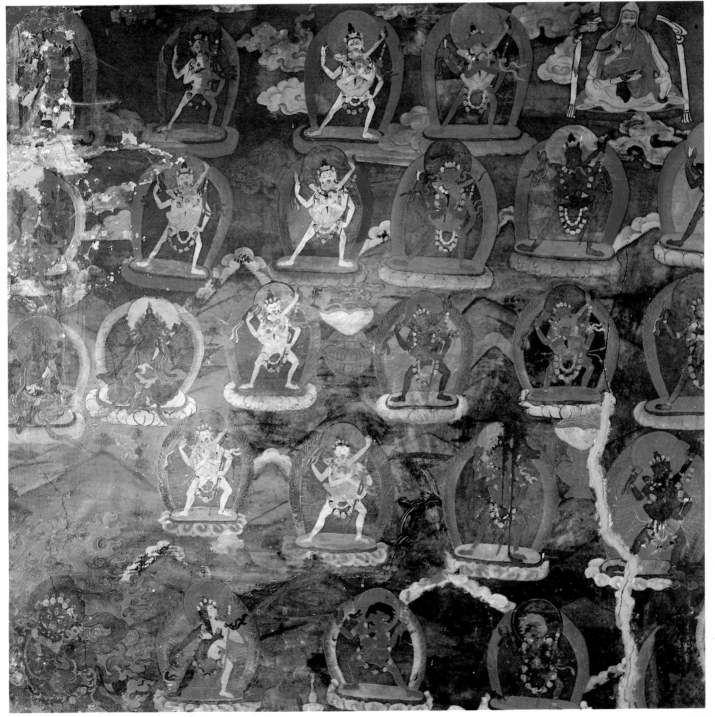

107

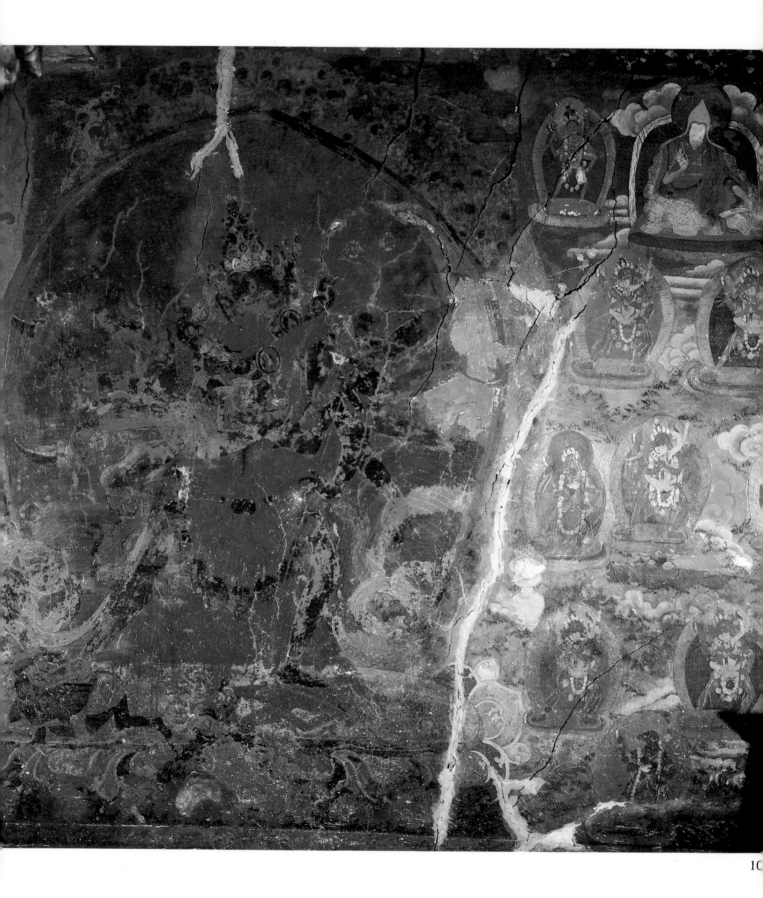

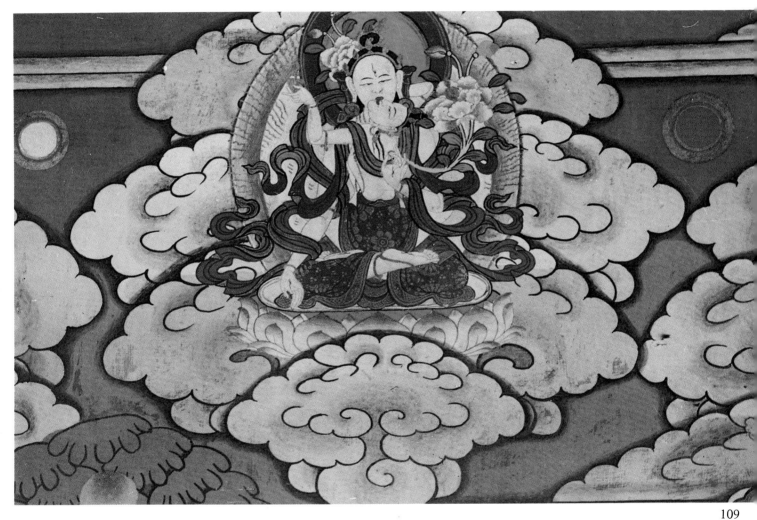

108. The Śambara Vajra. A section of "The 62 Attendant Deities of the Śambara" is shown at right. Fresco. The image is 61cm in height. In the Sera Monastery.

109. This is the Sitātapatra or White Umbrella (Tibetan: Dugs-dkar), one of the five Top Buddhas. A deity with his hair done in a double bun is called a Top Buddha. The white umbrella signifies "the all-embracing pure virtues of the Buddha", and "the great compassion of white purity that covers the dharmadhatu". This picture shows the haloed deity of yellow colour holding lotus flowers in his hand with the umbrella spread out behind him. He has three eyes in the face and one each on the palms of his hands and the soles of his feet. Fresco. The image is 18cm tall. In the Sagya Monastery.

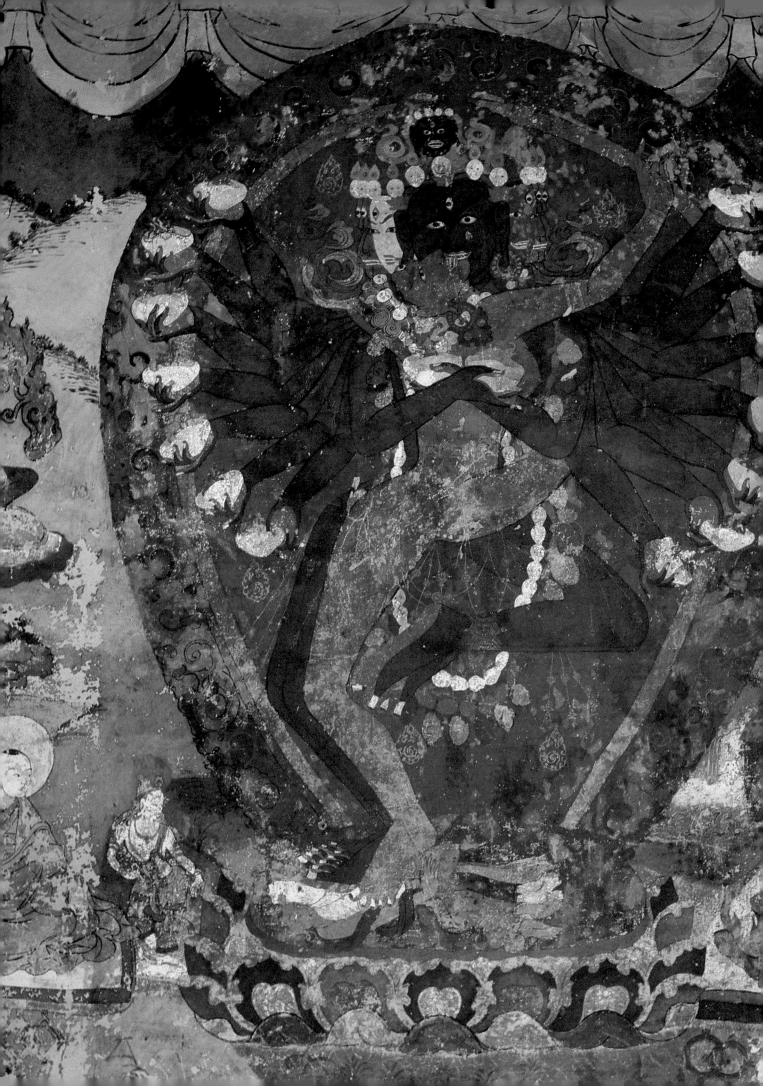

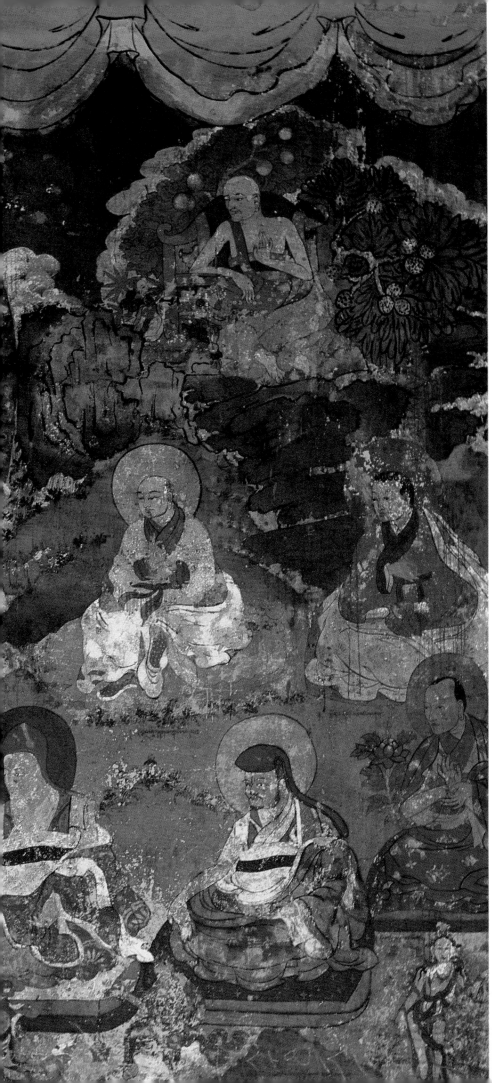

110. The Smiling Vajra. Fresco. The image is 2,000cm tall. In the Sagya Monastery.

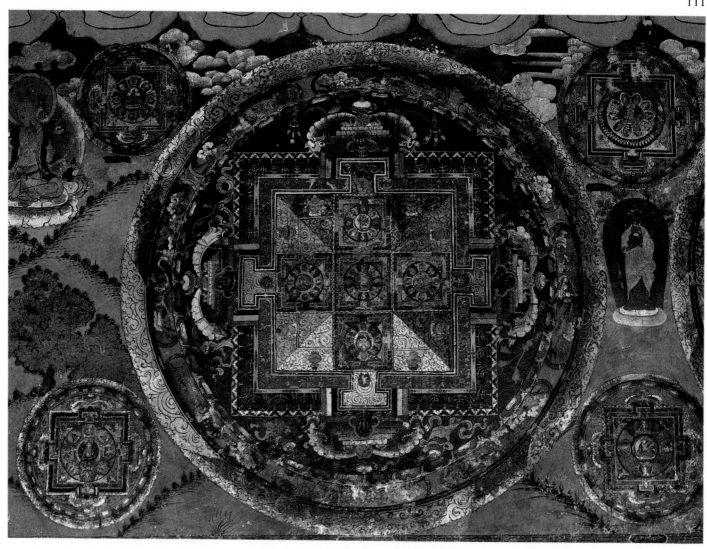

111. The maṇḍala comprising five kinds of ḍākinīs of vajrapāniara. This maṇḍala is highly venerated by Tibetan Esoteric Buddhists. Fresco, 200cm tall. In the Sagya Monastery.

112. This is Avalokiteśvara (Tibetan: Spyan ras gzigs). He holds a lotus flower in his left hand and a rosary in the right. Around the head he wears a string of human skulls and the devī embraces him around the neck. The Tibetan at his feet reads "Devoted to Avalokiteśvara of the Sea of Victory", a tribute by the painter. Fresco. The image is 30cm tall. In the Qoikang Monastery.

113. The Yamāntaka, one of the Thirteen Mahābhairava Vajras. He holds a skull-topped sceptre in his right hand and a vajra in his left, and stands on a green ox. Fresco (detail), 61cm tall. In the Drepung Monastery.

114. The Lakṣmī Śrī (the Auspicious Devī), or the Auspicious Goddess Mother (Tibetan: Dpal-itan iha-ma). The deity is known by 100 names, each of which has an image attached to it. This one in Tibetan means "Dmag-zor rgyal-mo", or the Supreme Conqueror of Enemies. She has a wrathful image and a peaceful one. In her wrathful image she rides a yellow mule which has an eye in the buttocks, and is of dark blue colour, with three eyes in the face, a halo behind and sagging breasts. According to legend, she used to be a deity of India's Brahmanism before she became a dharmapāla of Buddhism and was made the wife of Vaiśravaṇa Mahārāja, one of the four deva kings. She is also said "to benefit all beings with her meritorious virtues". January 1 is the day she is honoured because on this day she travels around the world on sunbeams and stores the sunlight of the day in her stomach. Fresco (detail). Size unknown. In the Drepung Monastery.

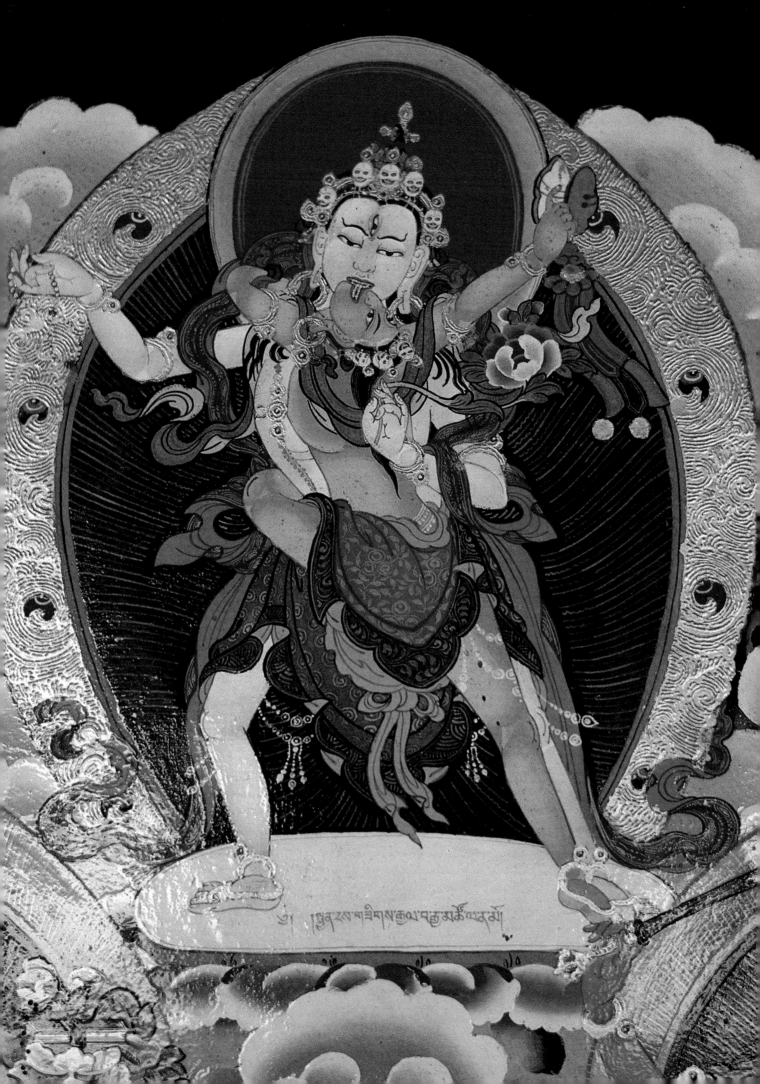

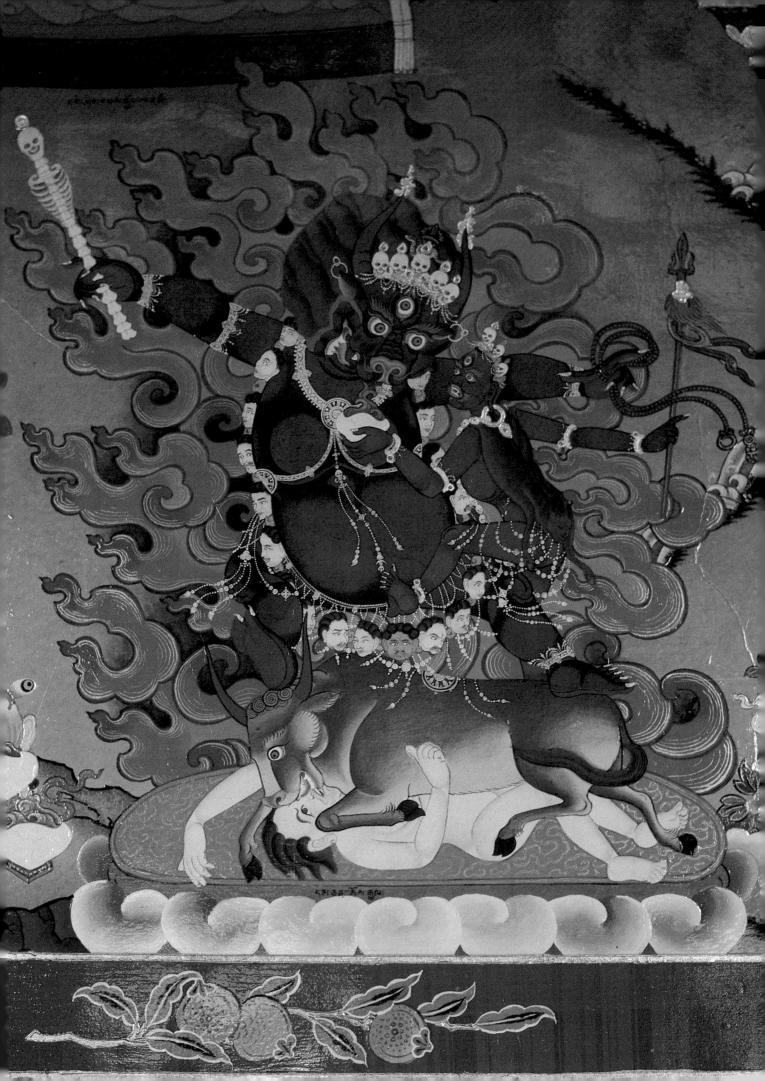

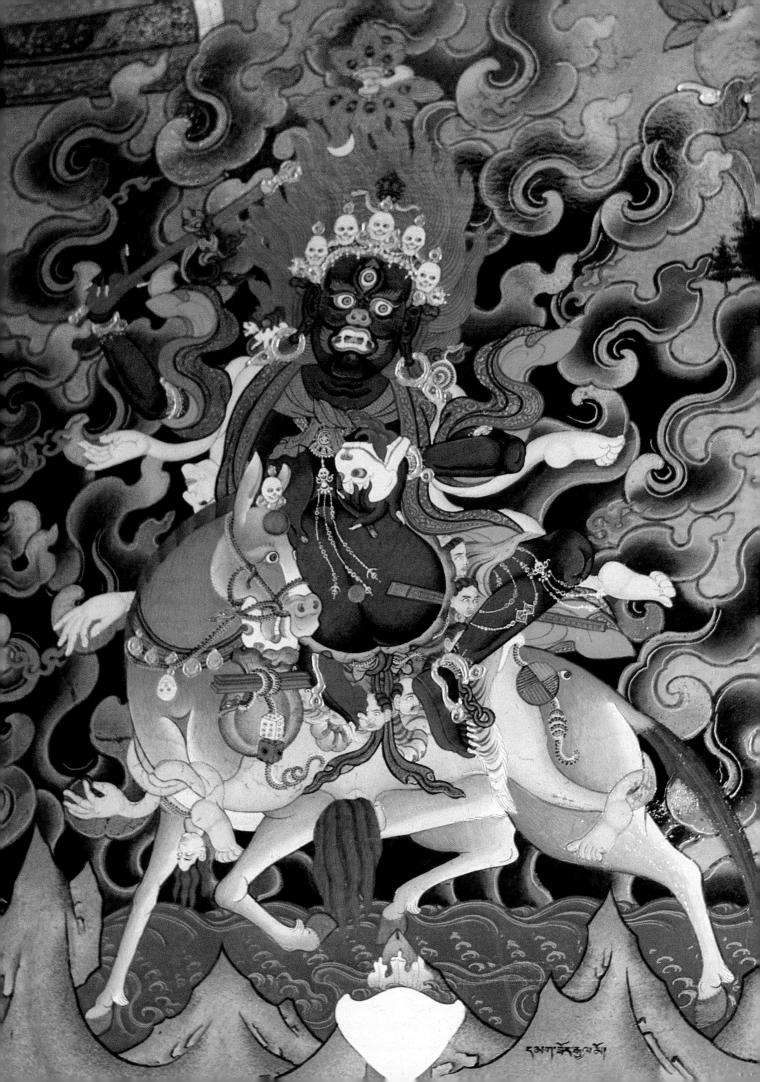

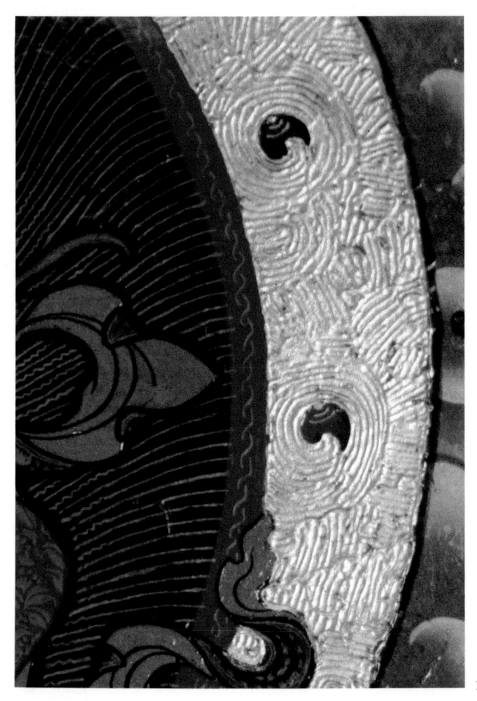

The devarāja Vaiśravaṇa (Tibetan: Rgyal-chen rnam-sras), one of the four deva kings. According to Buddhism, he is the guardian deity of the north and lives on the northern side of the Sumeru Mountain. He appears in many different images.

115. Part of the devarāja Vaiśravaṇa in picture 116.
116. This one shows him holding a streamer in the right hand, a rat with a pearl in the mouth in the left and he is riding a white lion with a green mane. Fresco. In the Drepung Monastery.

117. The Vajra of the Earth (Tibetan: Brtan-ma rdo-rje grags-shal-ma) is one of the guardian deities of Tibet. The yellow deer she rides is the animal she has vanquished. Below are the protecting devīs of the deity. Fresco (detail). In the Drepung Monastery.
118. The Dharmapāla-on-a-Goat. It is also known as the Vow-defending Dark Blacksmith (Tibetan: Dam can mkar ba nag po). He holds in his hands a hammer and a bellows of tiger skin for weapons, and is a vowed defender of Buddhism. The goat he rides is the source of his life. Fresco (detail). In the Drepung Monastery.

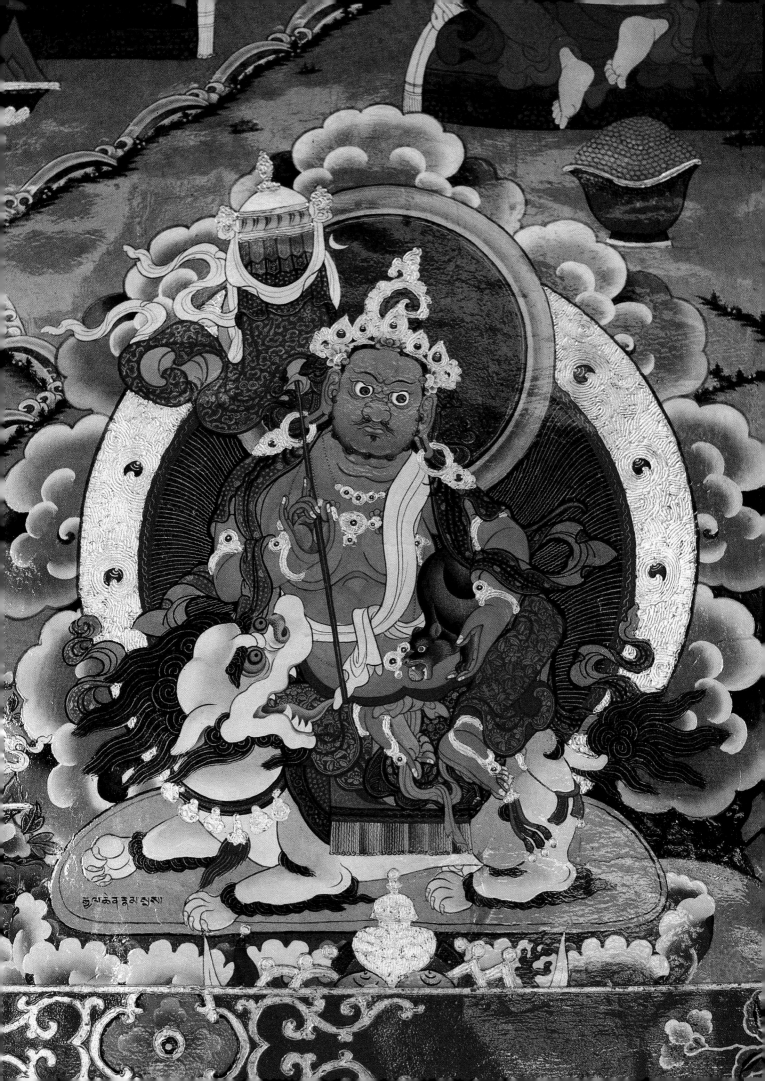

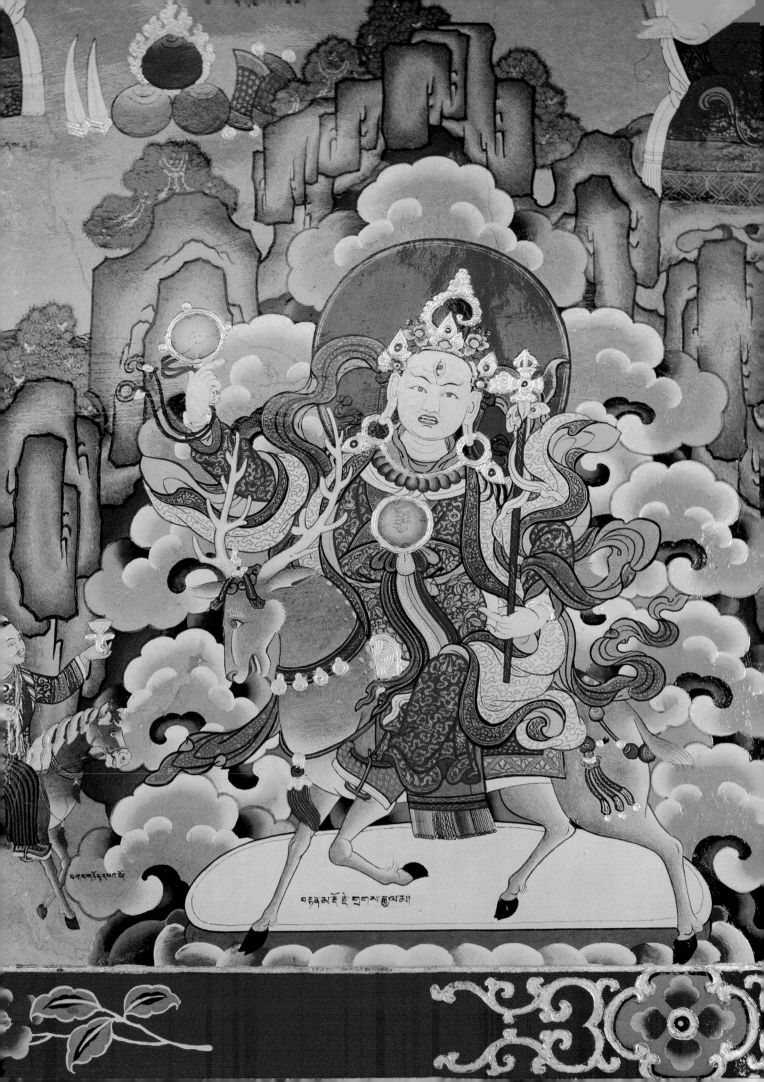

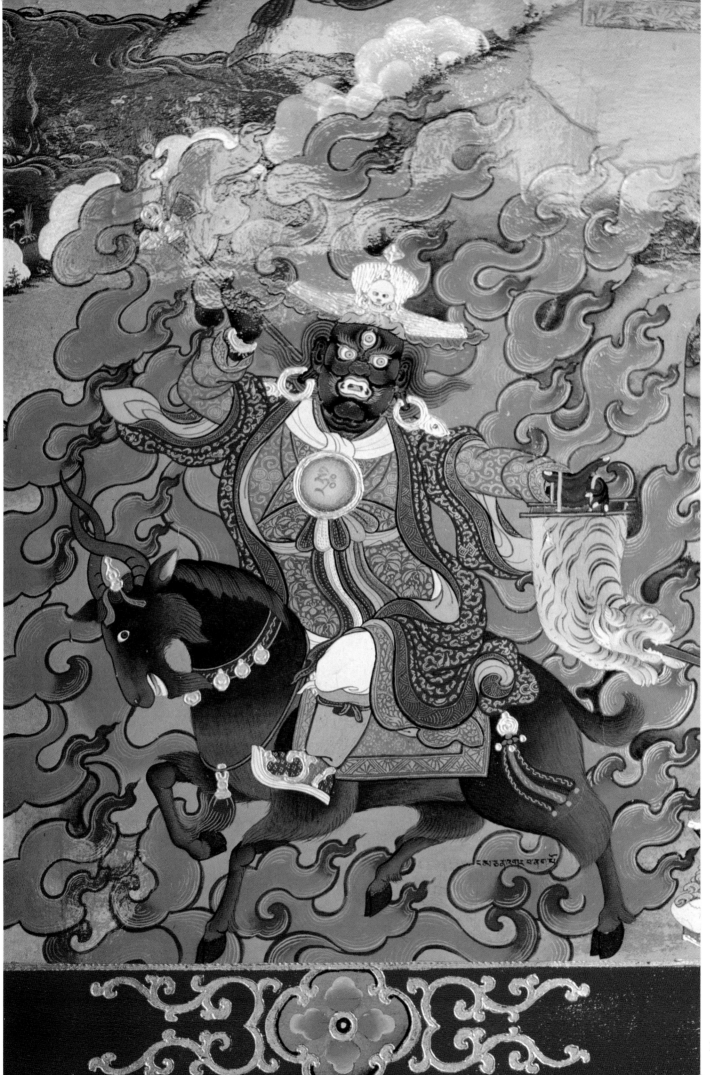

ངམ་ར་རུ་འཛིན་དཀར་ནག་པོ།

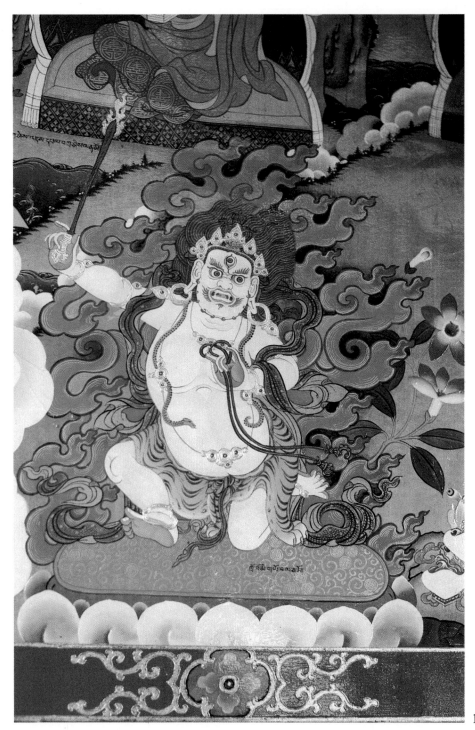

119

119. The Firm-footed Wrathful Vajra, also known as the Firm-footed or the Wrathful Firm-footed (Tibetan: Khro bo mi gyo ba), is one of the wrathful deities at the four gates. He has no female counterpart. Fresco (detail). In the Drepung Monastery.

120. The Mahākāla (the Great Black Deva), or the Six-armed Dharmapāla (Tibetan: Mgon po phyag drug pa). According to Tibetan Esoteric Buddhism, the deity is the form in which Mahāvairocana appears when he subdues a demon. He is of green colour, with six arms stretching an elephant skin behind him and wearing a skull-studded crown — features that are shared by the various images of him. In ancient times, the Mahākāla was worshipped as a war deity, a morale builder that ensured victory. He is regarded among the people as a deity of happiness, and is worshipped with incense and food. Fresco (detail). In the Drepung Monastery.

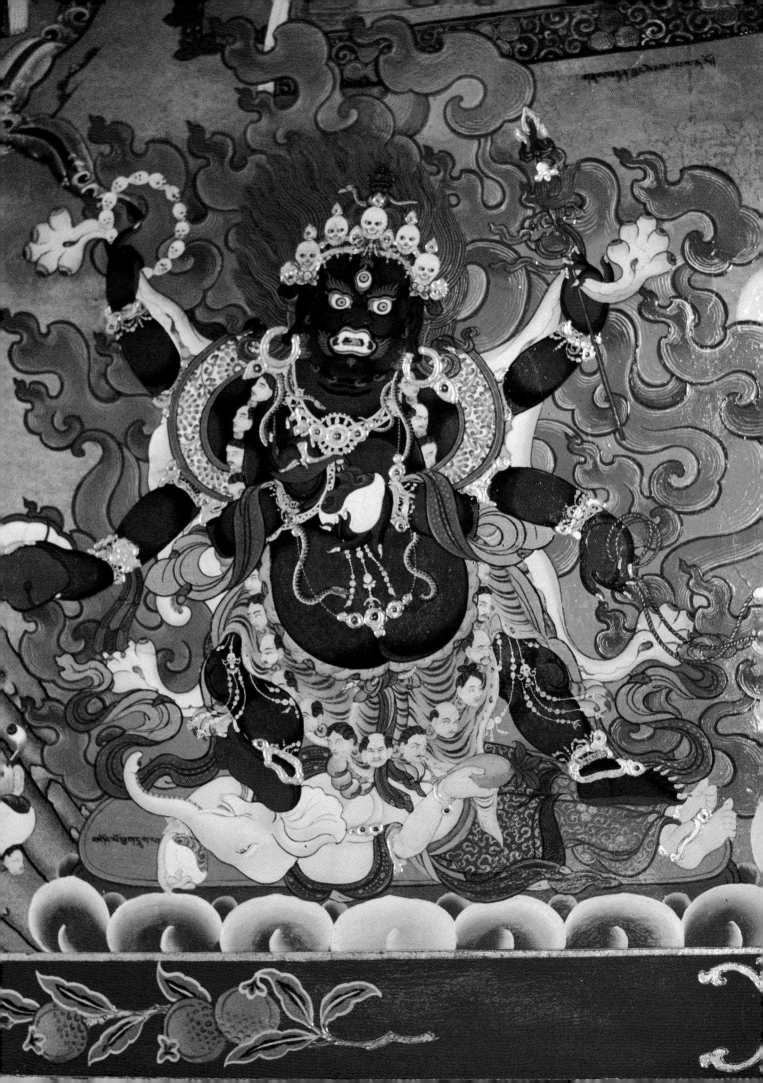

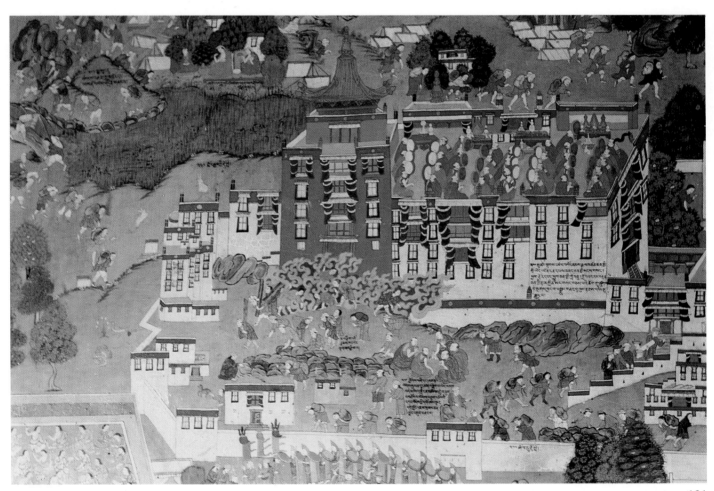

121

121. The painting shows the Potala Palace being extended in the 17th century. Fresco. About 300cm in height. In the Potala Palace.
122. The Potala Palace after the extension – the Potala as we see it today. The painting shows people celebrating the occasion with song and dance. Fresco, about 300cm in height. In the Potala Palace.

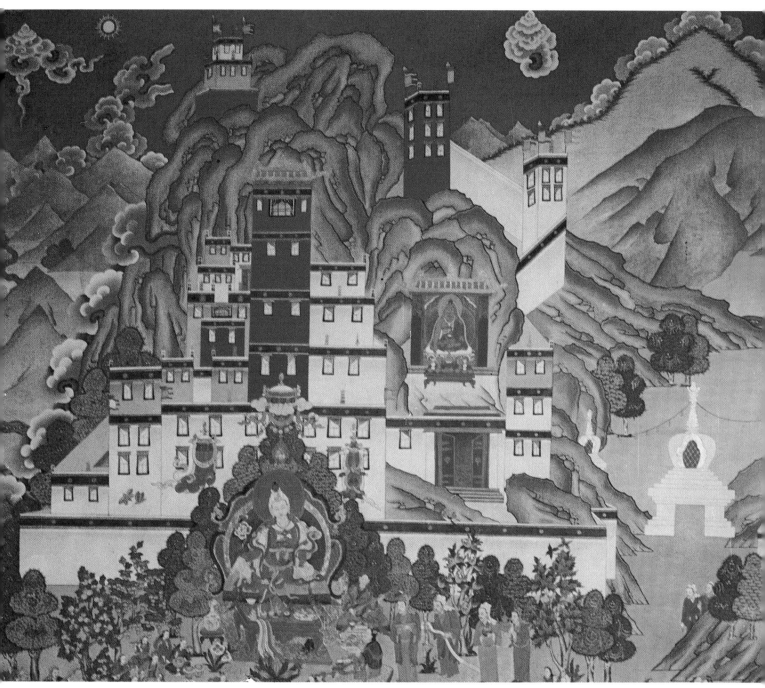

122

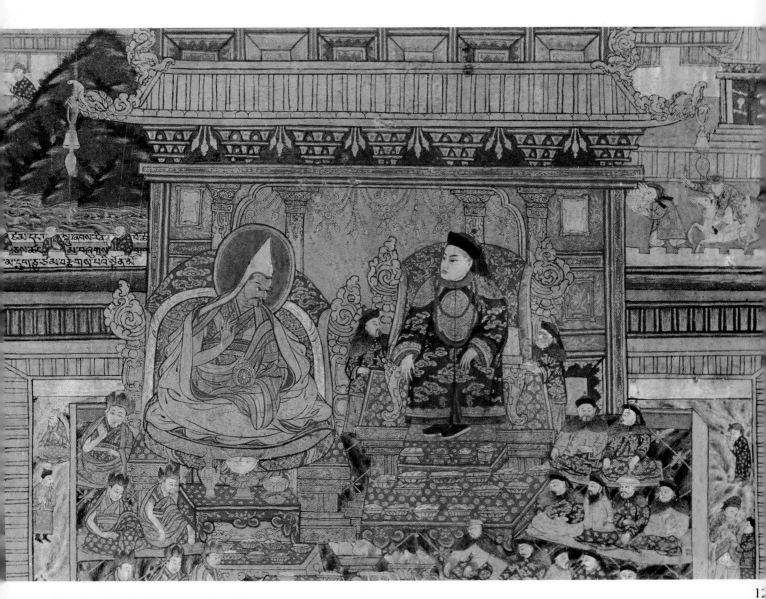

123. The Fifth Dalai Lama meeting with the
Qing emperor Shunzhi. In 1652 the Dalai Lama
went to Beijing to pay homage to the emperor,
who conferred imperial titles on him. The
painting shows the Dalai Lama sitting to the
right of the Qing emperor. Fresco, about 300 cm
tall. In the Potala Palace.

CLAY MOLDING

CLAY MOLDING

Clay molding of miniature Buddhist images, called "phyag-tsha" or "tsha-tsha" in Tibetan, represents a form of artistic expression in Tibetan Esoteric Buddhism. As the moldings are not difficult to make and the material is easily obtainable, such objects of art are turned out in large quantities by the natives. They can be found almost everywhere in Tibet.

In the making of clay moldings pure loess is first ground into fine dust which is then mixed with a small quantity of thin, short plant fibre. Water is added to this fibre-dust mixture to form a thin paste, which is stirred until it is evenly mixed and becomes tough clay. The clay is then pressed into wooden or stone molds and is left to dry in a well-ventilated place. When half dried, the moldings are slightly trimmed with a burin, and after the totally dried moldings have been painted in colour, they become objects of art.

Most of the clay moldings show images of Buddhas and deities. Small in size, they are usually placed on domestic altars, or carried along by devotees of Buddhism for instant worship so that "the perfect body of the Buddha" may be achieved sooner. They are also believed to have the power of protecting the carriers against the attack of demons and evil spirits.

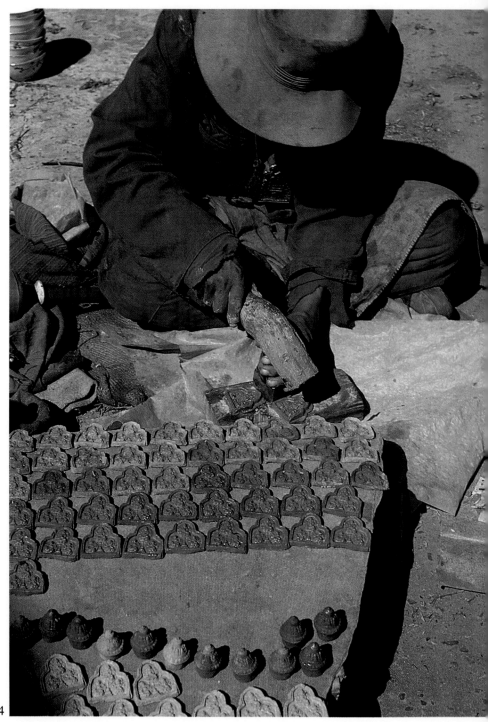

124

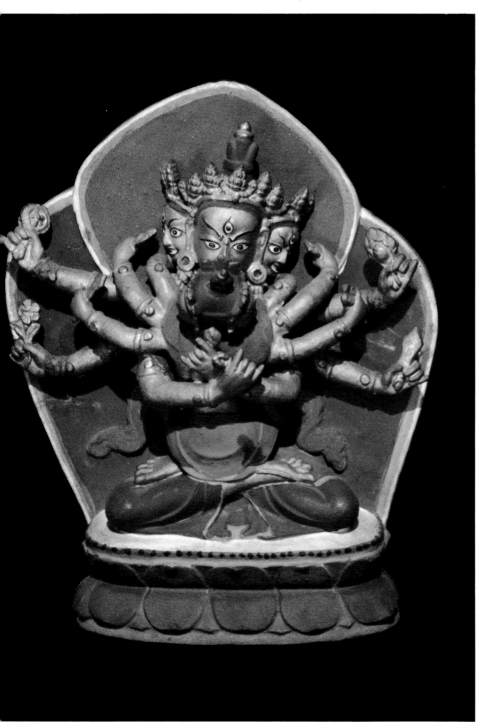

124. The craftsman making clay moldings.
125. The Guhyasamāja. Clay molding, 19cm tall. In the Drepung Monastery.
126. The Śambara Vajra. Clay molding, 15cm tall. In the Drepung Monastery.
127. The Śambara Vajra. Clay molding, 15cm tall. In the Drepung Monastery.
128. The Bhairava Vajra. Clay molding, 21cm tall. In the Drepung Monastery,
129. The Bhairava Vajra. Clay molding, 25cm tall. In the Drepung Monastery.

125

171

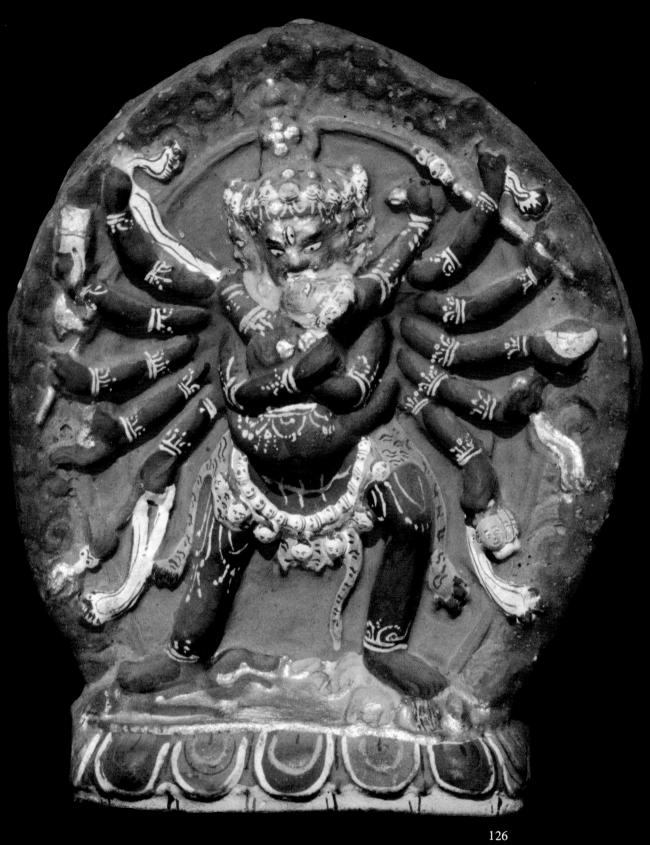

126

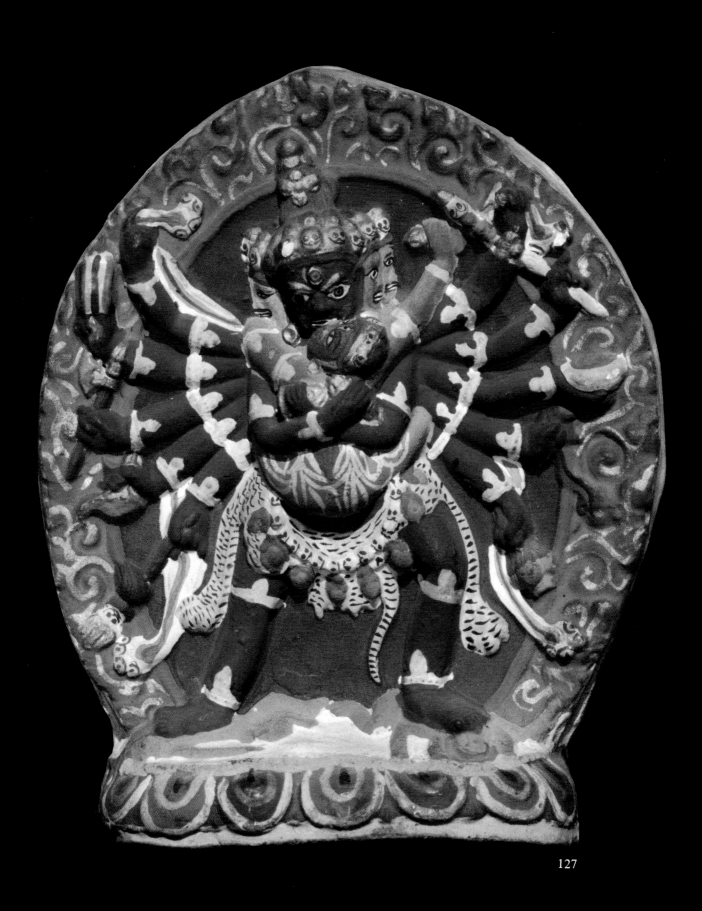

127

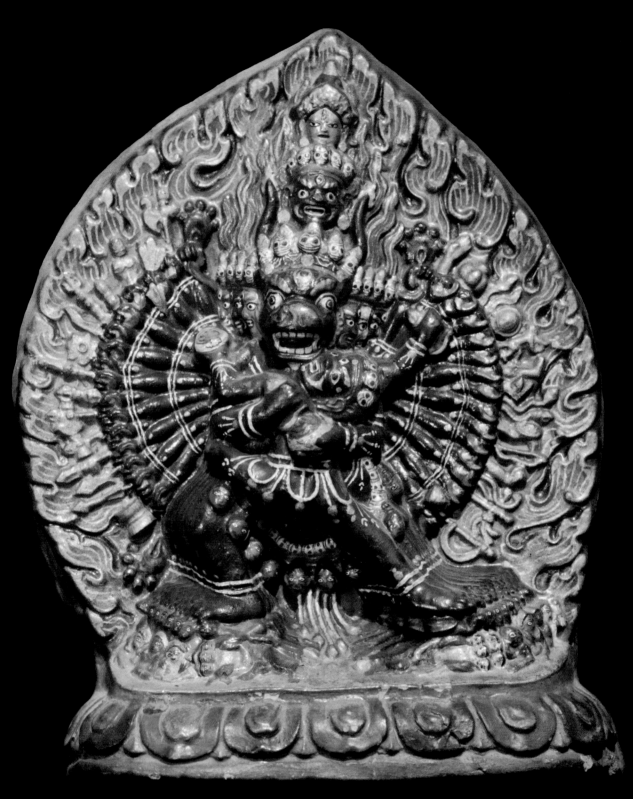

128

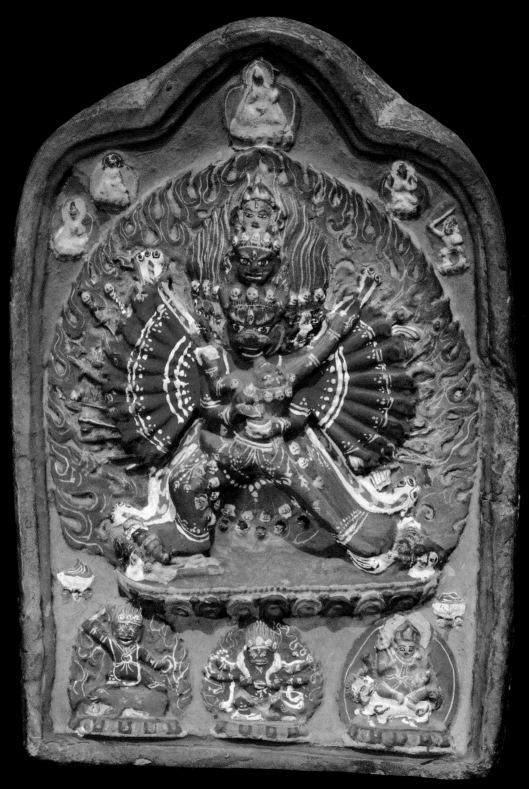

129

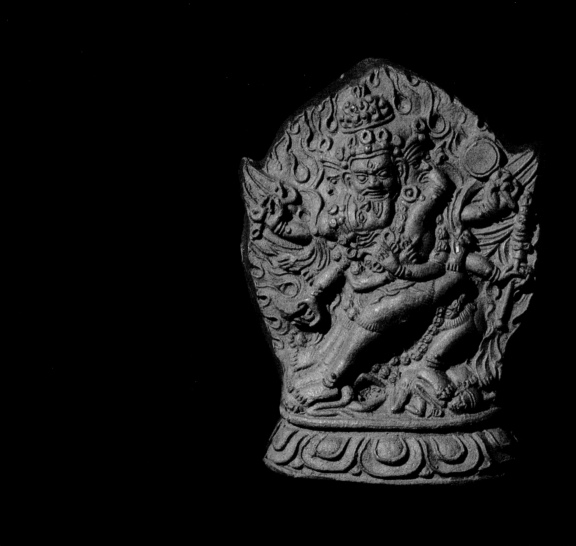

130. The Protector of Life. Clay molding, 5.5cm tall. In the Sagya Monastery.

WOOD CARVING AND
WOODEN TABLET PAINTING

WOOD CARVING AND WOODEN TABLET PAINTING

Tibetan Esoteric art abounds in wood carvings. These beautiful engravings lavishly decorate the columns, beams, doors, windows and cross-beam supporters in Tibetan monasteries and temples. The carvings on the wood columns in the prayer hall of the Drepung Monastery and those in the main hall of the Sera Monastery are representative of this Tibetan art. Shrines, platforms seating deities, altars, stūpas and some ritual objects are often adorned with wood carvings. Wooden statues of the Buddha and other deities are to be found in even greater numbers. However, small, exquisitely carved twin images of deities are rare objects because Tibetan monasteries and temples generally do not have them. Printing blocks of Buddhist texts cut in various historical periods are found in large quantities and they are equally valuable items of wood carving. These carvings show a great variety of cutting methods which successfully combine bold lines with elaborate ones; the craftsmanship also excels in the hollowing-out and picking technique.

Wooden tablet painting represents yet another branch of Tibetan art. Its subjects and pictorial composition are similar to those of *thang-kas* and the difference is that the pictures are drawn on wooden tablets of various shapes. Some of them have handles attached to them for holding and hanging.

131. The Śambara Vajra. Wood carving, 19cm tall. In the Sagya Monastery.
132. The Bhairava Vajra. Wood carving, 44cm tall. This one is a single image carving which shows the deity without the devī. In the Sagya Monastery.

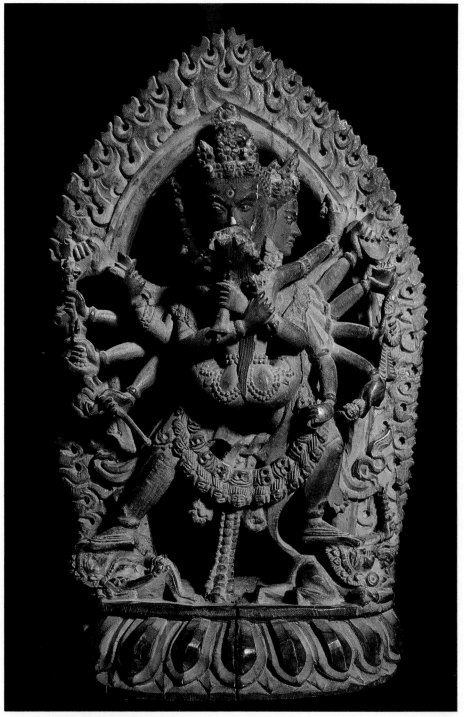

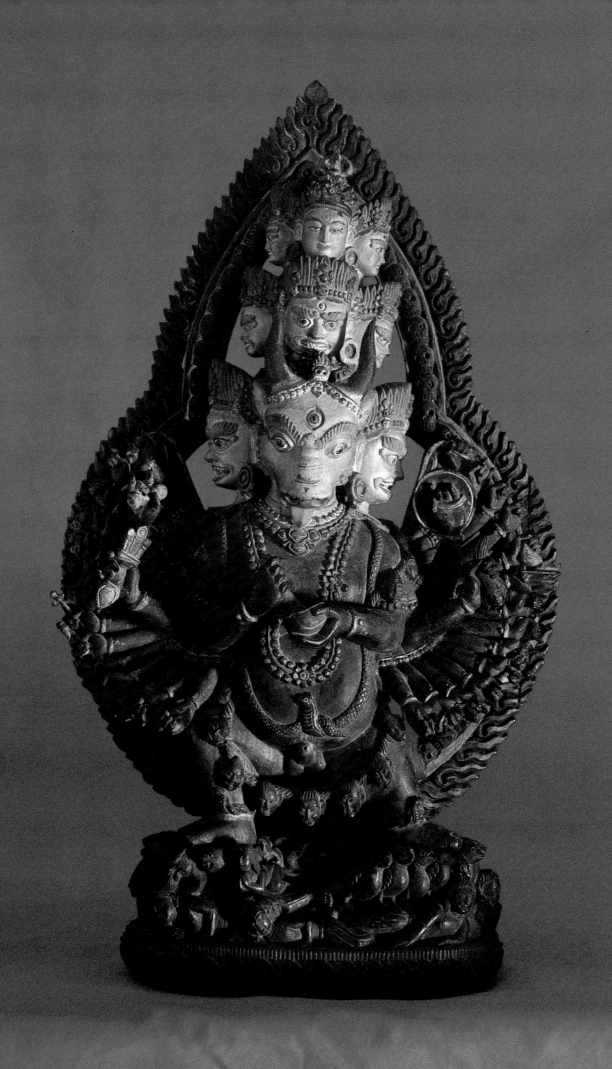

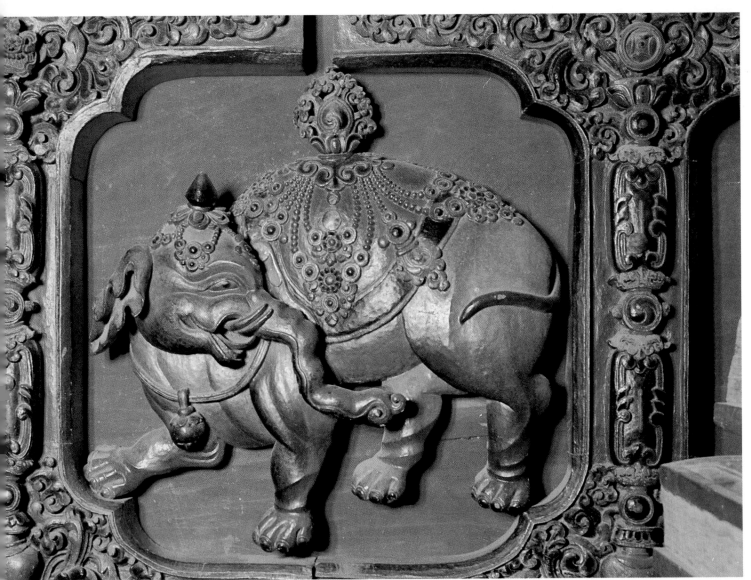

133. A carved wooden holy elephant in the
Potala Palace, 30cm tall.

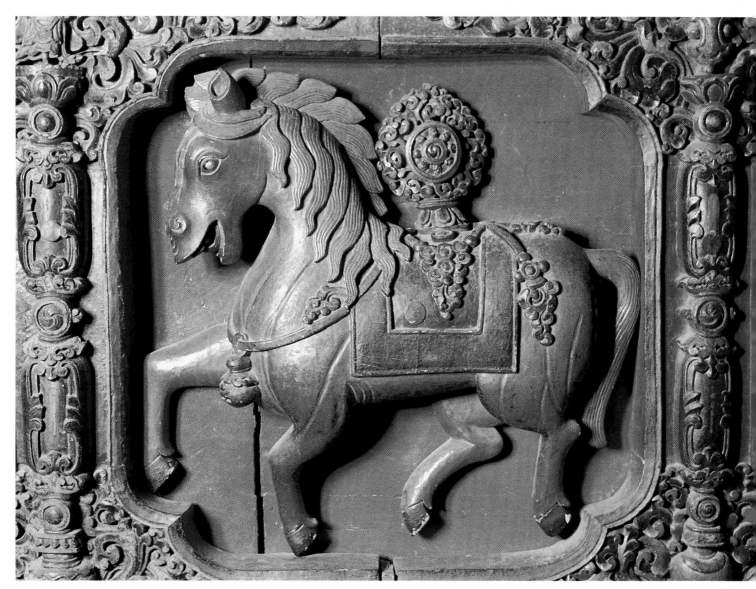

134. A carved wooden holy horse in the
Potala Palace, 30cm tall.

The Dharmakāya Samantābhadra
(Tibetan: Chos-sku kun-tu-bzang-po) is
one of the Buddhist Bodhisattvas.
According to Buddhist interpretation,
"saṁantā" means universal and "bhadra"
kindness, that is to say the deity possesses
the universal kindness for all beings. In
Exoteric Buddhism he is regarded as the
counterpart of the Mañjuśrī Bodhisattva,
and an attendant deity of Śākyamuni. In
Esoteric Buddhism, Samantābhadra has
two manifestations: one in the form of a
senior vajra among the attendants of
Mahāvairocana, the other in the same
form as the Exoteric Samantābhadra
serving as a senior attendant of
Mahāvairocana.

135. The Dharmakāya Samantābhadra.
Wooden tablet painting. The image is 14cm tall.
In the Sagya Monastery.
136. The Hayagrīva Vajra (Tibetan: Rta-
mgrin), wooden tablet painting. The image is
14cm tall. In the Sagya Monastery.

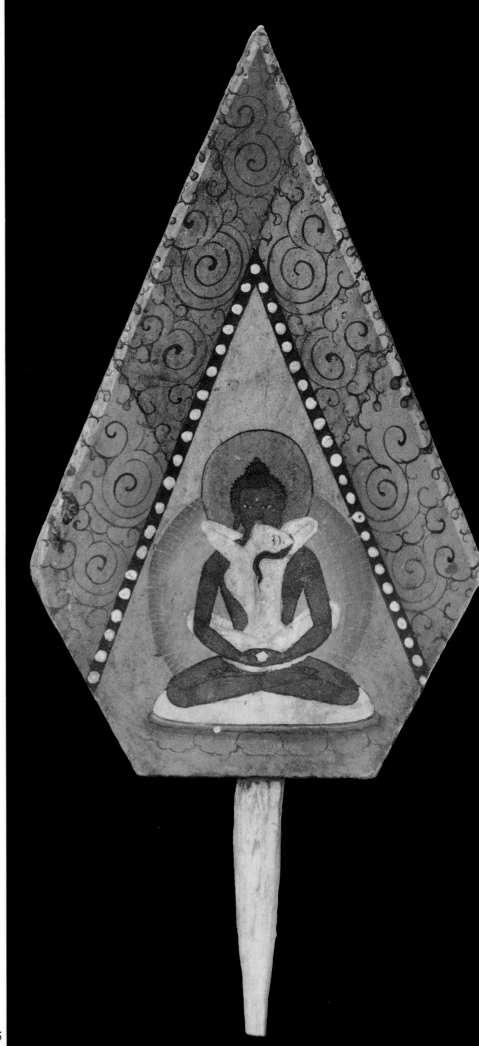

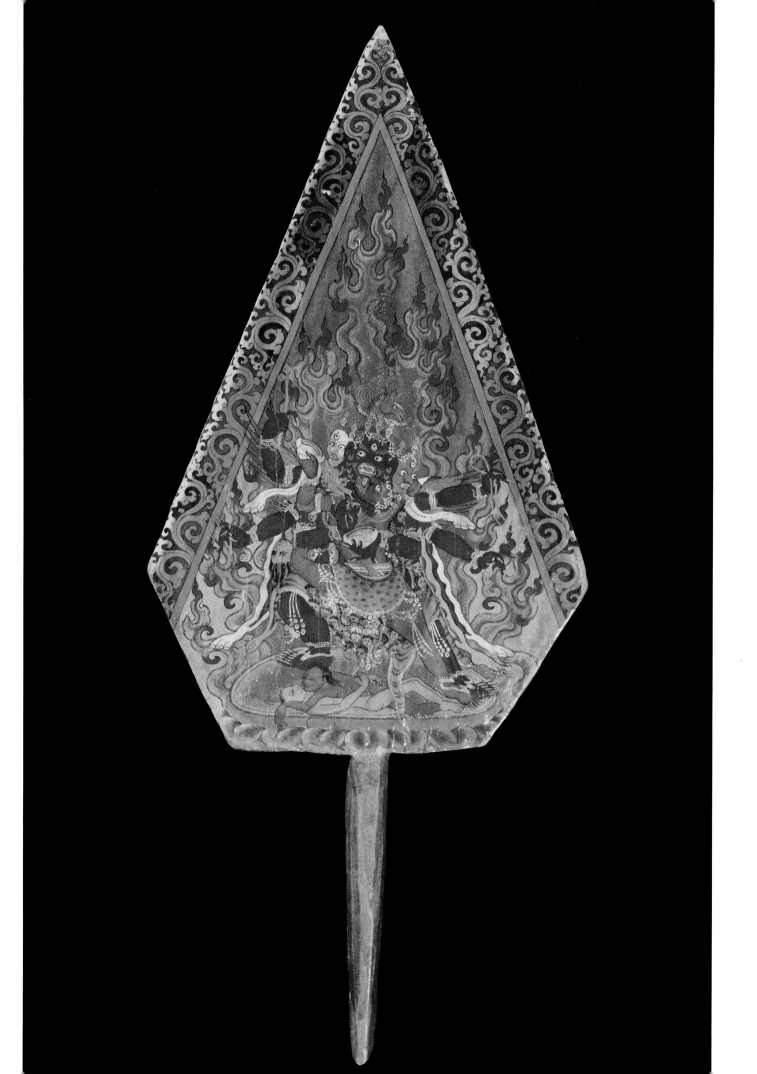

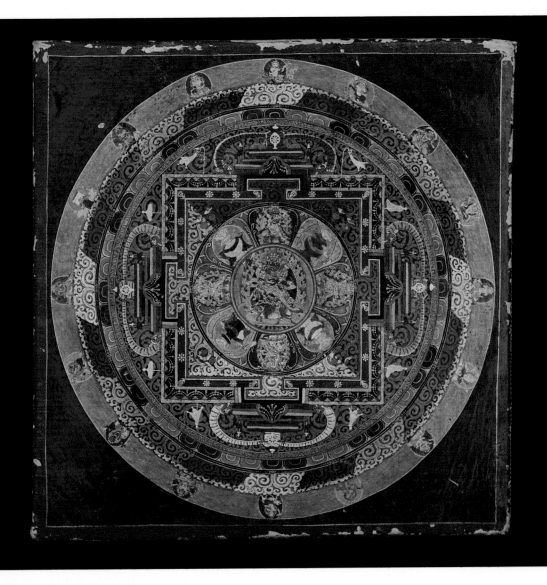

137. The maṇḍala of the Red Yamāntaka.
Wooden tablet painting, 30 × 30cm. In the
Sagya Monastery.

STONE CARVING

STONE CARVING

Stone carvings exist in great numbers in Tibet, and they can be found almost everywhere. They include Buddhist stone statues in the monasteries, reliefs of Buddhist deities on mountain cliffs, the maṇi (prayer stone) piles with the "Six-Syllable True Teaching" engraved on them, large stone slabs bearing engraved Buddhist texts, and stone lions guarding the entrances to gardens. Some of these carvings are cultural relics and works of art which date far back in history.

The stone Buddhist images in monasteries and temples are either reliefs or carved in the round and some of the reliefs have the inside hollowed out. These Buddhist stone carvings usually show single images; those with twin images on them are rare. Most of the Buddhist images carved on the mountain cliffs and the Six-Syllable True Teaching engravings are found along the roads leading to holy places, mountains or lakes. They line these routes, appearing individually or in groups. Some of them are painted in colour, or given coloured outlines. When pilgrims see them at a distance, they will start praying and counting the beads of their rosaries, as they walk up to them. Then they will perform prostration ritual. By doing so, the pilgrims, as if with the help of the deities, will instantly feel relieved of their fatigue, and be given new strength to continue with their journeys.

Tibetan stone carving is characterized by the simplicity of its art. However, it also suggests a sense of power. Works of early times are bold in style, while those of modern times are more elaborate.

138. The Kālacakra Vajra. Stone, 12cm tall. In the Sagya Monastery.
139. The Kālacakra Vajra. Stone, 10cm tall. In the Sagya Monastery.

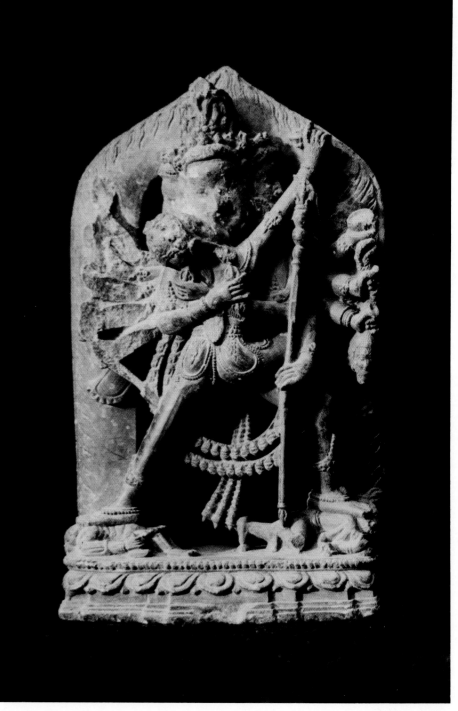

138

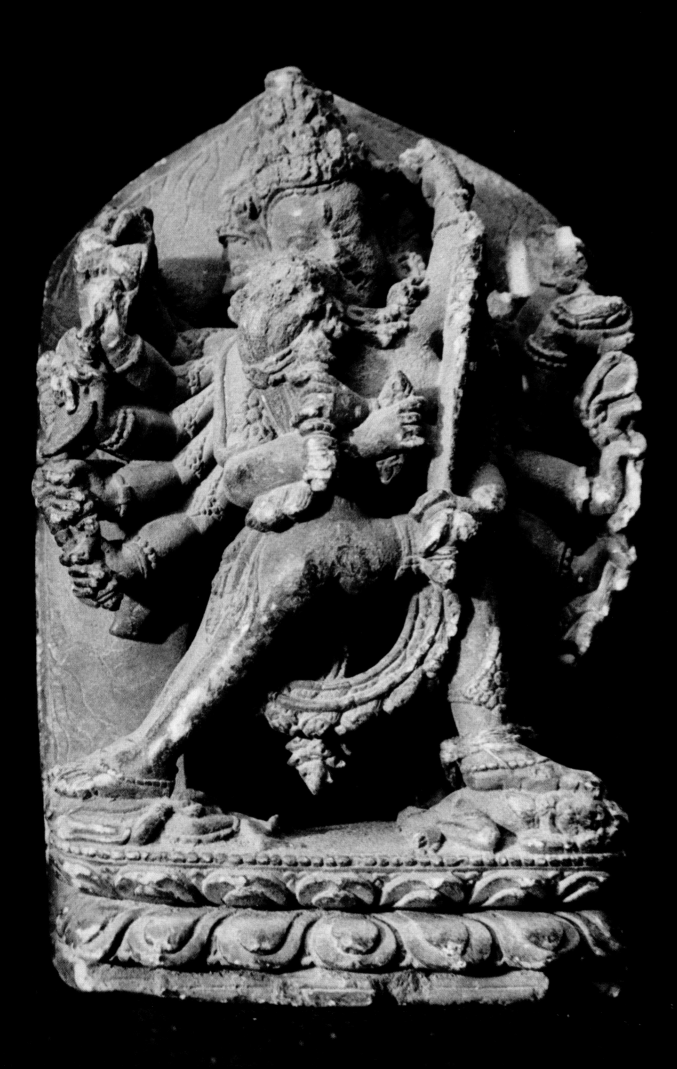

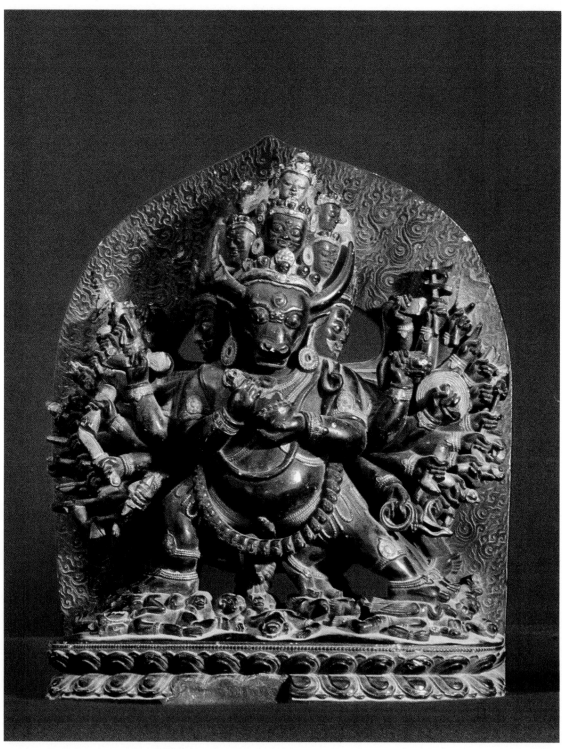

140. The Bhairava Vajra. Stone, 20cm tall. In the Sagya Monastery.

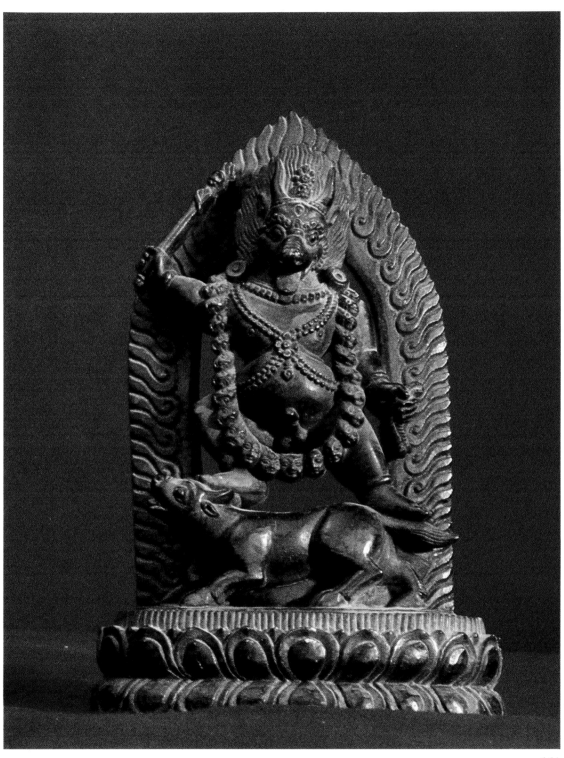

141. The Bhairava Vajra. Stone, 19cm tall. In
the Sagya Monastery.

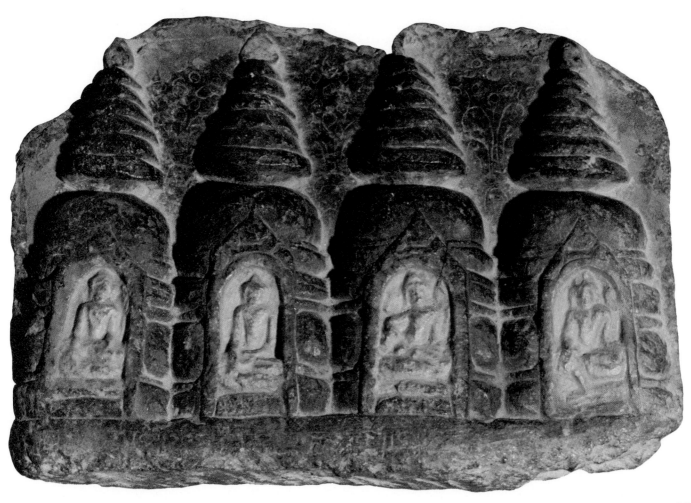

142

142. These stūpas seem to stand out from the stone slab on which they are carved. About 50cm in height. In the Xalu Monastery.

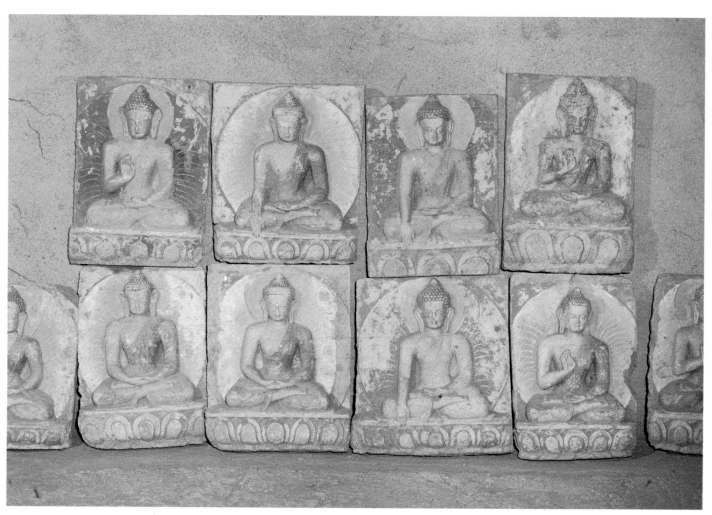

143. Buddha images carved on a stone slab.
About 40cm in height. In the Samye Monastery.

143

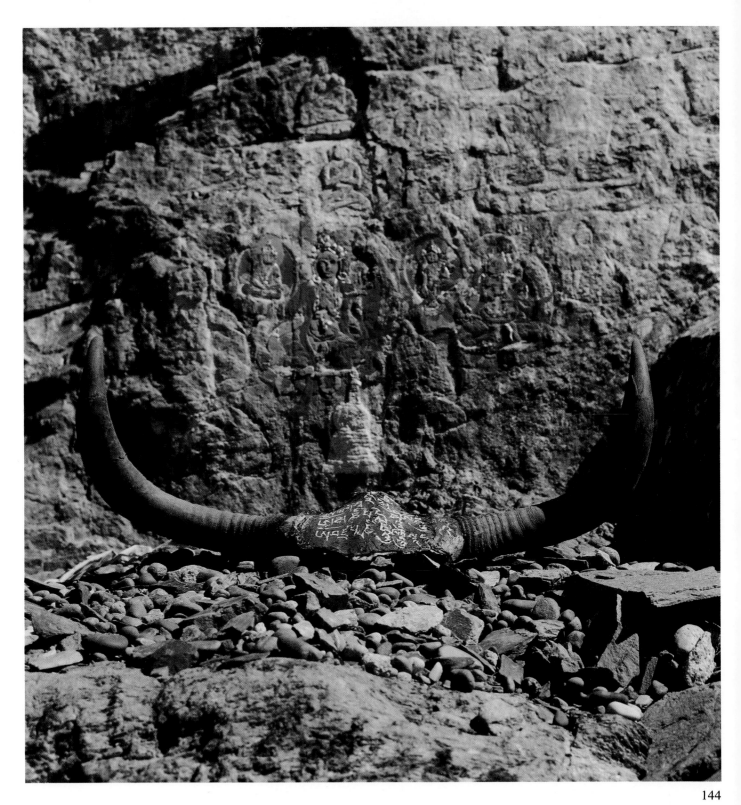

144

144. Carving on a mountain cliff. Such carvings of deities are usually found on the routes to holy places and they appear in individual or group images. This one is a group image carving. The yak horns are offered by Buddhist followers and bear the inscription "oṃ, ma, ṇi, pod, me, hūṃ", each of the syllables representing a Buddhist text.

145. Stone carvings on the mountainside behind the Sera Monastery. The image of Byams-chen chos-rje, founder of the monastery, appears at the top with those of Esoteric Dharmapālas and Bhairava Vajras below him.
146. Buddha images carved on the mountainside behind the Drepung Monastery.

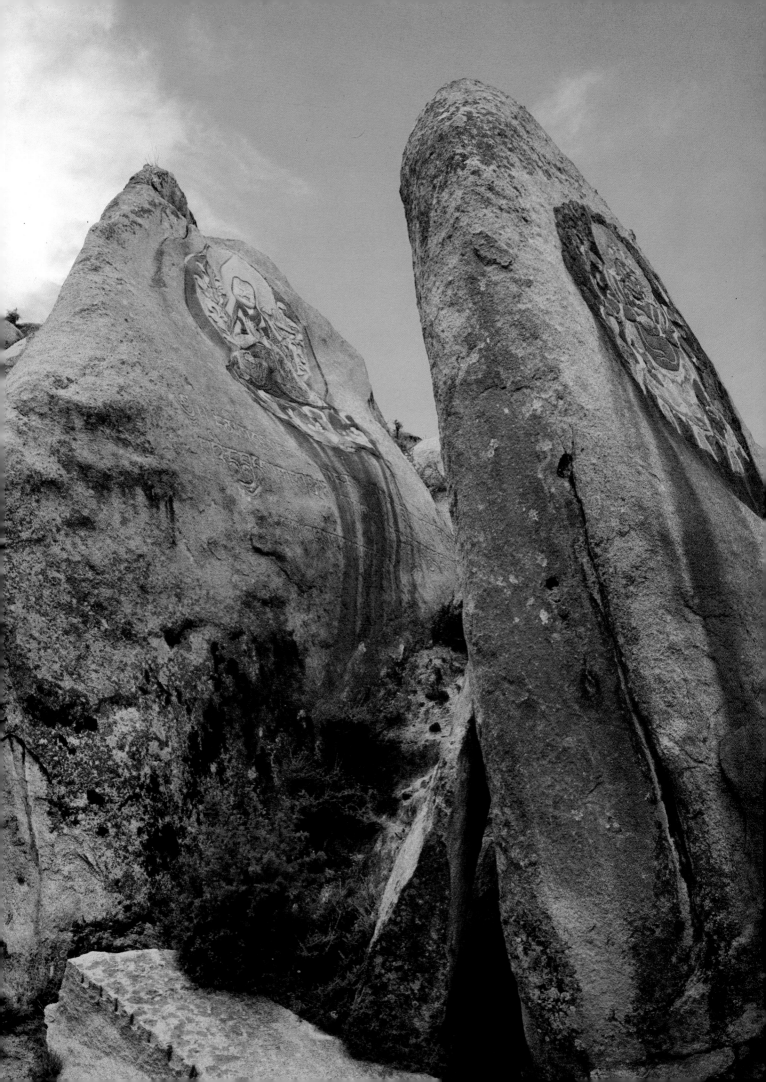

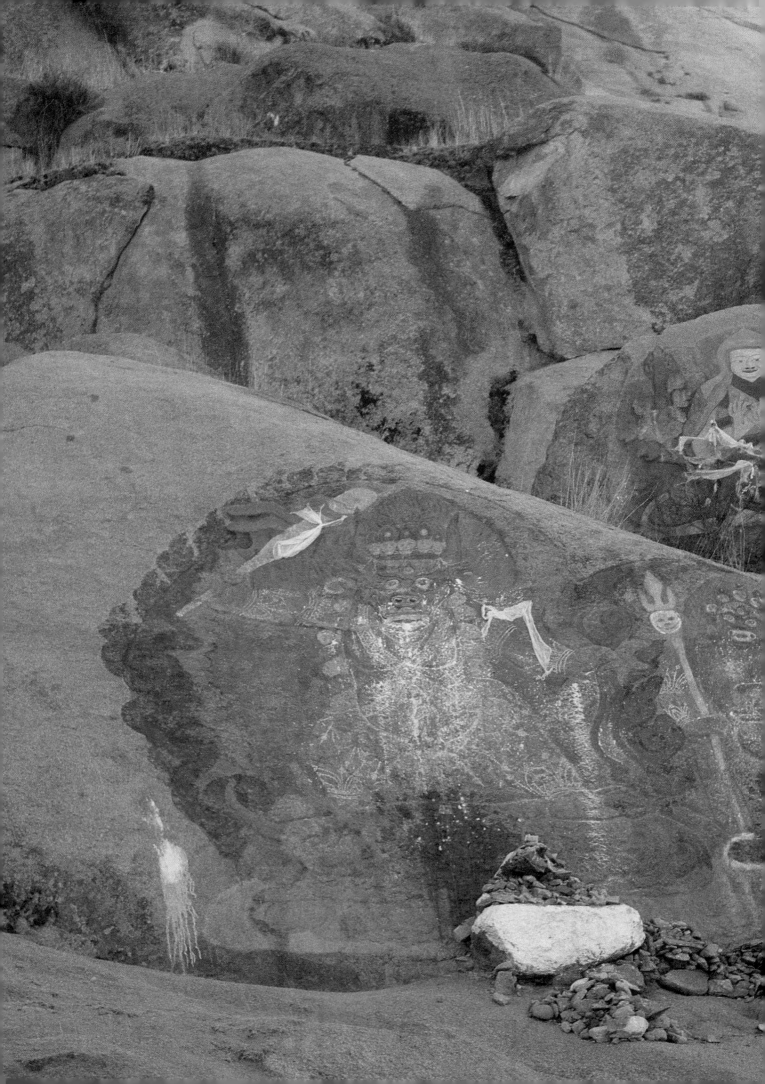

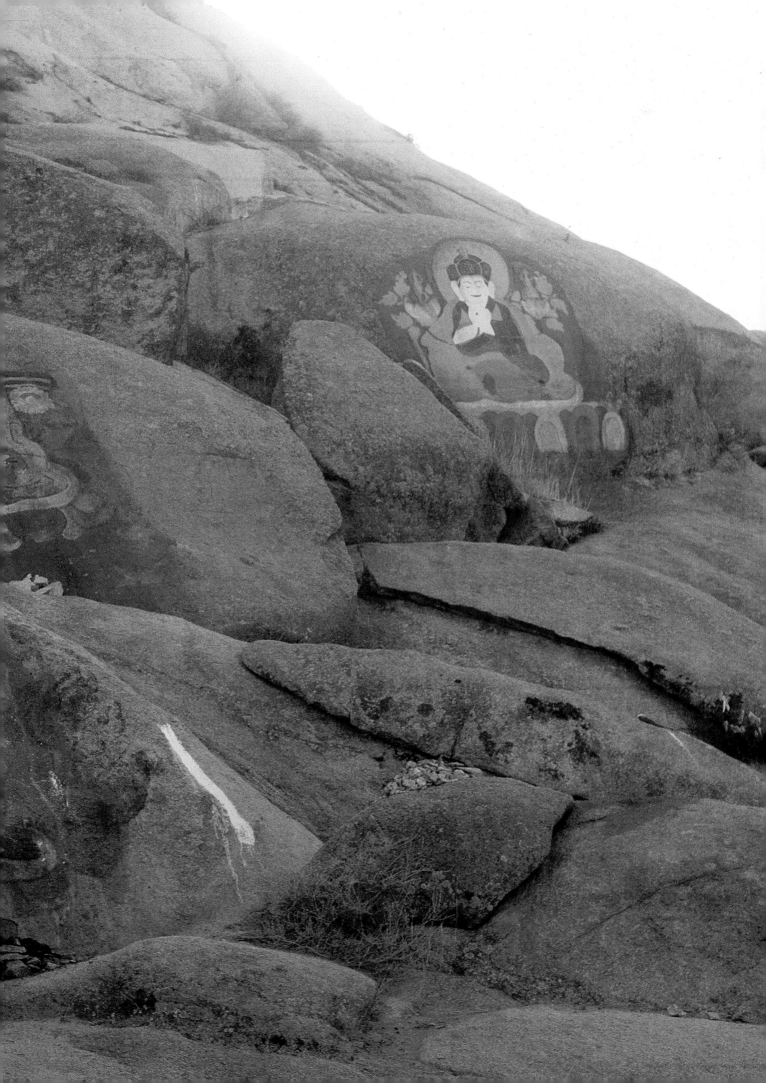

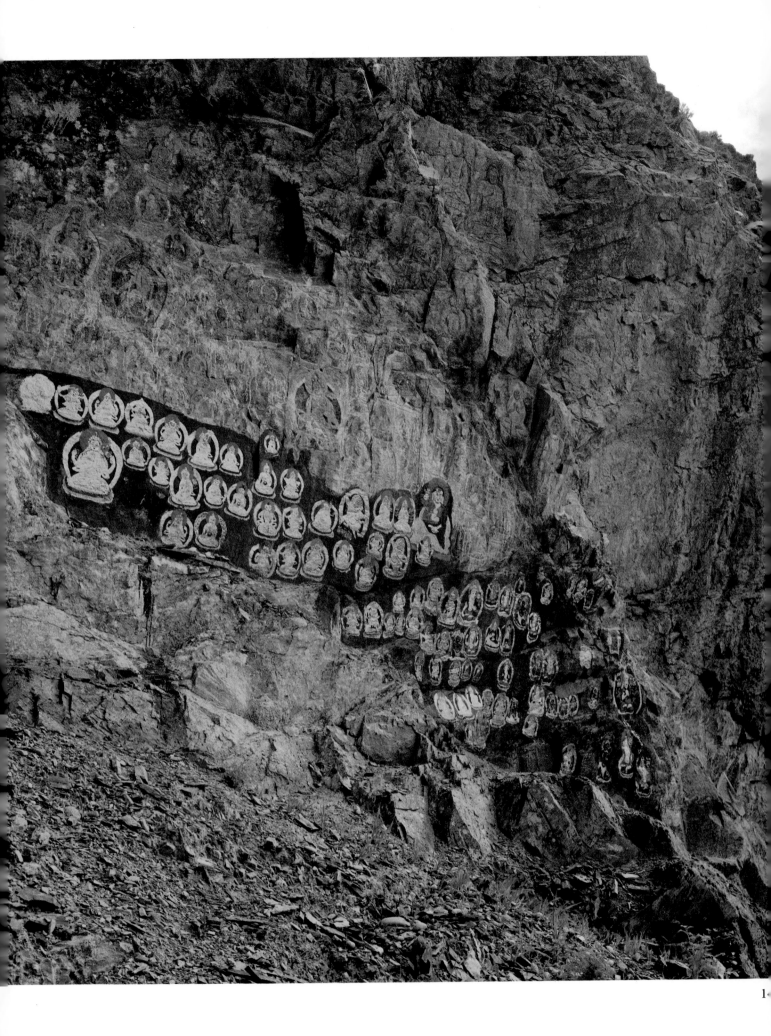

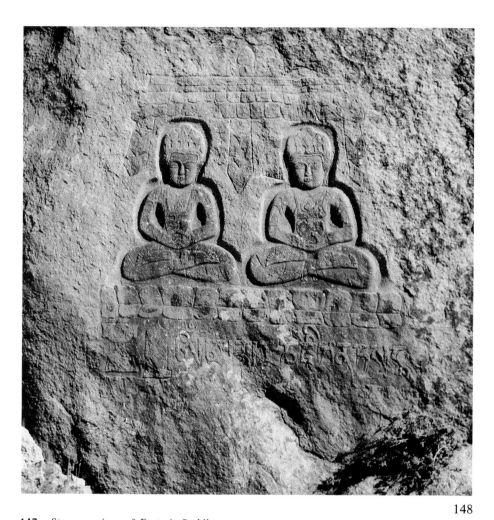

148

147. Stone carvings of Esoteric Buddhas on the King of Medicine Hill in Lhasa.
148. Two carved Buddha images, about 2 metres in height.

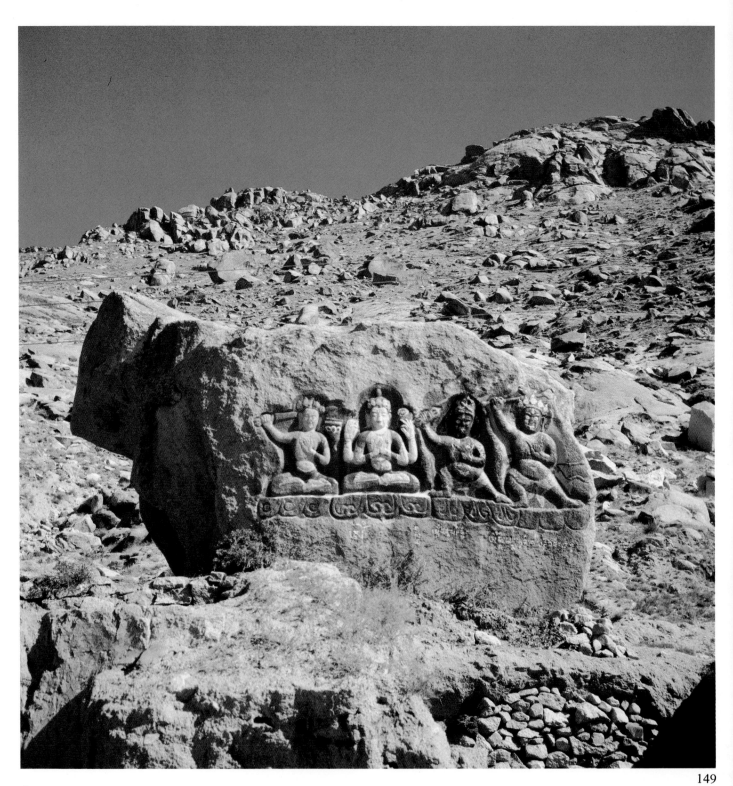

149

149. Mountain-cliff Buddha carvings near Lhasa representing (from left) Mañjuśrī, Avalokiteśvara, Vajradhara and Hayagrīva. Two metres in height.

150. This dharmapāla, with his hair standing on its end and his eyes showing extreme wrath, is going to break through the mountains. His head measures about 30cm in height.

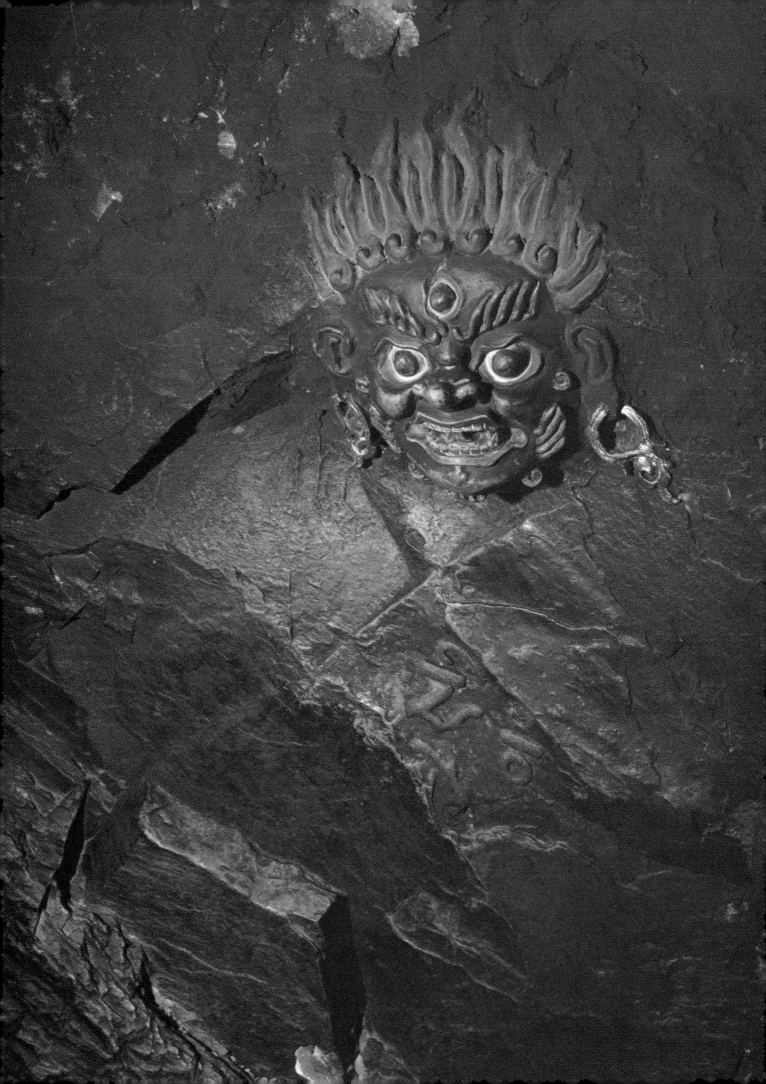

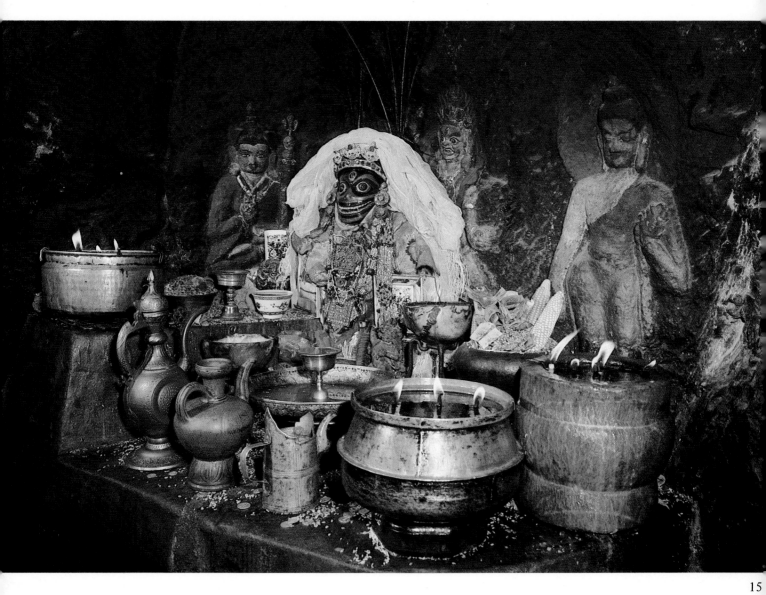

151. Carved images of Buddhist deities in a cave. The one in the front represents the Laksmi Sri, a deity highly revered by Esoteric Buddhism.

RITUAL OBJECTS

RITUAL OBJECTS

The numerous ritual objects of Tibetan Esoteric Buddhism may be divided into six groups symbolizing respect, praise, attendance, devotion, protection and guidance. Kaṣāyas, necklaces and *hatas* (ceremonious scarves) are symbols of respect. Bells, drums, bone flutes, and six-string lutes symbolize praise. The Buddhas' thrones, water vessels, flower baskets, and canopies belong to the attendance group. Rosary beads, the fish-shaped wooden percussion instrument, sceptres, bells, and initiation vessels are used to show devotion. Images of protecting deities, and written secret messages signify protection. Wheels, cylinders, tablets, banners and stones with the "Six-Syllable True Teaching" on them symbolize guidance. These ritual objects are made of various kinds of materials and are highly refined works of art which have gone through the process of casting, carving, insetting, weaving, stitching, and polishing. For instance, some of the flower baskets, woven with gold thread, and valuable as they are for that reason alone, also fully demonstrate excellent workmanship. The beads of necklaces, made of more than a dozen different kinds of materials, show that advanced processing techniques had already been mastered by Tibetan artists centuries ago.

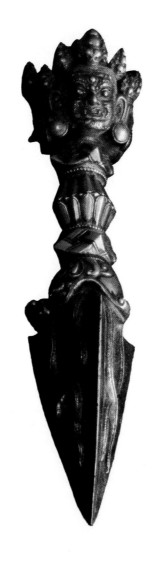
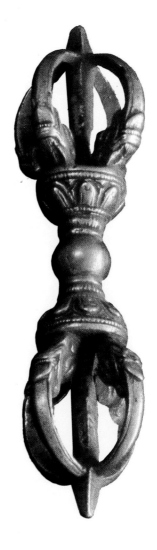

152. Group of the ritual objects of Tibetan Esoteric Buddhism: the vajrakilas (top row) and the vajras. In the Sagya Monastery.
153. The skull vessel. It is made of a human skull with silver trimmings and it is resting on an elaborately carved copper base. The skull vessel belongs to the devotion group and is used to hold wine during initiation ceremonies. In the Potala Palace.

152

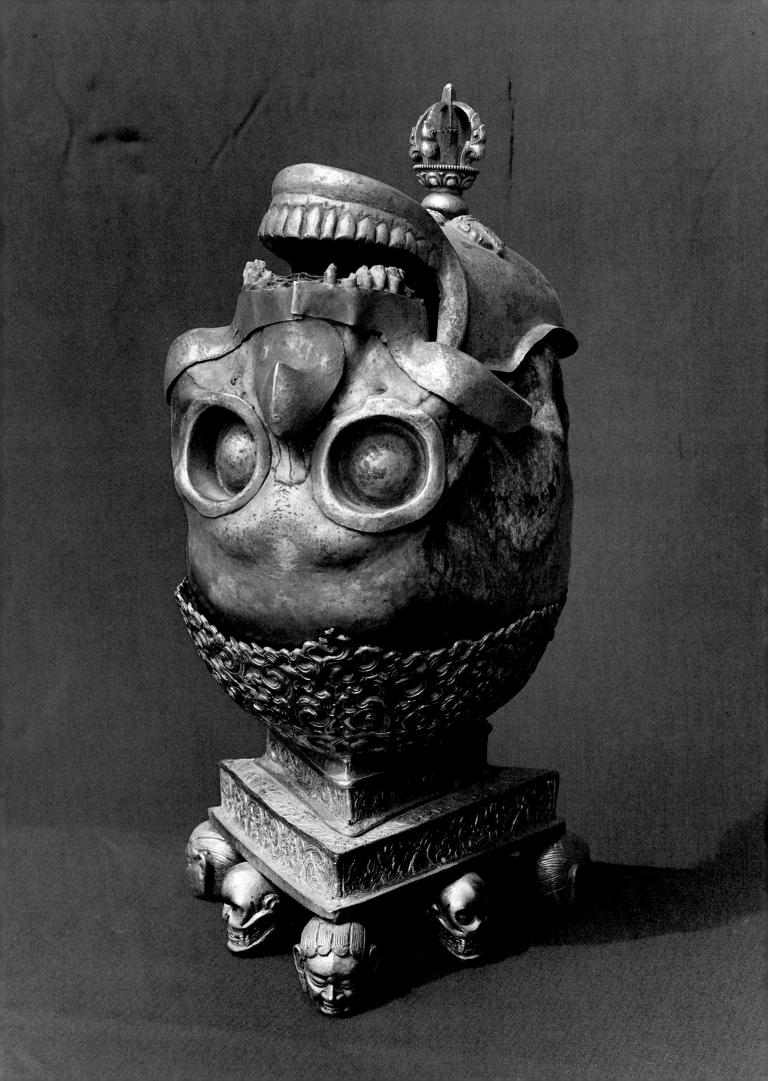

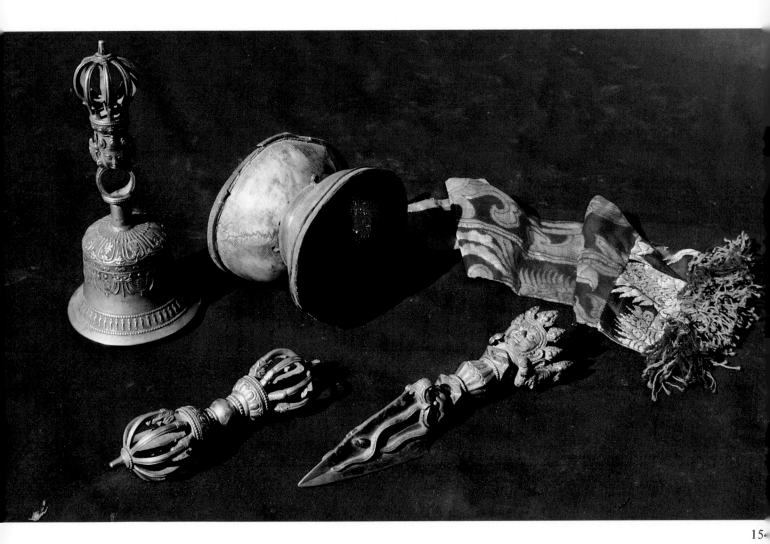

154. Another group of the ritual objects of Tibetan Esoteric Buddhism. Those in the top row are, from left to right; the bell, the hand drum, and the cloth bag for holding ritual objects. The two objects below are the vajra and vajrakila. Like the vajra, the vajrakila was a weapon in ancient India and it later became a ritual object of Esoteric Buddhism. It is also carried by the Satyadevatās of the Esoteric doctrine. In the Sagya Monastery.

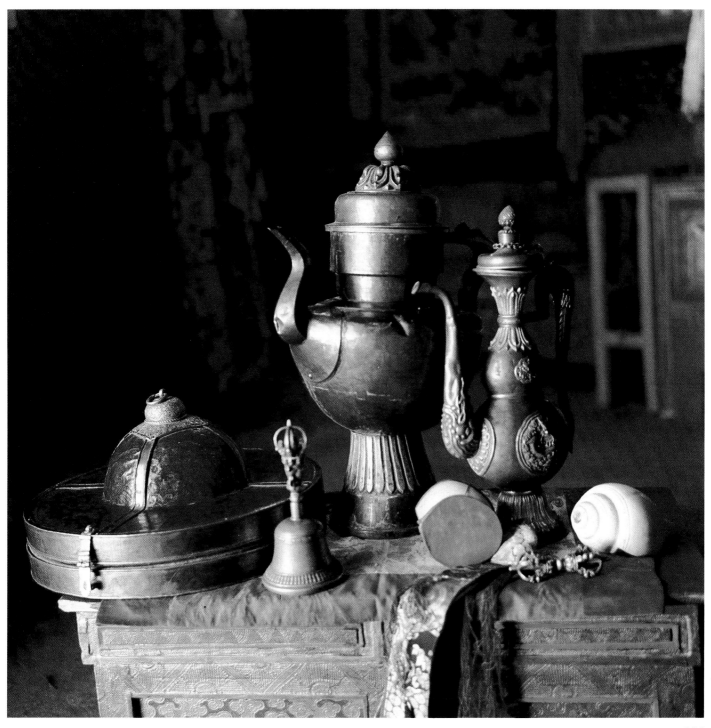

155. Ritual objects of Tibetan Esoteric Buddhism. From left to right: cymbals, of the praise group, used during prayer ceremonies; the bell, of the devotion group, is also one of the hand symbols of Tibetan Esoteric Satyadevatās; the initiation vessel, also of the devotion group, used during initiation ceremonies. The guru bathes the head of his disciple with holy water from the vessel while the disciple drinks wine from a skull vessel. This is a ceremony observed in connection with indoctrination by the guru. Such rituals are believed to make the initiated intelligent and pure. The drum as shown in the illustration is made of a sheep skin stretched over two human skulls which are joined together. The other ritual objects are: initiation vessel; the vajra, of the devotion group, a ritual object that the Satyadevatās of Esoteric Buddhism often carry when they are instructing the dharmahuta. The vajra was a weapon in ancient India, and it later became a ritual object of Esoteric Buddhism. It might have only one prong but it could also have 3, 5 or 9 prongs. At the far right is the conch, of the praise group. In the Sera Monastery.

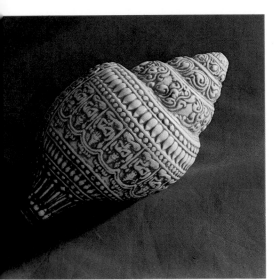

156

156. The conch, of the praise group. In the Sagya Monastery.

157. Tunres, of the protection group. They are carved out of ox horns and carried by chos-rgyals (grand lamas).

158. A lama praying with a ritual object in his hand. Behind him stands a prayer wheel with the inscription of "the Six-Syllable True Teaching" on it.

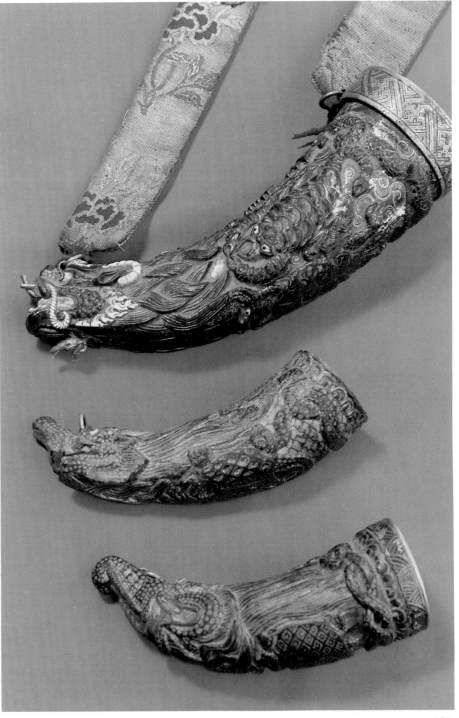

157

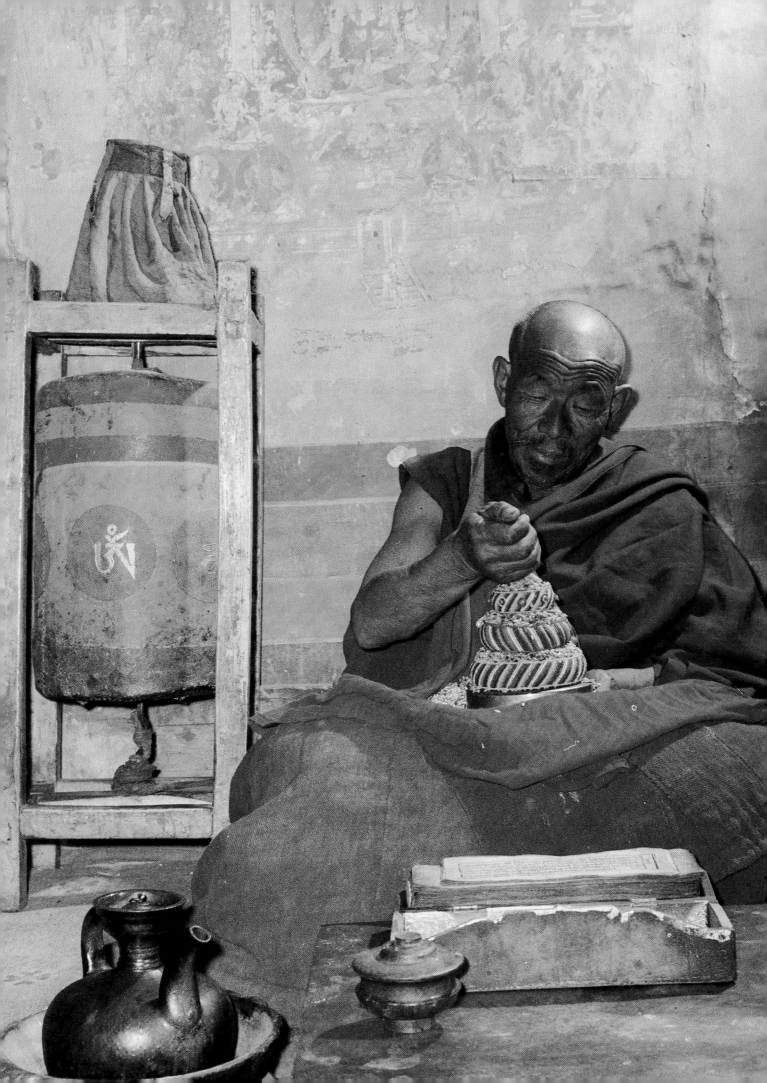

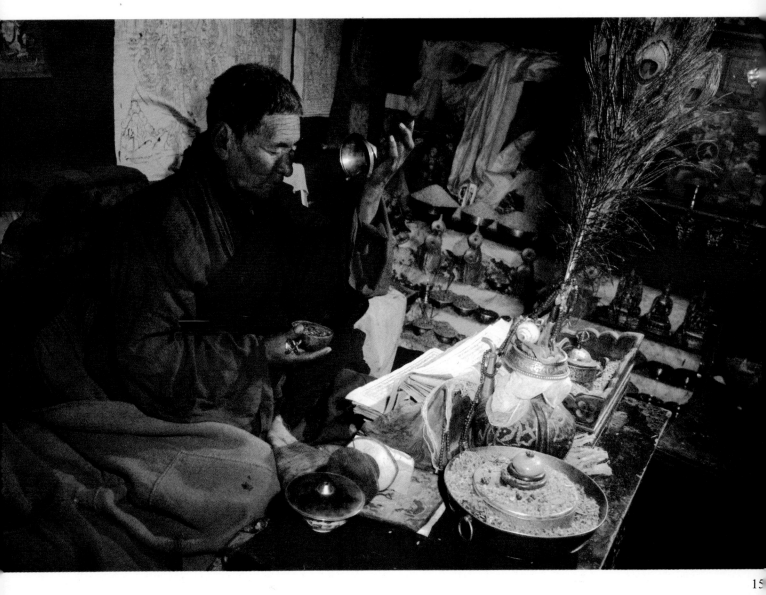

159. A praying lama ringing the bell with ritual objects in front of him.

APPENDICES

Appendix I

Thang-Ka Paintings

Tan Xiyong

1. Schools of Tibetan Painting

The *thang-ka* is an important type of Tibetan painting more widely seen than frescoes and sculptures. To an untrained eye, all *thang-kas* look the same, but in fact there are several schools of *thang-ka* painting in Tibet. The following pages are a brief guide to this form of Tibetan art.

The many schools of Tibetan painting may, in my opinion, be classified geographically into the Eastern Tibetan, Middle Tibetan and Western Tibetan types. (This is explained more fully in my article "Schools of Tibetan Painting", the *Cultural Relics Monthly of the Palace Museum,* No. 14, May 1984, published in Taibei.)

The styles and techniques of the Eastern Tibetan School, the oldest of the schools of Tibetan painting, was heavily influenced by those of the Han nationality. In this school, the artist finds it comparatively easy to develop his individual style, but as religious painting it lacks discipline, and sometimes tends to be too free. Take the painting of the Bodhisattva Mañjuśrī in Plate 87. The trees in the background behind the halo, the sun and the moon are inappropriate in a Tibetan religious painting. The trees show signs of Tang landscape painting styles.

The Western Tibetan School began after the Indian master Atisa came to Tibet in the 11th century, at the time of Emperor Ren Zong of the Song Dynasty.

Dissatisfied with the *thang-kas* of the Eastern Tibetan School for their lack of religious dignity, Atisa brought Nepalese painters to Tibet. They did away with the landscape background and replaced it with what is called "the assembly of holy ones in the sacred city" with the Satyadevatā, the principal Buddha or bodhisattra of the *thang-ka,* sitting in the centre. In the *thang-kas* of this school, with the exception of the Buddha, all the bodhisattvas, ḍākinīs, dharmapālas and gurus appear in the Ajanta "triple bend" posture. The Black Wrathful Devī in Plate 99 and the ḍākinīs in Plate 61 are perfect examples of this: their heads are inclined to the left and the bodies to the right while the centre of gravity of the feet is slightly to the left.

The Middle Tibetan School is an integration of the other two. While the Eastern type shows obvious traces of Han painting, and the Western Tibetan is heavily influenced by Indian art, the Middle Tibetan School is the most indigenous of the three. The Śambara Vajra in Plate 67 may be taken as representative of this school of *thang-ka* painting. There is no background landscape, but the painting contains in the foreground trees and rocks, representing the earthly world as against that of the saints. The image of the Satyadevatā, however, follows the strict prescriptions for Tibetan religious painting; the clouds behind the halo and the lotus throne give the *thang-ka* a more solemn atmosphere than landscape would have done. The composition is thus a compromise between the other two schools.

This school produces gold-embroidered and gold-painted *thang-kas* in addition to conventional colour-painted ones. As this is the type of *thang-kas* most favoured by the monks of the Sa-gya-pa Sect, they are also known as *"thang-kas* of the Sa-gya-pa Sect" or "gold *thang-kas".* The one showing the Smiling Vajra, painted in gold and thin colours against a black background (Plate 57), is strikingly Middle Tibetan. The images of the Sa-gya-pa gurus in the top half are unmistakably Han in style, but those of the Smiling Vajra and his female counterpart show Indian influence — graphic examples of the "compromise".

2. The Composition of the *Thang-ka*

A *thang-ka* consists of three parts: the Satyadevatā is in the centre of the picture with the realm of space above and the realm of earth below. As the realm of space is inhabited by Buddhas and bodhisattvas, it is also called "the realm of the holy ones"; accordingly, the realm of earth is referred to as "the realm of mortals" because it is where ḍākinīs, dharmapālas or monks reside. However, there is no hard-and-fast line separating holy ones from mortals in *thang-ka* painting. Sometimes a master who is believed to have achieved Buddhahood is placed in the realm of space; and at other times, when there are too many holy ones in the sacred city to admit any more in the realm of space, even a bodhisattva has to be put in the earthly realm.

The Buddha immediately above the Satyadevatā in the centre of a *thang-ka* is generally called "the upper Buddha", of whom the Satyadevatā is the attendant deity.

The colour-painted *thang-ka* showing the Kila Vajra (Plate 75) is an example of the composition of a typical *thang-ka.*

There are three Buddhas in the realm of space. The one in the middle directly above the vajra is Samantābhadra, one of the Dharmakāya Buddhas, who is seated on the lotus throne with his female counterpart in his arms. To the right of Samantābhadra is the Vajrasattva, a Sambhogakaya Buddha, with the vajra in his right hand which is held against his chest, and the bell in his outstretched left hand. On the other side of Samantābhadra is Padmasambhava, founder of the Rnying-ma-pa Sect and a Nirmānakāya Buddha. He wears his usual lotus crown, and his red cloak reveals the deva garment underneath. Under his left arm he carries the heavenly sceptre; in his left hand there is a kapala filled with blood, and in the right hand held against his chest a vajra.

With these three incarnations of the Buddha in the realm of space, the realm of the holy ones is represented in its entirety.

The Kila Vajra with his female counterpart in the centre is the Satyadevatā of the *thang-ka*. Together with the dharmapālas around him, he makes up the main part of the painting.

The five dharmapālas arranged in two rows underneath with the lower halves of their bodies shaped like a vajra, are the guardian deities of the five spheres, who are special to this Satyadevatā. The many ḍākinīs mounted on various kinds of animals at the bottom represent the realm of earth.

Let us look at another colour-painted *thang-ka* for comparison: the one shown in Plate 83 with the Protector of Life as the Satyadevatā.

In the upper part of the *thang-ka* representing the realm of space, in addition to the three forms of the Buddha that appear in the *thang-ka* described in the previous passages, we find the images of Sa-gya-pa masters of all generations included in the realm of the holy ones.

In the part representing the realm of earth, we find dharmapālas, ḍākinīs and, in the lower right corner, two Sa-gya-pa monks each accompanied by an attendant. The Sa-gya-pa masters are thus presented as holy ones in this *thang-ka*.

The *thang-ka* shown in Plate 93 with Bhaisajyaguru, the Buddha of Medicine, as the Satyadevatā is quite different in composition. The occasion it shows is called "the assembly on five platforms". On the platform in the centre is Bhaisajyaguru; the three platforms above and on either side of the central one are occupied by masters and the accomplished

monks of the Dge-lugs-pa Sect. The platform below the central one is crowded with holy ones, including the 12 Spirits of Medicine in the front row with successive rows of ḍākinīs, arhats, bodhisattvas and Buddhas behind them. Right at the back are dharmapālas.

This *thang-ka* also includes the two realms, but as the part occupied by the Satyadevatā has expanded to include all five platforms, not much space is left for space and earth.

The *thang-ka* with the Fearful Guardian (the Blue Mahābhairava Vajra) (Plate 63) belongs to the simplified type as it shows only the Satyadevatā without the two realms and their residents.

3. Images in the *thang-ka*

While the religious symbolism of the *thang-ka* may occupy the main attention of those who do research into this form of art, those who are not Tibetan Buddhists may find the significance of *thang-ka* images more interesting.

The images of the Satyadevatās come in three types: peaceful, wrathful and a combination of the two. The peaceful type refers to those deities who have a compassionate countenance, one head, two arms, two feet and two eyes; deities of the wrathful type have many heads, arms, feet and eyes: and those of the combination type, being halfway between the two, symbolize both compassion for human suffering and their physical prowess as dharmapālas.

Satyadevatās of any of the three types may appear in the *thang-ka* alone or in the act of union with their female counterparts as rejas with their devīs in *thang-ka* paintings. Let us look at some examples.

Tsong-kha-pa in the *thang-ka* shown in Plate 92 is of the peaceful, unaccompanied type.

The dharmapālas in the lower part (the earthly realm) of the *thang-ka* in Plate 91 that shows the Supreme Heruka are typical of the unaccompanied, wrathful type, especially the one in black at the right, with three triple-eyed heads, six arms and two feet.

Padmasambhava, who appears in the *thang-ka* shown in Plate 90 above the Supreme Heruka in the realm of space wearing his lotus crown and carrying the heavenly sceptre, is representative of the combination type. His glaring, angry eyes and the vajra that he holds in his right hand, which makes the anticipation mudrā, represent his wrathful aspect, while the dew-filled kapāla in his left hand and the smile he wears symbolize his peaceful aspect. (See also his image in Plate 9.)

The serene Avalokiteśvara, with his female counterpart clinging to him in the act of union (Plate 112), is a good example of the accompanied, peaceful type.

The accompanied, wrathful type is perhaps best illustrated by the colour-painted image of the Supreme Heruka in Plate 88. The Satyadevatā has 21 heads with 3 eyes in each of them, 18 arms and 2 feet. With his female counterpart wrapping her legs around his waist while holding his neck in her right arm and the kapāla in her left hand, the deity appears in a perfect yab-yam (union) posture.

The colour-painted image of the bodhisattva Mañjuśrī in Plate 87 is representative of the accompanied, combination type. The devī in his arms who is making the demon-subduing mudrā with her hand, symbolizes wrath, while the compassionate countenance of the deity represents his peaceful aspect.

Generally, dharmakāya Buddhas like Samantabhadra, and sambhogakāya Buddhas such as the Deity of Longevity, are of the peaceful type; they may appear

213

alone or accompanied, but nirmāṇakāya Buddhas (Śākyamuni, for instance) always appear alone and with a peaceful countenance.

All bodhisattvas (such as Avalokiteśvara and Mañjuśrī) look peaceful, with or without their female counterparts: rajas and dharmapālas are always wrathful-looking, whether they appear alone or accompanied.

Images of bodhisattvas that have a special significance may be at the same time peaceful and wrathful. Padmasambhava, for instance, belongs to this type because when he preached Buddhism in Tibet he fought the Bon-pos.

4. Sitting and Standing Postures, Mudrās, Thrones, Etc.

A survey of the imagery in the paintings of Tibetan Esoteric Buddhism must also include the seated and standing postures of the Satyadevatās, their mudrās or hand gestures, the thrones they occupy, their haloes and ritual objects, and what they symbolize. As space is limited, what follows is only a brief explanation of some of them. Haloes and ritual objects have unfortunately to be omitted.

Sitting and standing postures –

(1) Cross-legged posture: sitting cross-legged with the soles of the feet facing upward. See Tsong-kha-pa in Plate 92, and Bhaiṣajyaguru in Plate 93.

(2) Cross-legged lotus posture: the sitting posture of a devī embracing the Satyadevatā. The Guhyasamāja Vajra in Plate 78 sits cross-legged, while the devī he embraces is in the cross-legged lotus sitting posture.

(3) Enjoyment posture: one foot touching the ground with the other leg bent and resting on the throne. This is the posture of the Black Wrathful Devī in Plate 99.

(4) Cakravartīrāja (Wheel-turning King) posture: one leg resting horizontally on the seat of the throne and crossed by the other leg, slightly bent. This is the posture of the first deity from the left in the second row in the realm of space in the *thang-ka* of the Supreme Heruka (Plate 88).

(5) Relaxed left (or right) leg posture: similar to the Cakravartīrāja posture except that the legs do not cross each other. See devarāja Vaiśravaṇa in Plate 116.

(6) Dancing posture: standing on one bent leg with the other leg, also bent, extended outward. This is the way the Smiling Vajra stands in Plate 57. A vajra is usually seen in this posture when he appears in his peaceful aspect.

(7) Straight left (right) leg posture: standing on one straight leg with the other one held up. This posture is characteristic of wrathful deities, such as the Fearful Vajra in Plate 62.

(8) Cross-footed posture: the way the bodhisattva Mañjuśrī sits on the lion with his feet crossing each other in Plate 87 is an example of this unusual posture.

(9) Kneeling posture: kneeling on one leg and standing on the other leg, which is also bent. This posture, halfway between sitting and standing, is the one in which the rāja is represented in Plate 119.

Mudrās –

(1) Wrathful mudrā: the middle and ring fingers are bent against the palm with the thumb over them, and the index and small fingers held straight. It is also called the "anticipation mudrā". In Plate 63 this is the mudrā of the Fearful Vajra and that of other vajras holding ritual objects in their hands.

(2) The Vajra Hūṁkāra mudrā: two hands in the wrathful mudrā cross each other in front of the chest. This is the mudrā of Śambara Vajra embracing his female counterpart in Plate 67.

(3) Joined palms mudrā: the palms are joined together with fingers extended. Ritual objects may be held between the palms. See the Kīla Vajra holding the vajra in this mudrā in Plate 76.

(4) Preaching or wheel-turning mudrā: the thumb and the index finger are joined in a ring with the other three fingers straight. This is the mudrā Tsong-kha-pa makes with his left hand in Plate 92.

(5) Demon-subduing or ground-touching mudrā: all the fingers are held straight with the middle one touching the ground. The right hand of Bhaiṣajyaguru (Plate 93) is held in this mudrā. If the palm faces outward, this becomes the wish-granting mudrā.

(6) Bestowing mudrā: the palm is held up against the chest. The right hands of the three lamas in the second row below Bhaiṣajyaguru (Plate 94) are held in this mudrā. The other three lamas in the first row hold their hands in the preaching mudrā.

(7) Fixed mudrā: the palms are placed on crossed legs with the thumbs touching each other. The fourth from the left in the circle of Buddhas (Plate 94) shows this mudrā.

Thrones and mounts –

(1) The lotus throne: this is the throne normally used by Buddhas or bodhisattvas. The part for sitting on is called the sun seat, but as it is surrounded on the outside with lotus petals, it is generally referred to also as the lotus throne. The throne is to be seen in many *thang-ka* paintings. Sitātapatra (White Umbrella) occupies one such throne (Plate 109). His right hand shows the wish-granting mudrā and the left hand is held in the preaching mudrā. He sits cross-legged with his devī in the cross-legged lotus posture.

Deities may sometimes appear standing on a lotus throne as in Plate 119, in which the rāja stands on one leg on such a throne.

(2) The living souls throne: this is the throne on which the Satyadevatā in a *thang-ka* stands on heathen deities and ghosts with one or both feet. The Śambara Vajra and the Kila Vajra often appear on such a throne.

(3) Bird and animal mounts: the mouths for Satyadevatās may be birds or animals. The mount of the bodhisattva Mañjuśrī in Plate 87 is a lion, and the ḍākinīs below the Kila Vajra in Plate 74 are mostly riding birds or animals.

The images of Buddhas and bodhisattvas, the adornments they wear (crowns, rings, bracelets, tassels, rosaries, etc.), and the ritual objects they hold all have their religious meanings. The five-Buddha crown, for example, symbolizes the five kinds of wisdom while the crown with five skulls represents the five kinds of anger; flowers held in the hands are symbols of the accomplishments of the dharma outside this world, jewels signify its accomplishments in the immediate world, and weapons mean the end of demons and obstacles. But, for those who are not followers of Esoteric Buddhism it is hoped that detailed information in this respect will not be necessary.

However, there is one thing which needs a little explanation, and that is how the concept of Yin and Yang is expressed in *thang-ka* paintings of Tibetan Esoteric Buddhism.

Not only is this notion represented by the Buddha parents and rājas and their devīs, but ritual objects are also associated with it. The vajra is a symbol of Yang, while the bell stands for Yin; the heavenly sceptre and the arrow signify Yang, while the kapāla and the garland represent Yin. This notion of matching the two polarities, which has to do with both fertility cults in Indian culture and the Han theory of Yin and Yang, may offer us clues to understanding the links between Oriental cultures.

The author is the editor-in-chief of the *Weekly Economic Review,* Hongkong, an Acarya of the Rnying-ma-pa Sect of Tibetan Esoteric Buddhism, and deputy-chairman of the Society of the Diamond Vehicle, Hongkong.

	English	Chinese	Reference	Page no.
	Appendix II			
1.	Amṛtakuṇḍalin	甘露明王	Deity	14
2	Anuttara Yoga Tantra	無上瑜珈密	Doctrine	20
3	Atīśa	阿底峽	Translator	24
4	Avalokiteśvara	觀音	Deity	156
5	Bhaiṣajya guru	藥師佛	Deity	132
6	Bkah-bragyud-pa	噶舉派	Religious sect	21
7	Bkah-gdams-pa	噶當派	Religious sect	22
8	Bkah-hgyur	甘珠爾	Buddhist text	30
9	Bkra-shis Khye-dren	扎喜曲珍	Tibetan woman	20
10	Bla-ma dbu-mdsad	喇嘛翁哉	Monastic office	42
11	Blood-drinking Vajra	飲血金剛	Deity	90
12	Bod	吐蕃	Dynasty	14
13	Bodhimargapradipa	菩提道燈論	Name of book	24
14	Body secret	身密	Special term	32
15	Bon-po	本教	Religion	14
16	Bram-za Sham Kara	香迦惹	Indian master	14
17	Bstan-hgyur	丹珠爾	Buddhist text	30
18	Byan-chub Iam-gyi rim-pa chenpo	菩提道次第廣論	Name of book	24
19	Byan-rtse-chos-rje	絳孜却結	Monastic office	42
20	Canons	儀軌	Special term	10
21	Car-rtse chos-rje	夏孜却結	Monastic office	42
22	Conch	法螺	Ritual object	245
23	Dākinī	空行母	Doctrinal title	36
24	Dar-ma	達瑪	Tibetan king	22
25	Devī	明妃	Deity	18
26	Devotion to Buddha	皈依佛	Special term	42
27	Devotion to Lamaism	皈依喇嘛	Special term	42
28	Devotion to monkhood	皈依僧	Special term	42
29	Devotion to the dharma	皈依法	Special term	42
30	Dgah-idan Khri-pa	甘丹赤巴	Monastic office	42
31	Dge-bshes	格西	Degree of Monastic study	40
32	Dge-lugs-pa	格魯派	Religious sect	22
33	Dge-skos	格貴	Monastic office	42
34	Dharmakāya Samantabhadra	法身普賢	Deity	182
35	Dharmapāla	護法神	Deity	18
36	Dharmapāla-on-a-Goat	騎羊護法神	Deity	160
37	Esoteric Buddhism	密宗	Religious sect	10
38	Exoteric Buddhism	顯宗	Religious sect	10
39	Green Tārā	綠度母	Deity	142
40	Grva-tshan	扎倉	Monastic institution	40
41	Gsan-snags lam-rim	密宗道次第廣論	Name of book	24
42	Guhyasamāja	密集金剛	Deity	116
43	Guhyasamāja Vajra	密聚金剛	Deity	116
44	Happy Vajra	歡喜金剛	Deity	60
45	Hayagrīva	馬頭金剛	Deity	118

Appendix II

Principal Terms in English and Chinese

Appendix III

Principal Tibetan Buddhist Monasteries and Temples

Buddhist Monasteries and temples are found almost everywhere in Tibet. According to a report submitted by the Seventh Dalai Lama to the Qing court in 1737 (2nd year of the reign of Qianlong), the number of the monasteries of the Yellow Sect (Dge-lugs-pa Sect) alone amounted to as many as 3,477. This number would have been much greater if the monasteries of the other sects had been included. The following is a list of Tibetan Buddhist monasteries and temples that are often found in historical documents:

Monasteries	Location	Years of Construction	Names in Chinese
Qoikang	Lhasa	Between 7th and 10th c.	大昭寺
Ramoqe	Lhasa	Between 7th and 10th c.	小昭寺
Potala	Lhasa	Between 7th and 10th c.	布達拉宮
Samye	Zhanang	Between 7th and 10th c.	桑耶寺
Gaqu	Gaqu	Between 7th and 10th c.	瓜曲寺
Wuxangdo	SW of Lhasa	Between 7th and 10th c.	烏香奈寺
Chazhug	Nedong, Shannan	Between 7th and 10th c.	昌珠寺
Gacai	Maizhokunggar	Between 7th and 10th c.	迦采寺
Yerba	Dagze	Between 7th and 10th c.	葉爾巴寺
Toling	Zhadag, Ngari	Between 10th and 11th c.	陀林寺
Tangboqe	Qonggyai	11th c. No longer in existence	塘波且寺
Wubalung	Wubalung	11th c.	烏巴壟寺
Tubdain	South of Lhasa	Towards end of 16th c.	多吉扎寺
Minzhoiling	Zhanang	Mid-17th c.	敏珠寺
Gatog	Baiyu, Sichuan Province	12th c.	噶陀寺
Zogqen	Dege, Sichuan	1685	佐欽寺
Xeqen	East of Zogqen Monastery	1746	西欽寺
Baiyul	Baiyu, Sichuan	17th c.	貝域寺
Razheng	Lhunzhub	1056	熱振寺
Qeika	Maizhokunggar	11th c.	怯喀寺
Jilbu	Ngamring	1164	基布寺
Qayul	South of Dapo	11th c.	甲域寺
Sangpu	West suburb of Lhasa	1073	桑浦寺
Sagya	Sagya	1073	薩迦寺
Ngamring	Ngamring	14th c.	昂仁寺
Gambo	Talagambo	1121	崗波寺
Gamedainsa	Gama	1147	噶瑪丹薩寺
Curpur	Doilungdeqen	1143	粗朴寺
Gamalhading	Riwoqe	14th c.	噶瑪拉登寺
Deqendeng	Rongdiqelung	14th c.	德慶登寺
Nenang	Pumodan	1333	乃囊寺
Yangbajain	Yangbajain	1490	羊八井寺
Caiba	East suburb of Lhasa	1175	蔡巴寺
Kungtang	East suburb of Lhasa	1187	公堂寺
Baroi	Ngamring	12th c.	拔伐寺
Dainsatil	Nedong	1158	丹薩替寺
Zetang	Zetang	1351	澤當寺
Zhikungtil	Maizhokunggar	1179	止貢替寺
Daglung	Lhunzhub	1180	達壟寺
Riwoqe	Riwoqe'	1276	類烏齊寺
Longdoi	Near Lhasa	12th c.	隆多寺
Ralung	Ralung	12th c.	熱壟寺
Zhuggain	SW of Lhasa	12th c.	主寺
Kanqu	Lhozhag	13th c.	噶曲寺

Monasteries	Location	Years of Construction	Names in Chinese
Goicang	Goicang	1226	郭倉寺
Sara	Zharao	12th c.	索熱寺
Daglung	Nagqu	1180	達壟寺
Nartang	Nartang	1153	納塘寺
Qonang	Lhaze	13th c.	覺囊寺
Zecogba	Nedong	11th c.	則錯巴寺
Xalu	Xigaze	11th c.	霞魯寺
Kautam Ledu,	Qinghai Province	1392	瞿縣寺
Qambaling	Huzhu, Qinghai	1612	佑寧寺
Yasang	Shannan	1206	雅桑寺
Chopug	Chopug	12th c.	綽浦寺
Xugseb	Niepu	1181	修賽寺
Qomonang	Lhaze	13th c.	覺摩囊寺
Dagdain Puncogling	Lhaze	1614	達丹彭錯林
Gadain	Dagze	1409	甘丹寺
Drepung	Lhasa	1416	哲蚌寺
Zhaxilhunbo	Xigaze	1447	扎什倫布寺
Qoikorgyai	Jiemeiduotang	1509	羣科杰寺
Ngarichacang	Zetang	1541	阿里僧院
Gubum	Niezhong, Qinghai	1577	塔爾寺
Qambaling	Qamdo	1437	絳巴林寺
Sera	Lhasa	1418	色拉寺
Goinlung	Huzhu, Qinghai	1612	袞壟寺
Tegqen Qoikorling	Tumd, Inner Mongolia	16th c.	大乘法輪洲
Gundeling	Lhasa	1794	功德林寺

Appendix IV

Index

223